HONESTY:
A MEMOIR

<<<<<<<<>>>>>>>

HONESTY: A MEMOIR

Walking the Walk

✧✧✧✧✧

A memoir told as a story – a story so twisted
that it took seven books to tell

Book 6 in the Powerless series

LELA FOX

Cover designed by Queen Graphics
Photos via Deposit Photos; Photoshop editing by Creative Global
Contributing Editors: Teri Eicher and Noah Lloyd

Honesty is a 97-percent-true memoir; names of people and places have been changes and some incidents are used factiously or may be products of the author's imagination. Any resemblance to actual events, locales, businesses, organizations, or persons, living or dead, is entirely coincidental.

Visit the author's website at LelaFox.com
First Printing November 2019
ISBN: 9781711366982

TABLE OF CONTENTS

<<<<<<<<>>>>>>

DEDICATION

I dedicate this book to a long line of women...

To the AA sponsors I've had over the years:
Jenny, Oakley, Vickie, Nanci, Tami, and April.

To my sponsees, who helped me more than I helped them:
Tami, Amanda, Neal, Glenna, and many more.

And to the string of therapists who helped me get my head straight:
Connie, Kate, Sarah, Brynn, Mo, and more

<<<<<<<<<>>>>>>>>>

Only now do I understand how incredibly wise these women are.

<<<<<<<>>>>>>

WALKING THE WALK

"Honesty is the only way to fight the inner demons."

—SETH SMITH

ПINE LIFETIMES PER LIFE
HOW I GOT HERE

I've had nine Lifetimes in my life, each a 180-degree turn from the one before it. So my memoir is structured around these Lifetimes.

My first Lifetime, my childhood, is unwritten – who wants to read about the happiness and honey of my picture-perfect upbringing? Honestly, to write about it would make me hang up the keyboard because sappy stories aren't my style.

According to my tee-totaling parents, the moon and stars revolved around me and my two sisters. They allowed no alcohol in the house because both their fathers were lousy drunks, screwing up their own childhoods. The "new and improved" Fox family would be different, they pledged, so they built a life only found in 1950s do-gooder movies, white picket fence and all.

As the youngest, I received the most-liberal encouragement of their small-town version of "you can do anything," and Daddy, especially, made me believe I was Queen of Everything and could do no wrong.

But I did a lot of wrong. Over and over again.

Despite sobriety, I did stupid things until my final Lifetime, Number Nine, both the hardest and most serene of them all. But a lot happened before I could get there.

My memoir series begins with Lifetime Number Two and my first drink; my life changed in a flash as I drank four beers in a gravel alley with two albino sisters. The experience of near-instant addiction and the horror of high school became the book *Powerless*.

Lifetime Number Three encompassed college and my hurry-up-and-grow-up first marriage, destroyed by Bi-Polar swings and gallons of wine. You'll find the details in the follow-up book, *Denial*. The wonderful product of that Lifetime is now 37 years old with a family of his own.

The divorce prompted Lifetime Number Four where I partied like hell on non-custody weekends, and soon married a scoundrel of a man who loved my son more than he loved me. I wrote about it in *Chaos*. By that point, my drinking was a 24/7 affair.

I spent Lifetime Number Five with a man who turned out to be a callous, vengeful crook, but I had drunkenly agreed to most everything that happened, unaware of circumstances. He added almost $10,000 to my Visa card, paying mere tidbits when I sobered up enough to notice and nag him. The good, the bad, and the funny of that Lifetime became the book *Unmanageable*.

It took being homeless to reach my alcoholic bottom, spawning Lifetime Number Six – the most dramatic change by far – when I went to rehab to sweat through early sobriety. My first year sober was perhaps crazier than the last year drinking, minus the homelessness, thus the title of the book that explains it all: *Insanity*.

I worked with a kickass sponsor and turned my life over to the care and comfort of a Higher Power I called Dude. I thought I'd found nirvana, but... no, several more Lifetimes were to come.

This book is the end of Lifetime Number Six and the beginning of Lifetime Number Seven. The transition comes as I travel north, full of the hopes and the dreams only a naïve AA newcomer can believe.

My rollercoaster life has taken many twists and turns. At each tumble... each roadblock... each 180-degree turn, I'd shout to the heavens: "This is not how it's supposed to end!"

And it didn't end until Lifetime Number Nine, which you can read about in the final book of the series, *Serenity*, available in mid-March on Amazon.

Buckle in, folks. Because I write the hard stuff. The real stuff. The honest-to-the-bone stuff that makes you cringe, and feel the sometimes-painful realities of being a drunk and a sober alcoholic.

Yep. I write the stuff that makes you squirm in your seat. Squirm along with me in this edition of The Life & Times of a Curious Drunk.

<<<<<<<>>>>>>

STITCH & BITCH

CHAPTER 1

"I'm walking the walk and doing all the right things! So how could *I* get fired? Why *me?* I mean... I'm six whole months sober! I didn't do *anything* to deserve it." I stabbed the embroidery needle through the linen fabric with more force than needed, huffing a frustrated sigh.

Murmurs arose from the forty-plus women in the AA meeting as if they challenged the "not my fault" statement. But I insisted, "Seriously, ask Jenny! It really wasn't my fault!" I looked at my sponsor, sitting close beside me in the circle and pushing her rimless eyeglasses higher on that cute, porcelain-doll nose. But Jenny's grimace offered no support or defense of my plea.

I continued, "And no matter how much I pray, I still can't find a job."

"Have you *looked* for a job, Lela, or just prayed?" Jenny's sponsor, Nancy, asked from the other side of the circle.

Of course, I knew her question was just the opening salvo of a lecture on patience. My eye-roll spoke my disgust for her approach, and I refused to reply because I hadn't had time to look for a job yet. Nancy's snippy tone made it obvious she thought I was just a whiny newcomer, and her "harsh" judgement pissed me off, so I snapped, "It just happened yesterday, dammit!"

But that was a lie; it had happened three days ago and knocked me backward two days.

7

All the women laughed, and Nancy added, "Maybe you should look a little longer before you fuss." That snarky comment brought even more laughs.

"But what if there *aren't* any jobs for a washed-up advertising writer? West Palm Beach isn't that big of a place, you know. And what if there are no jobs – that's my fear. Y'all, my rent is due! I have a Visa bill! 'Woe is me,' as my dad would say, because I'm in a world of hurt."

"Your bitching time is up, Lela."

"But I'm not finished!"

"You actually went over. No matter how serious your issue, newcomers get a max of three minutes. So pass the needlework to the left, please."

"That's another thing! I want to bitch about this stupid meeting. I thought it was funny and cool at first, but you guys give me so much grief that I don't even feel welcome here, y'all! How can Jenny call this her homegroup? You guys are flat-out MEAN!" A curl fell forward on my forehead as my body jerked in time with my words.

Chuckles all around, even from Jenny. I clenched my jaw and thrust the embroidery hoop to the next woman, who shot me a look of pity, then deftly picked up the needle. She cooed, "I have only gratitude to share today, so thirty seconds will do." Then she spouted some happy-ass news about something at work, something I cared about NOT ONE BIT.

I leaned in closer to whisper to Jenny. "These women don't believe I have real problems, Jenny, and I *do*. How can you stand this butterflies-and-lollipops meeting?"

"Sounds like this would be a good day for you to just listen, hon. Listen and learn."

I rolled my eyes. *I just need a job... a job worthy of my advertising degree and decades of experience. After all, I deserve a certain level of respect as an award-winning writer... a professional.*

As the embroidery hoop passed from woman to woman, each shared honest wisdom about how to live sober; powerful wisdom because this meeting attracted women with long-term sobriety. Only a few struggled with life the way I did. On good days I admired them but doubted I could ever be sober enough to need just thirty seconds of stitching. Yet I continued to come, every Wednesday before a study session with Jenny at the Subway in Pompano Beach, home of the famous Goodyear blimp.

Getting fired had been a smack in the face, and I still felt buckets of anger toward Smyth Software in general and my boss Dale in particular.

8

Plus, I guess I felt a touch of Shame for not standing up for myself, and for not seeing through his plot to get me fired.

In my eyes, Dale had made me look like a fool, just like my ex-husband Stuart had, and I'd played right into his hands. Now I'd suffer without a letter of reference from my most recent job.

"Actually, I'm double-screwed, Jenny. And I can't let it go. My sense of peace is gone, and I'm out of control of things."

"Again?"

"What do you mean 'again?'"

"Sorry... I shouldn't have said that."

"Quit making it worse, Jenny!"

"Your stack of colored notepads isn't helping you sort through options, Lela?"

"Not this time."

"You can't put things in alphabetical order?"

"Hell, I can't even *recite* the alphabet! Nothing has happened yet, but nothing is listed on the job sites or in the classified ads. And the real problem hasn't come yet. See, I drank through the technology revolution in the advertising business. I'm out of the loop, and a forty-year-old can't exactly offer a fresh perspective for today's fast-paced ad agencies."

"Something will come around. Keep looking."

I said sarcastically, "I'm glad you're so sure of that, Miss Ma'am. Send some of that assurance my way, please, since you're so in control of it."

"Don't get smart with me, Lela. All you need to do is keep walking the walk. You'll get there."

A growl of frustration shot through my lips. "You just don't get it."

"I get that you're upset, I really do. But I can't help you do this, Lela. I can't make it go away for you. Why do you seem to expect *me* to fix the problem?"

"You *always* fix my problems."

Jenny threw her head back and laughed – loud enough that other Subway customers turned their heads. "You only *think* it's me, Lela! All your progress in sobriety?" I nodded, hoping for a pat on the back. "All that progress has come from *your own hard work*."

"Really?" I glowed with pride.

"Definitely. So keep working hard and you'll continue to make progress. I'm sure of that. But I don't know what else to tell you."

"Maybe something will show up in the classified ads this Sunday."

"Do you have your résumé ready?"

"The guts of it, and it's ready to customize for whatever job I'm shooting for."

"A cover letter?"

"Ditto. Ready except for the fill-in-the-blank parts."

"Then you're prepared... what are you bitching about?"

"I have nobody to address the résumé to! Don't you get it?!"

"First, keep your voice down. Second, do some research on how long people look for a job. I bet you'll find that you're not *supposed* to get a job in the first month of looking."

"A *month?!* I can't wait that long! I have bills! My Visa!"

"Then get off your high horse and start bagging groceries! Go to the mall and fold clothes... anything, Lela! Why are you so against that?"

I put my head down, knowing I should do exactly as Jenny suggested, but I honestly believed it was beneath me. *Quick comeback, Lela. Think!* I said, "It would be so temporary... is that really fair to the grocery store? Or the clothing store?"

"That's not the point. The point is you're a snob. A job snob."

I looked at my watch, trying to avoid this line of questioning. "Oh, shit! I'm going to be late for house arrest! I gotta go right now!"

"How convenient." Jenny didn't move, but I gathered my papers and jumped up in a frantic rush.

I kissed her left cheek. "See ya next week at the Stitch and Bitch!"

"Call me," she yelled at my back as I bounded out the door.

<<<<<<<<<>>>>>>>>>

A job snob! How DARE she call me that!? I'm just a down-to-earth alcoholic trying to find my way. And I have a lot to offer! My talents are sure to be an amazing asset to ANY ad agency, right? As long as I realize it may take a while for my salary to reach the six-figure point, I'll be fine.

The right side of my brain argued with the left side, and I defended myself out loud. "It doesn't *matter* how long ago you earned those awards! They're still on the books. National superlatives don't go away."

The doubting side of my brain countered with a separate problem, which I answered curtly. "No! It doesn't *matter* how long it's been since you've been a copywriter! Advertising is advertising. The basic rules don't change."

Another pause, another defense.

"Someone of your caliber can't work for minimum wage. It's unhealthy and likely to throw you into a deep Bi-Polar depression. Nope, you can't do that."

You can prove your talent, Lela. It's there in the closet, waiting for you.

I didn't know why I'd avoided putting my portfolio together for so long, but on that frantic ride home, I decided to use my anger for a good cause. *Make that portfolio sing, Lela. Show 'em what you're worth.*

Night had fallen as I unlocked the door to my apartment, and I heard the strange, distant buzz-ring of my GPS box, checking the whereabouts of my house arrest ankle bracelet. I'd barely made it home in time.

Too close for comfort, Lela. That's all you need now, huh? To go back to jail for breaking probation. I said aloud, "Yeah, that would help you find a job, for sure. Then bagging groceries would sound pretty damn good."

<<<<<<<>>>>>>

THREE PICTURES
CHAPTER 2

I gave myself only an hour for self-pity, refusing to call Mom for comfort. *Besides, Mom has heard so much of your insanity that she's sick of it! Grow up, Lela!* And I'd become very protective of my parents and didn't want to worry them.

I took a deep breath and opened the storage closet off my bedroom. Once again, I spotted the box labeled "Lela's Portfolio" on the top shelf... and once again, I cursed the movers under my breath. *Why would they put such a heavy box on the top shelf!? I'll hurt myself getting it down; I can see it coming.*

I'd already hurt my back in that apartment, repainting the dining room after my ex broke in and spray-painted graffiti on my walls. His timing had been purposeful, too... more evidence of Stuart's determination to squash my spirit. I'd been in jail for thirteen days and came back to his "gift" of destruction and theft of my new place.

Quit thinking about that, Lela. As Jenny says, his actions can't determine yours. But my anxiety remained off the chart. The sonofabitch Stuart Weinstein continued to harass me, and every time he contacted me was like a punch in the gut.

Enough! No matter how much he wants to keep you down, you are worthy and strong, so get that portfolio and hold your head high!

I'd borrowed a step stool from Jenny for the specific purpose of getting that damn box from the closet shelf. It housed my credibility – a rich leather binder with clear sleeves for print samples, plus audio and videotapes of my best broadcast work.

Younger writers would have transferred things over to CDs, I knew, but Lela Fox was old-school by necessity. I didn't know how to upgrade, didn't know who could do it for me, nor did I have the money for such luxuries. Fingers crossed; I hoped a potential employer would appreciate quality work over presentation format.

Too many pieces crowded the portfolio; I knew that. Weeding it down would take some time. I wrote most of the stuff decades ago, and most had been designed by husband number two and master-creative Miller McKeown. The famous (*and* infamous) Augie Highfield directed almost all the TV and video.

Despite their faults, Miller and Augie were still some of the best talent in the Southeast. Those two names, along with my own, were the cream of the crop in the creative field back in the day.

Yeah, until your drinking brought you down... until your clients couldn't depend on you... until you beat your head against the wall and still couldn't come up with an idea.

Of course, nobody in the West Palm Beach area knew of my reputation, neither the good part or the bad part, but the contents of that box would prove my excellence; it *had* to. My future depended on it.

Balancing on the stool, I reached to tip the bottom of the box up from the shelf. *Oh, shit. It's too lightweight! What happened? Is there another portfolio box I haven't seen?* The box, literally, fell into my hands. I stepped down from the stool and carried it to the bed.

Shaking the box, I heard a rustling sound and no more. *Oh, hell! I think it's empty! How can that be?* Then I ripped the not-sticky-anymore tape and opened the flaps. In the bottom, one measly envelope labeled "Sorry for your loss." *What the hell?*

Inside the envelope, three pictures.

1.) The leather binder licked with flames, a layer of firewood beneath it

2.) The cassette tape and videotape; soon to melt on top of the binder

3.) Stuart Weinstein holding a lighter, an evil grin on his red face

My entire body froze in shock, the pictures fell through my fingers and onto the bed, face up. I stared at them, drilled my eyes into their detail. *How could Stuart do this? How did he know the worst possible thing to do to me? The cruelest way to hurt me? Now I have no future at all!*

14

My hand shook as I wiped the sweat from my forehead and upper lip; it had appeared though it was plenty cool inside. Somewhere deep inside, my mind cracked into another sphere, another realm. And as stupid as it sounds, I saw my life flash before my eyes: scenes from my career in advertising.

After envisioning my PR photo with the Best of Show award at the Southeast Region Addy award ceremony in Atlanta, I flashed to what I assumed was a premonition: a gray-haired me wearing a blue and yellow Walmart vest, struggling to put a plastic tricycle in a bag.

I couldn't process the thoughts at the speed they came to me, didn't realize I'd flopped onto the bed and cried a puddle of tears. But I vowed to stop the emotional rollercoaster that had left the station. *Get your shit together, Lela. Don't let yourself be immobilized! That would be the worst.*

Denial seemed to be a way to cope, or so my mind decided. *This simply isn't happening. It's a hallucination, a horrible dream.* Minutes passed before I could fathom the reality. *I'm doomed. Fuck you, Stuart. Fuck you very much.*

As if in a daze, I walked to the kitchen and opened the fridge, then drew a blank. *What was I looking for?* I looked in the pantry, hoping to give myself a clue, then figured it out. *I've come for a beer. Oh, hell! I NEED a beer, a hundred beers, a thousand! A fifth of vodka and a truckload of lime. And a gun.*

<<<<<<<<<>>>>>>>>>

I had to dial the number twice; my vision had blurred with tears. And Jenny couldn't understand me at first because my throat diameter was so small, my voice squeaking nothing but incoherent syllables.

She was livid when she heard the news, and more livid when I told her about my robot-walk to the fridge. "Don't you let that sonofabitch make you drink! *He's* the loser, not you! Let *him* drink... and rot in hell for all I care. But don't you *dare* let him win, Lela Fox! No way. Got it?"

"But Jenny! Now I can't get *any* advertising job! Something I've done all my life, and now I have nothing to show for it." My voice was flat, ethereal, matching my emotional numbness.

"I'll make you rephrase that, you know."

A whine. "Oh, stop! Don't do this to me tonight, please! Your little teaching tricks won't work this time. Without a portfolio, I have no job. No history despite a lifelong career–"

"You didn't do it all your life."

Shocked, I stopped. "True, but–"

"And why did you *stop* writing?" Jenny drew her words out and up in tone, like a patient first-grade teacher trying to lead her student to an understanding. It was her way of forcing me to answer logically and honestly.

"Yeah-yeah... because I drank my freelance business away."

"And before that?"

"I got mad and quit my job."

"And that's called..." The rise in her voice went off the scale.

"Dammit, Jenny! Wreckage of the past! But please, don't be so–"

"So *what?* Real? Practical?"

"So in-my-face!"

She laughed. "That's my *job*, Lela. Here's the truth: your problem is temporary."

"Burning my credibility is pretty damn permanent, Jenny!" Her nonchalance had fired me up again, brought my anger to the top of my pounding head.

"Make more credibility... a new portfolio!"

"Ha! Right. Create twenty years of award-winning work for make-believe clients? Get it all printed, produced, hire the models? You're crazy."

Jenny tried again. "Okay... maybe find an understanding employer."

"That's even *more* ridiculous! Can't you see the magnitude of–"

"Offer to start on a contract basis, to prove yourself. Just tell the truth and you may get the sympathy vote."

I stopped. *The sympathy vote? Could that work? The truth shall set you free?* Jenny continued with a string of possible fixes, all unrealistic in my mind.

Then she said, "Make a video... tongue in cheek, saying how un-friendly the divorce was, tell the truth but be creative about it. I mean..." She chuckled, "You two... you can't make that shit up. It's a soap opera!"

My heart was racing, my mind seeing possibilities. I closed my eyes, envisioning intro footage to a video. "It could *really* be a soap opera... 'As the Portfolio Turns.'"

Jenny hooted a laugh. "Perfect! I'll help you! I'll do whatever it takes."

16

"I could make it even funnier with cheap and cheesy production... on purpose, ya know?"

"Now you're talking! Be mega-creative! With no client to make changes that could ruin it. I know how you used to react to client changes."

Her voice continued in the background as I zoned out, reeling with ideas, kernels of hope popping like popcorn. "I think this just might work, Jen!"

"The creative Lela roars back to life!" After a pause, we both cracked up laughing. I laughed chock-full of creativity and confidence, and Jenny laughed, she said later, because I had so easily transformed from gloom to glee.

"Jenny, I can do it. I can!"

"And remember, the Sunday classifieds are coming. I wouldn't be at all surprised if a small agency needs a kickass copywriter. The boss is a woman..."

"A recently divorced woman..." My voice rose to a high ending, as Jenny's had.

"Who got screwed in the divorce..." Our laughter tinkled through the line.

"This will work! By being clever about the loss, I show more about what I can do than the portfolio ever could!"

"See, that sonofabitch can't keep you down."

"Hell no! I'm smarter than he is, Jenny. He's evil, but I'm smart."

"Absolutely. Get your ideas on paper, Ms. Writer. Do it now."

<<<<<<<<<>>>>>>>>

I worked until two in the morning, creating a script for a slap-your-knee-hilarious skit. To myself: "Tomorrow, I'll shop for props and make some calls. I need this done ASAP."

My prop-shopping list, carefully written on a blue pad, led me on adventures through Delray Beach and further into the depths of Boca Raton and West Palm. As I'd done in my hometown of Rockville when I produced commercials for a living, I created a little pouch for receipts. After the shoot, I'd return all the props left somewhat-intact, no matter how weird it was to return tiny purchases.

My shopping list:

    gold plastic wedding bands
    ugly wedding or prom dress
    false eyelashes, bigger the better
    ugly flower bouquet
    bandit face mask
    fake moustache (handlebar)
    men's black bow tie and weird hat – top hat?
    a joke lighter or fireplace matches, big!
    water hose
    yellow raincoat
    toy firefighter's helmet
    rope

Jenny would play the dastardly villain Stuart Weinstein and I'd be the naïve bride, batting her eyelashes and immersed in the sweet smell of the fake flowers. Our wedding... kiss the bride, blah, blah. Then he'd play cruel tricks along the way: throwing me over the threshold, rolling his eyes a lot, tripping me on a walk in the park, making fun of me behind my back.

Then, wiggling his eyebrows, he sets fire to a stack of paper and I run into the scene like a frantic maniac, dressed as a firefighter, to douse the fire.

In the end, the video goes to super-fast-speed as I chase him around the room, tie his hands to his feet, and stand with my foot on his back, raising my water hose in victory.

<<<<<<<>>>>>>

A FAX FOR A DEAF FOX
CHAPTER 3

I had an idea and about ten bucks. And a bushel-basket full of fear.

Email attachments weren't a thing yet; documents were printed and faxed, especially things like résumés and cover letters. The good news was fax machines had become affordable by 1999; cheap enough for home businesses.

And cheap enough for an unemployed writer in a shitload of debt.

I wanted one. A cheap, used one like you'd find in a pawn shop. But just the thought of a pawn shop made me shiver with Fear and Shame, and it would probably be even worse now that I was sober.

On that Friday, I held my breath, pumped out my chest, and walked into Boca Pawn as if I belonged there. My feelings of confidence lasted about five seconds, melting when the greasy-haired guy behind the counter looked at me and licked his lips. *Creep. Don't you dare come out here! Stay behind that damn counter.*

I resisted the urge to run, staying on task. With so much junk on the scarred floor, I zigged and zagged through the aisles until I found the business equipment section. Most of the machines were twenty years old and broken, but behind an old electric typewriter, I spied a fax machine. A tiny one. No bells or whistles, a missing paper tray, and a stretched out spiral phone cord. Perfect. And ten bucks. SOLD!

At the cash register, I avoided looking at the greasy-haired man, but he was determined to talk to me. At his second comment, I looked at him quizzically, pointed to my ears, then used both hands to "sign" a word in ASL that was not a word as far as I knew.

"Oh, you're deaf!" he said, loud enough to be heard in the next county. I nodded and repeated the "sign." The stupid ass kept talking but talked louder. At the end of the transaction, I ASL-signed something else and he SCREAMED, "Nice doing business with you!"

Idiot.

On the way home, I counted how much I'd save by faxing at home instead of going to the Fed-Ex store. It was a good purchase, another feather in Lela Fox's hat, according to a full-of-herself Lela Fox.

When I unlocked my apartment door, my GPS box was buzzing; I'd slid in on the last buzz/ring. *Cutting it too close again, girl. You're going to be busted if you don't be more careful.*

Even worse, Monday was my next probation officer check-in – ugh! And I'd have to tell the bitchy officer I was job hunting. Changes to my "out with permission" schedule were sure to come, and the thought of it turned my stomach.

I despised seeing that woman; she always asked if I'd gone within so many feet of Stuart Weinstein. It gave me the heebie-jeebies to be accused of doing the thing most opposite of my desires. And my complaints about Stuart contacting *me* didn't phase her. Once, I took a tape of his five messages for the month; she didn't give a damn. "I don't care what *he* does," she said, "My job is to keep *you* in line."

They just don't get it! I'm so innocent and so stuck.

Those appointments ruined my whole day; feeling misunderstood and powerless caused instant depression, like being a dysfunctional drunk all over again. I shivered with anger just entering the office and sitting with the losers who waited with me. I wanted to scream, "I don't belong here!" even knowing it would do no good.

"Six more weeks, Lela. You can do that, surely." I had to talk myself into keeping enough hope to survive the humiliation of house arrest. I knew my sobriety could never peak as long as I wore that damn thing on my ankle.

<<<<<<<<<>>>>>>>>>

Stuck at home for the afternoon, I called my friend Lola for a chat, knowing she was one of the few people who could take a call in the middle of the day, and the Lela/Lola friendship was still strong despite the distance between us. "Lola, you won't believe what he's done now."

"I guess I don't have to ask who." Her huffing sigh gave away her anger; she *despised* Stuart, forever loyal to me and our best-friend bond.

"Take that awful tone out of your voice, Lola. It's not healthy to hate somebody. AA says 'Hate only destroys the hater.'"

"So I'll be destroyed. The sonofabitch makes my blood boil. Is he still calling?"

My eyebrows raised in the pause. *Lie to her, Lela. It would officially be a white lie.* "No calls for at least a month. I guess he gave up."

"Good, and good riddance! But what did he do now, as you said?"

"He did it sometime in the past, but I found the pictures. He burned my portfolio."

"Portfolio?"

Of course Lola wouldn't understand; we'd worked together *after* my advertising career fizzled. "Reprints of all my newspaper ads, TV and radio spots... brochures and all that. A presentation binder of my work, and I can't get a job without it. Not in advertising, anyway."

"Oh, my God! He hits below the belt again, dammit! And for you, it's... I guess a totally new job search?"

"I'm planning something bizarre, Lola. Something that reminds me of how we used to be so silly together."

"Do tell."

"I'm making a video that both explains what happened and it's like a soap-opera thing. Really cheesy and..." I paused, searching for a word. "I guess 'absurd' is the best description. I'm nervous as hell about the production, afraid it will turn out to be more expensive than I planned. But I want a kickass ad-agency copywriter job. It's where my heart is."

"You gotta follow your heart, my friend."

"I just bought a fax machine for sending résumés, so I'm hot shit, and my heart agrees."

"Oh-la-la."

"But I gotta go. It's time to call Jenny for the fax test."

"Call me later."

"You know I will."

I set up the fax machine on my dresser and called Jenny at work; we'd set up the timing for her to stand by her office fax for the test. I wrote on a plain piece of paper: FOX IS A FAXIN' FOOL! Then, I pressed the green "send" button.

To confirm that it worked, she faxed me back: a smiley face and, in her perfect script: GO GET 'EM, TIGER!

How lucky I am to have Jenny! She even knows my Dad's famous encouraging words: Go get 'em, Tiger. Hell-yeah, I'll get 'em! And I may not let go!

<<<<<<<>>>>>>

GOLD COAST PRODUCTIONS
CHAPTER 4

On Sunday morning, I risked being caught out of the apartment by the GPS box but felt I had no choice. Moving fast, I threw on crappy clothes, dashed to 7-Eleven with four quarters I'd found under the sofa cushions, and opened the creaky newspaper box to grab a *Palm Beach Post*.

Though I'd lived in the area for nearly two years, I still marveled at how thick the Sunday newspaper was. It was 1991 – the hey-day for printed newspapers, but the *Post* was killer-big that day because it was "season," when all the snowbirds from Canada and New York caravanned to enjoy the happy sunshine of South Florida. The population almost doubled from September to May; traffic also doubled, and it was a pain to find a table at a decent restaurant.

It's not like you can afford a decent restaurant anyway, dumbass. You need a job before you can buy a burger at Mickey D's. I'd pledged to eat all existing food in my pantry before I bought a single thing at the grocery store, and I was down to the gross stuff.

I ate stale cereal with almost-spoiled milk and, between gags, opened the paper to the classified section, red Sharpie at the ready.

Of the dozen-or-so ad agencies offering jobs, five of them needed a writer. One was a tiny text-only ad, not worthy of my time, I decided. *That leaves four – only four!*

The target: female-owned agencies, knowing the bad-ex-husband video would be funnier to them. Two agencies made it obvious they were led by a woman, and another listed a female as the contact person. *Okay, that leaves three. One of these three agencies will be my next employer.*

I Googled background information and client lists for each of the agencies. The tone and attitude of the business showed on their websites, too, giving me a clue about what they were looking for. Armed with that information, I customized three résumés and cover letters and faxed everything around midnight, hoping to be first on the boss's desk.

Go get 'em, tiger!

<<<<<<<<<>>>>>>>>>

I saw the probation officer Monday morning, fighting the usual result of a dive into depression and rise to rage. I did it with a clenched jaw and repetition of a chant to myself *"She's just doing her job... she's just doing her job."* Another way to fight the fury was to chant the phrase *"Say moo... you're just one of the herd,"* something I learned in rehab to remind me I was no better and no worse than any other human being.

My snotty probation officer had to reference that I was jobless on sixty separate forms, it seemed. She said, "Your schedule remains the same, Ms. Fox, to allow full-time job hunting. Obviously, we're more concerned about your employment status than *you* are." *How dare you put me in the same category as your other clients!*

Each visit followed a format. After the discussion of my schedule, the probation officer would say, "You must control your urges for Mr. Stuart Marcus Weinstein every moment of every day," which pissed me off to the max. *Urges?! Shut the hell up, bitch.*

Next – I guess it was a requirement – she asked directly, "Have you come within fifty yards of Mr. Stuart Marcus Weinstein or attempted to contact him via mail, phone, fax, or any other electronic means?"

And every time, I answered with the same line: "I've told you! I want nothing to do with him, and *he's* harassing *me! He's* the one who should be sitting in this chair!"

Her reply was also a repeat from earlier sessions: "This is about *your* crimes, Ms. Fox. I don't care what *he's* doing. But you must resist your urges."

The dirtiness I felt during those meetings repeated each month, too. I left feeling like a cretin, and mad enough to fight a Grizzly bear.

But the good news was I was out of that nasty office before noon. At two o'clock, I'd meet Jenny at the production studio to film my video portfolio.

She had taken the afternoon off and would play Stuart's role; my sweet Jenny was fired up to do it, laughing about how she'd practiced evil facial expressions in the mirror.

She'd said, "I'll never be as mean as he is, but I've got a wicked eye and my eyebrows warmed up to wiggle. I'm ready!"

<<<<<<<<<>>>>>>>>>

I could only afford one hour of the studio's time. To keep rental time to a minimum, I used my well-honed producer skills to shoot an eight-minute video in that one hour. As it turned out, the cameraman was having fun with the silliness of the skit and extended the time, adding more shots and different angles without charging me.

Jenny said, "You're surprisingly good at this, Lela. I admit... I'm impressed."

"Seems like I have my head on straight these days. I'm getting better, don't you think?"

She thought I wouldn't see her rolling her eyes, I supposed. With a sigh, she said, "You have good days and bad days. But sometimes I think you're 100 percent sober-minded."

I gloated; that was a huge compliment. "I don't want to hear what you think on the other days, okay? I'm trying like hell, Jenny, but being unemployed has sent my anxiety through the roof."

We sat on a sofa at the edge of the warehouse-sized studio, waiting for the technician to confirm the tape was technically correct. He ran the footage on a real-time monitor, so I knew it would take at least an hour for him to finish.

While waiting, Jenny and I chatted non-stop, AA talk, mostly. Then the sound of a door opening in the back grabbed my attention. A man wearing a white shirt and khaki shorts stood with his arms crossed, talking to the technician, and looking oh-so-fine. "Penis alert, two o'clock!" I said to Jenny.

"Wow, nice! Those biceps..."

"And his thigh muscles are long and lean, like a swimmer. Yum, yum!"

Unaware of our lusty gazes, the man spoke to the tech like he was a friend. We couldn't hear him, but he pointed back and forth to the monitor and laughed. First, a chuckle that brought movement only to his mouth, then a more intense chuckle, then he threw his head back to laugh, and finally, an all-out guffaw.

He spoke to the tech again, who turned and pointed to Jenny and me on the sofa. The dreamboat man looked at us and... boom! Sizzle! My eyes locked with his, and I immediately begin to squirm.

Excitement mixed with the buzz of anxiety screaming between my ears. *But there's nothing to fear, Lela. He's just a good-looking guy, not an ogre! But – oh, my God – look at those eyes! Mesmerizing! And the muscles! And oh, shit! He's walking this way!*

Jenny whispered to me as he neared, spouting a series of warnings, including the bullshit about how I wasn't sober enough for a relationship, quoting my counselor from rehab who said my meat thermometer hadn't reached 165 degrees yet.

When the man neared the sitting area, I could smell his cologne, musky but not overly so. A manly scent that vibrated with confidence and sex appeal. His white teeth glowed as he spoke. "Hi. I'm Dawson Hupp. And you're Lela Fox, right?"

"Yes, I am." I paused, lost in his eyes for a beat, then remembered my manners. "And this is my friend Jenny Jenkins." Dawson barely glanced at Jenny, keeping his eyes drilled into mine. *Oh shit, could he be more flirty?* My blood pressure zoomed, reacting to my dual feelings: half fear and half exhilaration.

With a broad smile, he said, "I'm your video editor. Aren't we booked for tomorrow?"

"Yes. At two."

"It's going to be epic! You're obviously a talented writer, a great producer according to the tech, and I'm one helluva editor." I melted a bit when he flashed a sincerely proud smile. Not cocky or snooty; just the right amount of pride and fearlessness. *But why is he so fired up, so enthusiastic?*

"This video is hilarious, Lela. And well done. Did you really shoot all that in an hour?"

"A little over." My squeaky response shocked me; I didn't think I was that nervous.

Dawson (a name I found funny, like a soap opera star's swoon-worthy name), scratched his head and asked, "But what is the purpose? What kind of client would order that?"

"*I'm* the client, and it will be my portfolio. A substitute portfolio."

26

His exaggerated confused look made me laugh; obviously, he *meant* for me to laugh. Then he asked, "So some kind of handle-bar-moustache villain burned something of yours?"

"Ex-husband. He burned my portfolio."

His eyes became saucers. "What an asshole! That's a dagger through the heart *and* the end of a career. Some husband he was, huh?"

"If you only knew..." I shrugged, trying to act unaffected by such drama. "And this video is both the explanation and proof that I can be clever and creative with a non-existent budget."

"Damn-good idea. Ingenious, really." At last, his eyes turned to Jenny. "And I must say, you make a great villain. Love the eyebrows. Not many people can be so convincingly evil."

"I'll take that as a compliment, I guess," Jenny said. Her expression made it clear: she was also interested in the silver-tongued Dawson. Maybe Jenny had planned to take the lead, convinced that I wasn't ready, but I didn't intend to give up that easily. I wouldn't let her push me to the side, even with the fear building in my gut. There'd be no argument from Dawson's end, anyway; he made it obvious he was into *me*. Not Jenny.

His smile, a sideways grin accented by perfect dimples, sent a shiver down my spine. And what he said next caused even more fear... or was it intrigue?

His words: "I'd like to do something for you." I froze solid. That's when Jenny elbowed me again, surely a warning. Evidently, Dawson was no dummy and saw the writing on the wall. "No, no. I mean, uh, knowing you're unemployed and seeing how funny this video is, I figure you're a fun, creative girl. I can do you a *favor*."

Another elbow from Jenny. My response was tied to her displeasure, I guess, and to my now-piercing scream of anxiety between my ears. I warned, "Careful, Dawson."

He shook his head and put his hands up in mock defense. "Wait! No! It's not *that* kind of favor!" His innocence was genuine, it seemed, and after a beat, I laughed.

"Then tell me what kind of favor you mean, Dawson Hupp."

"Sorry, I guess I should've started with the simple offer: I'll do the editing free of charge if we can do it after hours."

After hours. House arrest. Not enough notice to change my schedule. Shit!

Instantly paranoid, I looked at the hem of my pants to make sure the damn ankle bracelet wasn't showing. It wasn't, but my embarrassment was. "Dawson, thanks for the offer. Unfortunately, I have to pass. I turn into a pumpkin at five o'clock."

"That's too bad."

Wait! What am I thinking? I have scheduled time off for a meeting with my sponsor on Wednesdays! I turned to Jenny. "Can we postpone our meeting this week so I can do the editing?"

"No," she replied, leveling a glare at me. I glared back.

Then I turned to Dawson and said in a tone full of smiles, "I can do it on Wednesday, around five." I heard Jenny huff in disbelief that I'd defied her.

"Wednesday it is! But let's make it 5:30."

"Deal!" *Yay, Lela! Go get 'em, tiger.*

Little did I know how much of that *Go get 'em* I'd need to get through that editing session.

<<<<<<<>>>>>>

REFRIED BEANS

CHAPTER 5

I arrived at Gold Coast Productions early and sat in the editing suite to wait for Dawson. The dim lighting and soft-jazz background music created an ambiance as romantic as it was mysterious. It reminded me of being in the editing suite with my Rockville video partner, Augie Highfield. The memory jarred me, feeling way too sleazy and slutty.

You and Augie sure made the editing suite a place for romance. But "raunchy romance" is a better word for it. Augie, my friend and my enemy, the one who liked me too much but treated me like shit.

I remembered the night we shared a fifth of tequila and streaked around the building at two AM. We came *this close* to sleeping together, but he was the one to put on the brakes. Couldn't cheat on his wife so easily, he'd said. The thought sent my Shame monitor into the red zone.

I'd tried to work through the Shame of my past sexual life with Jenny as my guide, but I just couldn't let it go. Maybe because my sluttiness was the polar opposite of what my mother expected of me. All around, my drunken behavior stood in stark contrast to my parents' morals, and I felt incredibly ashamed by it all.

As Jenny said, "This is getting old. Again, pleasing your parents isn't your primary goal in sobriety. You should be beyond that." But I wasn't "beyond it" at all. As ridiculous as it was, I wanted to be like my Mom – just as Goody-Two-Shoes, just as honest and pure. Bit I was far from it.

If I could only shake the horrible reality of my sexual past! It haunted me daily. Except for that subject, the stupid antics of my drinking days seemed so far away by that time... as if they happened in another epoch. But thinking of Augie had opened the can of continuing Shame; it churned in my gut like burning gasoline and turned into a torrent of self-hate.

So, waiting for Dawson, I formed a renewed sense of worthlessness and bombarded myself with negative thoughts to make sure I felt like shit. I *wanted* to feel the Shame, maybe, hoping it would stop him from beginning the seduction dance.

I knew from the other day that he liked me; he'd made it obvious. At first, it felt great, but now, it felt dirty. *Don't be what he wants! Be a loser! You're just a washed-up slut with questionable talent – how DARE you assume you're deserving of a man or a job or a day of peace!*

Tears came to my eyes, but I fought them, refusing to let my own bullshit interfere with the project at hand. Slowly, slowly... looking around at all the monitors and knobs and slider buttons, I relaxed.

Eventually, my eyes focused on Dawson's workstation. Like mine, the theme was funky and eccentric. Decorated like a tiny museum of the weird and twisted... stocked with silly kid's meal action figures, offbeat souvenirs (a rock with "Plymouth Rock" written in Sharpie), more visual puns... a full array of ridiculous objects. Like me, he'd probably amassed the collection over many years.

My favorite of his: a miniature can of Old El Paso refried beans, personified with arms, legs, and a long, thin neck. The can-man's round head sported googly eyes and curly black hair, his pipe-cleaner arms folded over a colorful strip of Mexican poncho fabric. I reached to touch it...

"Helloooo, Lela Fox! Come on dowwwn!" Dawson swept into the room and threw his briefcase on the client sofa, bouncing up the step to the studio space.

I smiled. "Hey there, Dawson! Just admiring your workspace. I surround myself with stupid shit, too."

"How dare you call my 'Museum of the Weird' stupid shit? Each piece is a masterpiece!"

"Funny."

"Especially funny today, my friend, because I have a special gift for you."

"You do? I think your editing magic will be gift enough."

He raised his index finger. "Just a sec," then he slid through a narrow door leading to a cluttered closet. I heard bumps and thumps, then an *ooooff* from Dawson.

Sixty seconds later, he tripped coming out of the closet but stayed on his feet, landing with a sly grin and his hands behind his back. "Creative juice!" he said, then presented what he'd hidden: a bottle of cold champagne and two flutes.

In a millisecond, my blood pressure shot through the roof. *Oh, no! Alcohol six feet from me! One-on-one and a celebration. What do I do? Dammit! No Lela, no-no-no. Don't drink it! Yes, somebody WILL know! YOU will know! But what do I say?*

I guess he saw my face fall. "You don't like champagne?"

My jaw froze, my mouth in a wide "O" and as dry as a desert. Words wouldn't come, only grunted syllables. *Come on, Lela! Say something! What do alcoholics say when someone offers them a drink? Oh, my God! Help! Jenny! Dude!*

Suddenly, my vision blurred. Dude appeared as if my mind had snapped to attention in a puff of clouds. And there he was: his jeans just as worn, his cigarette still perfectly half-smoked, but his eyes weren't smiling. In fact, he grimaced... saying no? *I swear he's telling me no! How can that be?* I tried to wish the vision away, catching the twinkle of Dude's eye as he disappeared from my mind. *Did Dude himself just tell me not to drink? Bullshit! My mind is tricking me big-time. Why did he even flash in my head? This is crazy.*

Dawson was saying my name, ending with a question mark. *But what do I say? Tell him my Higher Power told me not to drink champagne? Help! Somebody! Please help me! I haven't trained for this!*

I heard the end of Dawson's question, but the first few words came from inside a tunnel. I heard the end: "...but I hope this evening turns out to be special, so it's a *good* bottle, not my normal two-dollar brand."

Silence hung in the air like morning fog. Dawson's hopeful expression turned to one of confusion before I could find words. With a shaky voice, I said, "Thank you, Dawson, but I don't drink." Then my eyes rolled to the back of my head.

"Are you okay, Lela? You've turned white. What's going on?"

I tried to straighten up, focus on my bones. I saw my hands shake and sat on them so Dawson wouldn't see. "Yeah, I'm fine. But, uh, where is the ladies' room?"

Dawson raised both arms, the bottle in one hand and flutes in the other. "You don't look so good. Are you sick? Can I get you something?"

"Seriously, I'm fine. Just need to, uh, powder my nose, as they say."

No response, just a half-confused, half-pissed look. Obviously, I hadn't responded the way he'd expected.

I stood, pushing against the desk to steady myself. "Bathrooms off the lobby, right?"

His head rattled on his neck in gesturing yes, but his look was of utter confusion. I walked past him with weak legs and asked, "Do you have the footage cued up?"

"No... I thought we'd, uh, get to know each other first." A deflated Dawson Hupp squeaked his answer.

Somehow, I kept my shit together. "Well, Dawson, since I'm getting your services at no charge, I thought you'd want to keep it simple and quick." A long, five-second pause; evidently, he didn't plan to reply. I stared at him for a beat, then ducked and said, "I'll be back."

<<<<<<<<<<>>>>>>>>>>

The bathroom vanity was Italian tile, the recessed sinks a bright turquoise ceramic and a great contrast to my beige-ish burps of vomit. Luckily, blasts of hot water cleared the drain, but I stepped to the second sink to guzzle from the tap and splash my face with scoops of cold water.

The mirror showed a fragile child, mascara running in rivers to her chin, her lips swollen and slack. And the fragile child had wet her pants with the force of the purge.

What do I do, Dude? How can I go back in there and face him? A scared voice from an unknown source bellowed, "Run away!" I answered silently: *But I CAN'T run away. I can't!*

My imagination popped a sweaty Diet Coke bottle into view and brought a thin sense of calm. *Yeah, drink something else, something carbonated. Pretend a Diet Coke is what you wanted all along. Pretend you're a normal person who just doesn't drink. Isn't that what you want, anyway?*

I looked at myself from three angles. *Wash your face. Dry your pants. Get your shit together.* "Fetch yourself up sharply," *as Jenny would say. You're bigger than this, stronger than this. You're okay. You're okay.*

I repeated the phrase dozens of times, finally beginning the process of re-grouping my face and clothes. I knew I'd been away so long that Dawson would question me. *But you're the one in charge here, Lela, whether it's a favor or not. You came here to do a job. Something for your future. You have to be okay. You MUST! Find a way to fake it.*

I had a germ of an idea and enough lying experience to pull it off.

Go get 'em, tiger.

<<<<<<<<<>>>>>>>>

I stuck my head in the doorway before going in. "Is there a Diet Coke hiding around here somewhere?" My smile was meant to dazzle, and I thought I was doing a fine job.

"I'll get it for you. Come on up! You look better."

"I feel better."

Dawson's tentative smile inferred he wasn't so sure, but I didn't care; I'd pretend my ass off. *Focus on the project, Lela. Only the project.*

Dawson stepped past me. "One Diet Coke coming up. Is a bottle okay?"

"A bottle is exactly what I hoped for." I watched him leave and stepped up to the creative area and sat with a plop. There was no champagne bottle there, no flutes. I said to the can of refried beans, "See? Problem solved."

> This was the first of many times I was side by side with drinkers in early sobriety. It took a long time to feel comfortable with it, but anytime I felt tempted, I'd flash to a vision of the refried beans can for strength.
>
> In case you don't already know (duh), I'm a very visual person. Even after twenty years of sobriety, I use these conjured scenes to guide and calm me. My journal, still color-coordinated, includes many such drawings.
>
> When married to husband number four, I paid big bucks to a pen-and-ink artist for an original; it hangs above my desk to this day.
>
> You may have guessed; the artwork is the Refried Bean can, with watercolor washes of color. It helps me remember that taking a drink is still just a whim away, and something I must continue to fight.
>
> The true miracle is I don't think about taking a drink much these days, and for that, I am eternally grateful.

<<<<<<<>>>>>>

UNTIL THE FLASH
CHAPTER 6

I met him at the gate. "Hello-hello, Damon Toomey! How was your flight?"

"As uneventful as you want a flight to be!" he said, hugging me tightly after dropping a carry-on beside his Sasquatch feet. "My dear Lela! I'm so, SO happy to see you and your gorgeous sober face! A brand-new face!"

Surprised, I asked, "*New* face? I look different?"

"Like night and day. You don't look like a ghoul on downers anymore."

"If that's the only comparison, that's a pretty shitty compliment, Damon. I thought you'd be–"

My friend laughed and put his hands on my waist. "Calm down, babe. You look *fabulous*. Healthy. Clean. Happy. Your eyes are clear and bright, like you're re-focused and seeing a good thing."

A smile spread on my face. "It's true that my sober life is glorious. Not all a bed of roses, but happy. The worst part is that I'm still unemployed."

"That problem will solve itself in time." Damon's calming force on me hadn't changed. He was my best friend in many ways and had been for years. Our history was long; he'd been the one who stood up for me when I couldn't stand up for myself... when I was drinking a fifth a day and falling for Stuart Weinstein's bullshit.

Damon was my protector, but, unfortunately, just too nice of a guy to be my type in the boyfriend department.

He put his hand on the small of my back as we headed down the concourse toward the hub. "So are you sending out résumés right and left?"

"Yes! And I haven't told you yet! I have an interview on Tuesday. So you can be my coach this weekend, okay? Let me tell you how wonderful I am."

"You don't have to tell *me*. I'm already convinced of your wonderfulness. You still turn my crank, Lela Fox."

"And you're still a kickass good *friend*, Damon. F-R-I-E-N-D." I couldn't help but feel flattered that I "turned his crank," but he was barking up the wrong tree. He was like a big brother to me.

I looked at his profile as we walked. Damon's brown hair had softened in color a bit, and a few gray hairs gleamed within it. But his strong jaw and perfectly Georgian nose still created a nice-looking face. His body still showed a dedication to working out, too; he was fit and trim. All together, Damon created what any woman would call a prime specimen of a man. *He'll land a lady someday and find his place in paradise. Maybe I could fix him up with one of Jenny's friends.*

My thoughts broke my focus and I didn't hear his next comment. "Wait... what'd you say?"

"I said, the straight life suits you."

"Thanks, but... I'm boring now. Straight and boring."

Damon's goofy guffaw vibrated throughout the concourse. "I'm sure you're *far* from boring, my curly friend. And according to your e-mailed agenda, you won't let me be one bit bored this weekend."

"There's so much to do here! And so many people I want you to meet."

"I definitely want to meet the famous Jenny. Your guardian angel, it seems."

"No, Damon. *You* are my guardian angel. *She's* my life coach. Exactly what an AA sponsor should be."

He huffed, "*I* would've done the life-coach thing if I'd known how."

"It wasn't your job to get me sober! You were – and still are – my friend, Damon. And you don't judge me. That has helped more than you'll ever know."

"And I didn't drink with you, tried to steer you *away* from it, right?" Obviously, he was looking for confirmation of his prior helpfulness, and I accommodated him.

"Yep, you steered me away from the vodka, that's for sure." A chuckle. "Which is why I found you such a damn nuisance."

"Gee," Damon's lips twisted into a silly face, "Thanks."

I continued talking about how boringly stable I was, including the latest changes in my psych meds that seemed to take away even the smallest spikes in my mood. His comment cracked me up: "Better living through chemistry!"

We stopped at my car in the parking garage, and Damon froze. "You drive a white Jetta? What happened to the silver Nissan van?"

On the way to my place, I told Damon the story.

"The van was a lease, and I was waaaay over on mileage. So Stuart and his high moral standards replaced the odometer. I had to tell the truth, owning up to a fraud my ex committed."

"Oh, wow! And you're not in *jail?* How did you get away with *that?*"

I smiled. It was a bizarre story. "The Nissan guy didn't know how to handle it, he said, and just told me to leave, not worry about it." Damon gasped. "But I had to tell them because, as my sponsor said: 'Sober people are honest people.'"

"Wow! Do you know how *lucky* you are? I'd like to strangle that damn Stuart sonofabitch." He looked out the window, his jaw clenched. It bothered me that Damon seemed obsessed with hatred of Stuart. He may be right... maybe Stuart *was* "evil to the bone," but I'd learned to let my soon-to-be ex-husband's bullshit roll off my back. Anger got me nowhere.

As he looked around the interior of the Jetta, Damon said, "So how did you end up with a rattily piece of shit like this?" He pushed random spots on the dash and doors, trying to soften the sound of the rattles. His efforts didn't affect the noises at all. "What's up with these rattles? It's a nice car otherwise."

"Well, that's a whole 'nother story."

"I have time."

"Okay." *How do you summarize that stupid story?* "Because my son Bo got ketchup on the *other* car I was supposed to buy." Damon's confused look made me laugh. "Told ya, it's a long story."

Damon waited, then gestured for me to continue the story. "I discovered the Jetta's rattles on the way home from the dealership, but I couldn't take it back because I'd already pissed the saleslady off to the max. So I ended up with a shitty car. What can I say?"

"The trade-off is you didn't go to jail for fraud."

"Good trade. Dude was watching out for me."

"You mean *the* Dude? The Big Lebowski? Or *your* Dude?"

"Mine, for sure."

But Damon was still too focused on my ex. "That damn Stuart! What an asshole! And *all* the nastiness he's done to you! It makes me mad as hell! Is he still calling and bothering you?"

"A little." *Ha! No, a LOT.* But I stayed silent to keep Damon's anger at bay.

"Shit!"

So much for keeping him calm. Damon's anger is still off the chart. "Calm down... he doesn't know I got fired, or that I have a new car, or where my new job will be."

"The conniving bastard may track you to the ends of the earth!"

"Please, Damon. I don't need to hear that. And the best way to change the subject is... ta-da! Here we are!"

I pulled into the apartment complex, meeting another car on its way out. I saw a flash of the driver, wiry gray hair, glaring at me. *No, it can't be him! It's just that you were talking about him. Go away, Stuart!* Upset, I ran over the curb and we bounced down the boulevard for a while. "Sorry, I'm distracted, I guess."

Damon suspected nothing amiss. "It's me distracting you. And I'm the best-looking distraction of your sober life."

"Riiiight."

When we walked into my apartment, I spun around to show off my decorating skills. "Welcome to paradise. My sober place, furnished with side-of-the-road finds and the best of West Palm's second-hand shops."

He smiled. "Nice place, baby. But I see some of your old stuff in here."

"Just what I could salvage. My parents took a U-Haul to Stuart's house to get what the sonofabitch would let them have. They went there just after they dropped me off at rehab."

I cocked my hip, remembering a fact I seldom told others. "And you know what – this pisses me off the most of *anything* he's done: Stuart called my mother a word even *I* don't say. The C-word."

"A cunt?"

"Yes!"

"Oh, I bet your dad went apeshit!"

"Mom said she held him in place with a choke-hold on his belt loop, whispering how much worse it would be if he beat the snot out of the sonofabitch."

"I wish *I'd* been there to kick his ass," Damon growled, literally, and his face reddened. His reaction wasn't much different from that of others who loved me.

"Damon, try to back down on your anger, okay? If I allow myself to get that mad, or think of either revenge or self-pity, I risk my sobriety. So I shrug and chant what my sponsor says. 'This, too, shall pass.'"

"Yeah, but it may pass like a kidney stone." I cracked up laughing; we both did. "You're one strong badass, Lela Fox."

"I take that as a compliment, Damon Toomey." Mutual nods ended the topic, so I opened another.

"Tonight's activity: the dueling piano bar! Show starts at seven."

"I saw the venue's website. It sounds like so much fun! It's a new thing, you say?"

"New for me! Jenny recommended it, but with a warning."

"What kind of warning?"

"They serve alcohol, of course, but toward the end of the night, some people get crazy-drunk. Honestly, I'm not sure I can handle that part. And if not, we can just leave early, if that's okay."

"Of *course* that's okay! If you're not comfortable, just say the word."

I told him about the only other time I'd been around alcohol – in the editing suite with Dawson – and cried while telling the story. Damon's gentle, comforting touch moved me. Tears still brimming, I asked, "Why can't I just be a normal person who doesn't drink? People think I'm weird. And boring. I can't party like I used to and just go sans vodka. It's not the same."

Damon ooh'ed and aah'ed in soothing me. "First, you don't *know* what other people think. You don't *know* they think you're weird and boring. Just stick your toe in the social waters a bit at a time."

"Yeah, maybe." I sighed, ready to stop the drama-talk. "So get settled, and I'll make us a sandwich, with a side of your favorite Cheetos, my friend!"

"A gracious host... thanks."

<<<<<<<<<>>>>>>>>>

Damon and I began the night when he caught the joke of the venue's name; I hadn't said it out loud and fast, but Damon caught it instantly. We were on our way to Hugh Jorgun's Piano Bar.

We arrived early; the stagehands were busy, the performers absent. Two occupied tables spilled into three, and, as we found out later, seated the pianists and their wives and friends. Their rowdy antics and loud voices served as entertainment as we shared a plate of nachos.

The show began at the end of my first Diet Coke. Two men took the stage, wearing glittered red, white, and blue tuxedos and Alice-in-Wonderland-sized top hats. They flipped the tails of their coats backward with flair and sat at the pianos placed head-to-head.

They started with a simultaneous and exaggerated deep breath, then began ferocious playing loud and hard. The song: a rowdy *Great Balls of Fire*. They changed the lyrics here and there, forming a side-splitting performance for a full-hour set. I laughed my ass off, loving every minute.

We both hooted with laughter through such lively songs of Bon Jovi's *Living on a Prayer* and Garth Brooks' *Friends in Low Places*. Their rendition of Queen's *Bohemian Rhapsody* sent us to the moon, and I knew more of the words than Damon did.

As the night progressed, we elbowed each other when the pianists called for audience participation. He giggled and pushed me, "Go on up, Lela! It'll be fun!"

"No way I was going up there!" I answered. But my reluctance to be the center of attention puzzled me, too. The drunk Lela would have been first-up and loving it. When I shared my puzzlement with Damon, he said, "I like you better this way. Let the stupid people be stupid. Because, thank God, you're not stupid anymore."

Hmm. Interesting words. So "drunk" becomes "stupid" for me.

People were drinking; I noted exactly how many margaritas the women at a neighboring table downed and spied a mousy brunette with a liter of wine hidden in a bladder bag with a spigot. Squirming in my seat, I felt uncomfortable watching them get bombed and gave Damon a play-by-play as the servers brought drinks to the tables.

It was like I'd just quit smoking and forced to watch people smoke as if it was no big deal. *How DARE they?*

The second set was rowdier, and the bar crowded with over a hundred revelers. It seemed they got drunker and drunker by the minute.

I saw a woman howling like a wolf. Just like I used to do.

I saw a woman fall in the aisle. Just like I used to do.

I saw a woman making out with a man, standing between his legs as he sat on a barstool. In public. Just like I used to do.

I heard a drunk woman laughing ten times louder than the crowd. She was drunk and sloppy. Just like I used to be.

In the bathroom, I saw a falling-down-drunk woman sobbing, mascara pouring down her face, wailing about the way some guy "out there" had treated her. "He said I was too drunk to kiss," she howled. It was way too familiar.

Back at the table, I told Damon about the woman in the bathroom and the dirty feeling it brought to me. "This is the way *I* used to act, and it turns my stomach. Somewhere between sad and gross." I felt clammy, my skin tingling as if wrapped by porcupine quills.

Damon stood, ready to leave if that's what I decided. "Are you ready to go? You know it's cool, right?"

Do I let drunk people determine my actions? Our table is off to the side of the worse drunks; we're a bit insulated. I'll be damned if they can get the best of me! My answer: "Not ready yet."

But the scene got exponentially worse over the next half-hour. Third up, the pianists' audience-participation victim onstage proudly flashed her tits. The crowd went wild, and a flurry of bras flew in the air. That's when I looked at the ceiling; it was covered with bras, like 3D wallpaper.

The girl who flashed her tits turned to shake her ass at the crowd and I saw myself in a former life. Disgusted, feeling dirty and slutty, I croaked, "Let's get the hell out of here."

> **Being around calm people sipping wine is one thing... being in a crowd of drunk assholes is another. It wasn't long before my temptations disappeared, though. In fact, less than a year after this shaky incident, I felt comfortable going to a bar where 99 percent of the people were drinking. It's not for me to judge.**
>
> **But drunk people still disgust me; there's not one bit of "funny" in it. In fact, I worry about the drunks, concerned they may have this dastardly disease and not know it yet. And I wonder what problems they're running from.**
>
> **As the Big Book says, there's no reason to avoid "drinking establishments" if we have a good enough reason to be there, but I**

41

can't advise a newly sober person to venture into such places. Not even to a piano bar with a funny name for the purpose of a few laughs.

Mostly, I wonder how the performers feel about such sloppy people who do the same stupid shit night after night. To have a job entertaining drunks is like a recovering alcoholic being a bartender with a generous pour. Not for me, thank you very much.

I'll just keep writing for those outside of the fray.

<<<<<<<>>>>>>>

JENNY KNOWS BEST
CHAPTER 7

We met at a McDonald's near Pompano Beach, about fifteen miles south of my place. So excited for the two to meet, I proudly said, "Damon, I present super-sponsor Jenny Jenkins, my hero and savior!"

Damon reached for a handshake, but Jenny playfully smacked his hand away. "Screw that! I'm a hugger," then she reached to capture Damon's tall shoulders. Even with the height difference, Jenny had mastered the sideways hug, keeping her ample breasts away from Damon's body. She'd taught me that AA-hug trick, too.

Damon's voice took a gentlemanly turn, smooth enough to spread on toast. "I'm thrilled to meet you, Jenny! I've heard so much about you already. You're helping my girl, and that means the world to me. Your quotes, the ones she quotes to me – pure gold."

"Nah. I speak fluent bullshit."

"Sounds like magical sprinkles of wisdom – at least that what Lela says."

Touched, it seemed, Jenny wrinkled her cute little nose at me, then batted her eyes at Damon. "I've heard just as much about you, probably. But today I stand in as Lela's official judge of character. She's sober, but not so smart yet."

I laughed nervously. Jenny's so-called joke wasn't so funny to me; it sounded more like an insult and a threat to discredit me. Still, I laughed with the two of them, going with the flow.

When Damon turned toward me, Jenny pushed up her rimless glasses and scanned him top-to-bottom. Glancing sideways, she saw me watching her. I smiled, but she scowled in return. My brow furrowed in confusion, wondering what the hell could be wrong with my sponsor. *She disapproves before she even talks to him? She's made a judgement about him already? Why? How?*

My anxiety meter shot into the red. Typically, Jenny approached everything with acceptance and openness, maybe *too much* openness. So the scowl in response to meeting my friend scared me. It's not the way she rolled, in my experience.

As we chatted over burgers, Jenny was far from her usual chirpy self. Her bushy hair tied back in a knot at her neck exaggerated the severity of her attitude, and her tone was sharp... bitchy and terse. *What's going on, Jenny? Why are you treating my Damon like he's an enemy?*

Speaking as if from a throne on high, Jenny questioned Damon about his practically non-existent drinking habits. His answer: "I am a purveyor of dark ale, testing the brew of the month at my favorite pub on the first day it's poured. And that's it – one beer a month," he said laughingly. "But after I realized Lela had a problem, I stopped drinking even that one beer in front of her."

He winked at me, then turned back to Jenny. "She's important to me. Important to the *world*, in my book."

Jenny eyed him with hard, cold eyes. "Are you in love with her?"

Afraid he would answer honestly, I jumped from my seat, banging my thighs on the bottom of the table. "Jenny! Don't ask that! How *he* feels is none of your business."

Her glance at me spoke volumes; It was as if she said, *"I know what I'm doing and have a right to ask."* I snapped my mouth shut and sat back in the booth, pouting.

Damon hadn't answered Jenny's question, I noticed. Maybe he felt something bizarre coming down from Jenny's soapbox.

He was right.

Jenny laced her fingers together, elbows on the table, then she spoke to Damon as if he was a child. "Damon, I've advised Lela against relationships."

He answered immediately. "No problem. I agree, actually. It's too early in her sobriety to–"

Jenny ignored his comment, continuing. "And today I'll add that she must also avoid *unrequited* relationships. You love her. It's written all over your face."

Silence. Any comment from me would hurt somebody's feelings or push Damon and me further into the "children being scolded" box. My friend silently stared at Jenny with a surprised expression. It's like he couldn't figure out if Jenny was well-meaning or controlling.

And I wondered the same.

She rarely gave me orders, but this was a direct command. *Has she flipped on some kind of bitch switch? She's trying to run Damon off! Why? Why is she standing in as my judge?*

As the silence dripped with tension, I felt I must explain and spoke slowly. "Jenny, you don't understand the relationship I have with Damon. And while you know I love *you* – and almost always do what you say – this one is out of your wheelhouse. I've known Damon for ten years!"

"*Twelve* years, actually," Damon dared to speak from the sideline.

I ignored him, feeling bolder and drilling my eyes into Jenny's to emphasize my stance. "There is history and mutual respect here. He's a *good man* and good for *me*. You can't say one negative thing about Damon *or* our friendship because you'd be flat out wrong!"

Jenny rolled her eyes and shrugged, then spoke to the ceiling, "She's just a crazy baby, God, and a stubborn one. She pretends to listen, but she argues instead."

My temper rose. "Jenny! What the hell?! I know what I'm talking about and you're being completely close-minded! You say there are no 'musts' in this program, but you've said 'must' twice!"

Silence again. I'd never seen Damon eat French fries so fast. His head was down, but I saw his face, red as hell. That left Jenny and me to stare at each other with vibrating intensity. As if daring the other to make a move.

I squenched up my nose and mouth, making a snotty-kid face, letting it speak for my feelings. Inside, my anger built like a volcano. *Why has this woman suddenly become a bitch? She's overstepped her bounds... trying to control me. To hell with that!*

"Jenny, is this on purpose? Like some kind of conquest for you?"

"I know what I'm doing, you little nit-wit," she said. I gasped. *Name-calling? What is she DOING?* "Lela, you're not ready for even a friendly relationship with someone who is so obviously in love with you. Especially one who drinks beer!"

"*One* beer! And we've always just been *friends!* You're waaaay wrong, Jenny. About *all* of this." When she didn't answer, I continued. "And you're acting like a tyrant or something! Trying to *control* me. To hell with that shit!"

I glanced at Damon. His face had turned white, and he sat on his hands; my friend had never been good at hiding anxiety. I tried to ease it. "Damon, I'm sorry you have to hear this. Emotions run high when I'm with Jenny, no matter how much of her bullshit I believe. But this... this is..." I didn't have the words and blew a huff of air to show my frustration. "I'll just say she's *all* wrong about this. Wrong about you. And wrong about us."

Damon wiped the ketchup from his lips with a crumpled napkin and spoke in staccato syllables, looking directly into my now-teary eyes. "I'll do what Jenny says is best."

My voice was instantly at a fever pitch. "No! You *won't!*"

Jenny's eyes filled with fire in the flash of a second. Her tiny hands, usually so perfectly manicured and soft, seemed like claws as she shook an index finger at me. "Lela Fox, listen to me! Everything about your life has changed, and everything about your past has to *stay* in the past, Damon included."

"Bullshit!" I screamed; heads turned. I didn't care one bit. Not lowering my voice, I continued, "Damon stays. He's a positive for me. I can't believe you're being such a–"

Jenny's arms extended, palms up. "Whoa, whoa, whoa! What a train wreck we have here!"

I thought Jenny was backing down and trying to keep things calm, but I was wrong. Over the next sixty seconds, she sneered at Damon, shooting barbs of sarcasm and borderline-insults. Each time I objected, she barked at me, pointing out how little I knew about life, and how "bat-shit-crazy" newcomers were. Once, she said that nobody cared what I thought.

I couldn't believe what I was hearing. *What is wrong with Jenny?*

My tears began, first stinging my eyes, then flowing in rivers down my cheeks as confused thoughts churned in my gut.

Maybe she's right. No! She's not! But what do I do? I can't just tell her to go to hell, can I? She's my sponsor! My savior! But she's wrong about Damon and has suddenly turned on me. Oh, Dude! What do I do? She's on some kind of bender to keep Damon away and keep me feeling small.

Interrupting my thoughts, Jenny leveled her eyes at me and sneered. "Lela, it's Damon, or me. Your choice."

My jaw dropped. "Whaaat? No! You can't do this! You're wrong! And sponsors aren't supposed to–"

"But I know best. You've said it a hundred times."

"Not in *this* case! Saliva was flying; I was on a roll, my lips frothy with anger. "Not only that, you have no right to speak to Damon *or me* in such a condescending tone. And you don't give me orders, either, because you're not my damn boss!"

The only sound was my heavy breathing. Jenny looked at her burger, rolled her eyes, and spoke in a voice full of venom. "Right, because you don't *have* a boss, Ms. Unemployed Writer."

If I'd excused her earlier comments, the acceptance stopped there. I knew she meant to hurt me with that final line. Purposely hurt me. *What kind of sponsorship is THAT?*

I looked deep into her eyes and saw hate. *Hate! What the hell?!* I wailed, "Jenny, what's *wrong* with you?"

Her flat and emotionless words stung me again. "I should ask you the same."

Nostrils flared, I shot fire from my eyes, drilling into Jenny's used-to-be-kind brown eyes. Without looking away, I said. "Damon, we're going," and pushed my hip against his to nudge him out of the booth seat. Poor Damon didn't say a word, just stood aside to let me lead the way.

I stomped out of that cursed McDonald's and never saw Jenny Jenkins again.

> Until that moment, I believed Jenny had my back no matter what, wanted only the best for me, and glowed in 100 percent perfection. My basis: the typical, and perhaps necessary, blind trust of an AA newcomer.
>
> I'd never questioned her motivation in trying to help. But it was as if she told Damon to step away because she was jealous of him. A power-play with me as the plaything. As my anger ebbed, the pain came forward, crushing my soul. Jenny had betrayed me.
>
> I would soon find out why Jenny turned on me – she was drunk. She'd been drinking for two months. Yet she'd continued our weekly

study sessions and daily phone calls, where she wove a tapestry of AA wisdom.

My heart hurt as I struggled to comprehend it all. I didn't yet understand the nature of alcoholics: the character defects that flourish under our skin no matter how many chips are in our pockets.

And to show how little I knew about the program, I wondered how Jenny could have kept her standing in "sponsor school" when she could turn into a monster so quickly. I thought sponsor requirements existed. Perhaps they should exist.

Losing Jenny was my first bout of grief in sobriety. Somehow, I avoided the bitterness many would have felt. I can only thank Dude for keeping me on track.

Still dedicated, I studied the Big Book on my own, depending on Lela Fox to keep Lela Fox sober. Maybe that's why there's much more to the story of my recovery.

The evening of Jenny's meltdown, Damon flew back to Rockville. For the next several weeks, he called more often than his usual thrice a week and spoke more gooey-lovey language than usual, too.

I didn't fuss at him for being too nice as I usually did; I didn't even argue when he said he was worried about me. Because I was worried about me, too.

<<<<<<<>>>>>>

ELLIE CHERRY & ASSOCIATES
CHAPTER 8

"Burned it?!" Her enormous green eyes widened to the size of saucers.

"Yes. In a fireplace, then sent me pictures of it in flames. Nice guy, huh?"

I explained my dilemma to Ellie Cherry, owner of a trendy and growing ad agency in North Palm Beach. A New York transplant with a high-pitched nasal accent to prove it, she dressed like a modern version of a vintage Hollywood actress, her red hair coiffed just-so and an embroidered metallic jacket with an asymmetrical collar.

I guessed her to be about my age chronologically, but much younger and more famous in her swelled head. Yes, Ellie Cherry was a class-A bitch; I knew it at first glance. She reeked of pompousness and attitude.

She huffed, "Your over-formatted résumé doesn't show your aptitude for this position, Ms. Fox. Are you seriously here without a portfolio and expecting a job?" Her nose was high in the air; I nearly laughed out loud at the booger I saw cradled within her nostril hairs.

"No worries, Ms. Cherry. I have another way to present my abilities. A *better* way, actually."

Without taking her eyes off me, she raised a stick of Wrigley's gum to her tongue, folding it perfectly in thirds as they do in commercials. Neon-white teeth bit into the gum, and the chomping began, sending my anxiety two notches higher.

My hands shook as I cued up the tape on her AV cart, my voice broke as I explained my roles in the writing and production of the video that served as my portfolio. Ready to press PLAY, I peered at Ellie and her silent assistant, an older woman wearing a matronly dress and sensible shoes. "Are you ready?"

They both nodded, and I held my breath. Then I heard a squeal, the sound of a small animal, I thought.

Ellie shrieked nearly as high as the maybe-animal and twice as loud, adding an undertone of goo-goo baby talk. "Oooh! My sweet little Isabella is awake!" Then she turned her back to me, clucking like a mother hen as she leaned toward the floor.

What the hell? A damn CAT in her office?! Now, of all times?! Please tell me no. I need your attention, Ms. Bitch!

But it wasn't a cat. It was a teacup poodle, hardly the size of Ellie's palm. The boss scampered from behind her desk to set the pup on a pee-pad that appeared the size of a football field in comparison. Then she called the matronly assistant for help, sternly giving instructions, "Put Izzy in the *exact* center of the pad and make grunting sounds."

Ellie looked at me and gestured to the dog; I knew I had to pretend to love the pup despite the timing and stupidity of it all. Professionalism had gone out of the window.

But thinking the quickest way to her heart may be through her dog, I put on my best dog-mommy act. We spent at least ten minutes ooh'ing and aah'ing over the damn pup, and she'd warmed to me a bit, it seemed. "Only good people are dog lovers, Lela. So you must be a fantastic person."

"I'd like to think so."

"And, I'll have you know, only fantastic people work here. No jailbirds, tattooed cretins, or prima donnas allowed." I froze, now wondering if my GPS anklet had shown under my pants as I'd crawled on the floor with the puppy. Evidently, she saw my face turn pale and asked, "Is there something wrong?"

"Uh, no. Not at all. But I'd like to show you my portfolio at some point." *Oops, that sounded too snooty. Then again, she's cornered the market on snoot, so what the hell?*

"I suppose we *should* get back to business. But you see how cute distractions can be around here, huh?" Her smile faded as she straightened her jacket and returned to bitch stance. The softening of her character during puppy play disappeared as fast as it had appeared.

The matronly assistant spoke from the floor, "Let me get Izzy sleepy-sleepy on the pillow again, and then I'll be ready, too."

"Thank you, Prudence."

Prudence? Her name blew my mind, so weird and icky. *She's not even British! Prudence! The Matron-Servant of Ellie Cherry?*

Again perched on her chair at her boss's knee, Prudence announced, "She urinated but did not defecate, Ellie. I'll mark it on the log." *A dog log?! How anal she must be!* Then I chuckled at the pun I'd created. *An anal poop schedule! Ha!*

In a rush, Prudence pulled an extra-large bottle of Purell hand sanitizer from her bag, pumping three squirts on her palm and rubbing her hands together vigorously, like a cartoon character in double-time. The speed of her hands and "ewwww" expression made the scene even funnier to me, and I fought the urge to laugh out loud. But I guess my face gave it away.

"Is something funny, Ms. Fox?" Ellie Cherry asked.

Shit. Busted. "Actually, yes. Something is cued up and ready to be *very* funny. My portfolio video. Are you ready to see it?" *Good save, Lela.*

The two women sat back to watch, and, finally, I pressed PLAY. The first scene showed Jenny's hand and mine, wearing the gold-plastic wedding bands. Dawson had overlaid silver sparkles in the editing phase, and the Halleluiah chorus soundtrack helped set the stage. For the opening title and credits, I'd chosen soap-opera-style music from the 60's – dramatic and crackly.

I watched my interviewers' faces morph from boredom, to smiles, to chuckles. The final scene brought a thunderous laugh from Ellie but nothing from Prudence.

Oh, no. The ending isn't good enough! I've screwed up. This isn't going to work and, what the hell, why did I ever think it would? I'm such an idiot. Idiot, Lela! And now I look like a fool. How can I get a job with this piece of shit three-minute flop?

Hiding my shame, I turned to press EJECT and removed the videotape, not daring to look at my judges. I slid the tape back into my missed-a-dusty-spot briefcase and kept my head down.

After a pause, Ellie said, "Interesting approach, Ms. Fox. I admire your efforts." I looked up to see her studious expression and an unmoving, unreadable Prudence. *Do I have to impress Prudence, too, or is she more like a secretary?* I glanced at her growing sneer, then dared to look back at Ellie. To my surprise, she was smiling.

"A very creative solution. Shows ingenuity, resourcefulness. The script is great. The production is perfectly tacky... I don't wonder if that was an accident." *Is she saying she liked it? These are compliments? So I'm not dead in the water after all?*

Ellie's smile broadened, and I felt 400 pounds of pressure fall to the floor. *Maybe it worked!*

Ellie continued, "Maybe you haven't been quizzed on this issue, but it's the most important to me." I nodded, at full attention. "What was the production budget on the video?"

I froze. *Do you know the number, Lela?* "Hold on, let me do a bit of math. As you might guess, that's not my specialty." I grabbed a pad from my briefcase and scribbled some numbers, but my mind took a curve on the simple addition. A huff of frustration, too loud.

"An estimate will do, Ms. Fox. Don't argue with pennies."

I chuckled, "Sometimes pennies argue back, so I pay attention." I tried the arithmetic again and quickly checked my answer. "The total is $112.68 plus travel expenses."

Those green eyes widened again. "You did all that for 112 chachkies?"

"If that's dollars, then yes."

"That requires talent, Ms. Fox... almost as much as the writing and production planning. I'm impressed."

"I've never been applauded for being cheap, Ms. Cherry," I laughed, "but thank you."

"It shows what you can do with a tiny budget. And I've never been able to test that in an interview."

"Of course, that budget is with no field producer or prop-meister. I did it all myself."

"On what time frame?"

I shrugged, giving it my best guess. "A week. Eight calendar days."

"Excellent." She spun around in her chair, stopping with her back to me. *Quit messing with the dog, dammit! Talk to me! My future is on the line here!* Just as suddenly, she spun the rest of the way around to face me. "Print ads? E-mail blasts? Direct mailings?"

I could only assume she was asking about my experience in those media. "Eight years as a direct-mail specialist. And until the last decade of my career, print ads were close to ninety percent of my work."

Prudence the Matron scribbled away; I noticed it was shorthand – real, 1950s style secretary shorthand. *Who does that any more? This scene is such a weird mix of old and new.*

"Okay, the key question is…" Silence ticked for three seconds, maybe four, maybe a year. "Because I don't have examples of your print writing, would you be willing to start on a contract basis? Say, a two-month contract? Then if all goes well, we will negotiate a salary with the appropriate benefits. Would that be acceptable?"

Her words sent me to the moon. I wanted to turn flips across her fancy tile floor, jump through the hoop of her massive display of award trophies, and land on the puppy pad. *Log THAT, dear Prudence!* A series of tingles to my extremities brought the warmth of relief. *Hell-yeah that would be acceptable!*

Ellie cocked her head, obviously watching the power of my emotions as they washed over me, and a smile came to her face. "You're easy to read, Ms. Fox."

"I am?"

"Yes, you are. I take it as a 'yes.' Am I correct?"

"You are! Thank you! And very much!" *Whoa, Lela. Be cool. Play hard to get.* I cleared my throat, reeling myself back in. With the straightest, most professional tone I could muster, I said, "I'll consider the offer carefully, but I need a few more details, of course."

"Certainly." She turned to Prudence, who sat at-the-ready, her pen poised. "Prudence, look up Laura Gilmer's contract. Use that form but double the numbers for Ms. Fox. The two of us will finish up in the meantime."

Holy shit! Double the numbers! I just got a job offer! I'm not going bankrupt after all! But play hard-ball, Lela. Tell her there's competition, lie and say you have more interviews coming up. Yeah, three this week.

As my heart raced, Prudence and her sensible shoes left Ellie Cherry's office. I watched the door slowly close, somehow feeling it was closing on me. I furrowed my brow, wondering why the sense of doom had suddenly overtaken me. After all, it was an offer when I doubted having another for comparison.

Ellie visibly relaxed, and she sighed. "Thanks to Prudence, the office is run like a machine. They call her Führer Prudence, in fact. She's the office manager, work-flow manager, my personal assistant, Izzy's caretaker, and slave master to six underlings she calls the Pru-ettes. Nothing falls through the cracks at Ellie Cherry and Associates."

"Sounds great," I said, but I didn't mean a word of it. *Just give me a keyboard and creative freedom. The rest will fall into place.*

Ellie rubbed her two index fingers together, staring into space. "All the efficiency can drive you crazy, to be honest. But anytime you need a break from the pressure, come and play with Miss Isabella. I may have to auction time slots with her. I'm hoping she'll lighten this place up."

It shocked me to hear she felt her own company was "too efficient" but felt eased by her change in attitude with Prudence out of the picture. I asked, "Can I get another kiss from the pup?"

"Let's play!" She grinned like a toddler; her entire face involved in the fun.

On my knees, I played with the dog's tiny paws and bopped her nose as she bit my fingers with the spikes of tiny puppy teeth. In those two minutes, the dog stole my heart. *Aha! And this is the way to get in Ellie Cherry's good graces. Win-win.*

Prudence entered and sucked all the air out of the room. I stood, smoothing the wrinkles from my dressiest black pants as I saw Ellie's eyes fall to my ankles. *Oh, shit.*

I dashed to my chair, sitting quickly to pull the hem of my pants over the GPS anklet. *Oh, no. She saw it. Will she know what it is? Do non-criminals know what it means? Oh, God, please! Don't let her say anything. Dude! Help!*

With one eyebrow cocked, she watched me carefully, then oh-so-slowly pushed the contract Prudence had provided toward me. I reached to grab it, resisting the urge to snatch it and run. "Review this and let me know if you will sign. I have other people waiting for an answer as well, so please call me by Thursday."

"Oh, but I have other interviews scheduled this week–"

"By Thursday. Noon." The bitchy-Yankee-snob persona had returned with a vengeance, and I felt the sting of being reprimanded.

It's because she saw the damn ankle thing. Dammit! I'm doomed. But wouldn't it be illegal to discriminate because of it? Would it? Gotta research that. As if I'll have time. Now or never. But you have the offer. Get the hell out of here.

I didn't look at the handwritten numbers in the blank spots, just asked if it was negotiable. I'd snapped back to super-professional to match her change.

"No. Take it or leave it."

Our handshake was firm. "I'll call you on Thursday. Before noon."

On the way home, tears of relief flowing and my hands shaking with leftover nerves, I realized that Ellie Cherry might have turned cold after seeing my anklet, but she hadn't rescinded the offer. It was still valid, and that was all that mattered.

I swerved a little on I-95 South to retrieve the contract from my briefcase and scan the details. I hit my brakes when I read the first fill-in-the-blank entry. "Holy shit! Fifty bucks an hour! I don't care how squeaky-clean Prudence is or how bitchy Ellie Cherry can be. This job is MINE!"

The start date: 11/11... *what day is that? Monday. November 11. And ending 1/11. Cool, I'm all in. Way to go, Lela Fox!*

I set the contract aside and noticed the time. The clock read 11:11. *Cool. Elevens. It's meant to be.*

I took the Delray Beach exit and headed east to the POWERLESS club. *Better hit the noon meeting before you get too proud of yourself. And maybe find a new sponsor. Quit putting it off, Lela. You don't do well on your own.*

<<<<<<<>>>>>>

OLD HABITS DIE HARD
CHAPTER 9

On Thursday, a few hours after calling Ellie Cherry to officially accept the contract job, I called to share the news with Mom as I drove to the AA club. She cheered and told me I was wonderful, as my mom had done my entire life. I felt validated, ecstatic, and grateful as hell.

Suddenly, a torrential downpour blocked my view of the road and threatened to send me in a 90-degree turn. Such rains were typical in South Florida, but I still wasn't used to them. "I gotta go, Mom. Dangerous rain." I needed to say nothing more; she rushed through a "be careful" and hung up the phone. *As if I'm hell-bent on being careless, silly Mom! I just got an excellent job!*

I gripped the wheel with my windshield wipers on max speed and crept down A-1-A at 20 MPH, rolling in the parking lot five minutes after the meeting started.

The POWERLESS club boasted casual rules, though – too casual, in my opinion. People came in and out during the entire hour, and I found that "against the rules" according to what I'd learned in rehab. There, they taught me to stay in my seat, hold my pee, and listen with a keen ear.

Though I tried to relax such staunch rules, I still had disdain for latecomers and wanderers; it was ingrained in my program.

I slipped in quietly and sat at the back, my rubber sandals squeaking and my curls frizzed like a maniac on speed. I had no umbrella; I'd lost seven in seven months, so I quit buying replacements. But that day I felt ridiculous without one.

Think about it – you can't afford the cheapest umbrella yet, shit-for-brains. Not until you get paid, which can't come soon enough.

The contract from Ellie Cherry and Associates specified weekly paydays, but I'd still have to pay my rent on the last possible day and float the check. The Visa debt... I'd have to borrow from Mom to make the minimum payment. Finances made me crazy, and all my debt filled my gut with knots. *Your momma taught you better than that, Lela Fox!*

With my mind out of gear during the opening readings, I checked out who'd made it to the meeting. Charlie, my ex-roommate from the halfway house, was usually there, and I searched for her bouncy, top-mounted ponytail. *Ah! There she is! Near the front this time, and sitting next to Oakley!*

Oakley was a joyously sober woman with fourteen years clean, a snorting laugh, and bushels of self-confidence. I watched her and smiled. Bubbly, pudgy, red-headed Oakley always brought a smile to my face. She concentrated on the chairman as if she'd never heard the monotonous twelve traditions before. She'd be the perfect sponsor for me; I felt it in my bones. *And if you weren't such a chickenshit, you'd ask her.*

The ceiling-mounted clock blocked my view of the chairman on his raised dais, but the moment he opened the floor to discussion, I caught the time. 3:11. *There it is again!* Elevens had been showing up for the past three days; they began on the way home from my job interview. It seemed to always be 11:11 or 1:11, or eleven after whatever-hour. I wasn't watching the clock or looking for them; it was just a coincidence, supposedly.

But they happened too often to be a coincidence.

It wasn't only the clock that randomly showed elevens, either. My recovery books, for instance – all the good stuff seemed to be on pages 11 or 111 or something-11. At first, I thought I was going crazy. Then I thought it might be a sign, or Dude "talking" to me. Then I'd chide myself for having such superstitious beliefs.

But... damn. What could I do? It kept happening, and it had to mean something! I told Charlie, and she rolled her eyes at me, not seeing the significance I saw so clearly. So I shut up; to tell others would draw criticism or comments about being a "stupid newcomer," a label I hated.

Oakley was the third one to share in that meeting. She talked about her fourth step and how much it changed her life. I yearned to do a "real" fourth step, now doubting everything Jenny had done to help me. If she was such an ass at the end, I wondered if she'd been self-serving the whole time.

Will you ever open up to a sponsor again? Trust somebody enough to pour your heart out to her? On the other hand, if Jenny was only half-heartedly helping me, just think how much more you could learn and grow with a new and truly-sober sponsor.

Oakley brought the room to a rolling laugh when she said her fourth step proved resentments toward everybody she'd ever known, including the doctor who delivered her. I'd heard similar things, but Oakley had a way of making everything seem smart and original.

Bubbling with charisma, she was well-liked in the club and shared her vulnerabilities and struggles with ease. I'd never heard her say she was down about anything except when her mother died. And even then, she had asked for good vibes, not prayers. She wasn't a Jesus-preacher at all; I liked that.

I'd wondered if a sponsor would poo-poo my idea of Dude as a Higher Power, still fearing being made fun of for having a "vision." And that was just one reason I wanted a sponsor who believed in a similar "build-it-yourself" Higher Power. I listened closely for somebody to talk about their HP in a non-traditional way, and I'd been listening for a full month, knowing I seriously needed a sponsor.

The group's chant, "Thanks for sharing," roused me into paying more attention. And soon after, I once again caught the silver-haired, big shouldered guy looking at me. Damn, he was nice-looking! Silky hair, the perfect ratio of salt to pepper, and smooth, touchable skin. And still smoking the little cigarillo things with a white plastic tip.

His across-the-room smile was genuine, and a shiver raced down my spine; it was as if he saw deep inside me. *He likes me! And I think I like him! He'd be the perfect cuddle partner with those strong arms wrapped around me, yeah...*

My thoughts stopped abruptly when I imagined how long and hard Jenny would argue with me about not having a relationship so early in my sobriety. *Is smiling at somebody a relationship? Hell no! So, smile and let your mind wonder about being his girl. There's no harm in that.*

I didn't share in the meeting; it was all about the fourth step, and I knew my "practice round" was merely an exercise in being honest. Far from complete. Jenny had pointed out that I hadn't listed my soon-to-be-ex, the one I resented the most.

Afterward, in the parking lot with humidity hanging low and heavy, a group of women gathered near the door, including Charlie. "Wassup, Char! Hit me with the latest Serenity Sisters gossip."

"Oh, and so much to tell! Drama, drama, drama."

"Why am I not surprised?"

"Elsa relapsed."

"Oh, no! Not Elsa! She had almost eight months, right?"

"Nine. She got kicked out, of course, but still sneaks into my apartment like she lives there!"

"*You'd* get busted if they caught her!"

"Damn right! I've done everything but call the house manager – still Rhonda. Sometimes Elsa leaves immediately, but twice, she passed out at the kitchen table."

"Did you drag her out?"

"Absolutely. It took three of us, even as small as Elsa is, but we put her under the bushes on the far side of the parking lot. She'd disappeared by morning."

"Man, this disease sucks."

"Sucks cheese," she said. Her favorite phrase.

As usual, I made the joke. "Yeah, *Swiss* cheese." But this time, Charlie didn't laugh. I studied her carefully. "What's on your mind, my friend. You're not thinking right."

"No, I'm not." She kicked at a cigarette butt on the pavement with a faraway look. "Hey, you want to get a burger around the corner?"

"Sure. I have some time before my ankle catches on fire."

"When do you get that damn thing off? Soon, surely."

"Four more weeks." Then I asked a serious-as-hell question. "Charlie, you sure you have the cash for a burger? Don't stick me with the tab like you did last time."

"My fat wallet says I got paid yesterday. So yours is on me this time."

<<<<<<<<<>>>>>>>>>

Charlie's problems centered on living at the halfway house; I knew it, and I knew why. "That place kills people, Charlie. There are too many angry addicts and alcoholics there, and so much drama that a person can't ever rest. So save your money and get out of there! ASAP, girl!"

A waitress interrupted to take our order. Too early for a crowd, we sat at our bouncy booth that paralleled the wall of windows at the diner's front. Nice view; lots of activity to keep us entertained. Charlie put the menu in its slot and huffed a sigh. "Well, to be honest, I'm still mad at you."

"For what? I didn't do anyth–"

"You could've waited for me and been my roommate."

"I *told* you, Charlie. I've never had a female roommate in my life! Only husband-roommates. Seriously, I would *suck* at being a friend-roommate. Underneath all this social butterfly bullshit, I'm a loner and a homebody. Besides, do you really want Stuart Weinstein stalking *you*, too?"

"He's still at it, then?"

"It comes in waves. This week, just one creepy, crying message. But he knows I'm not working at Smyth Software anymore."

"How?"

"Hell if I know. The man has big-time connections, I guess. He still doesn't know my new car... or at least I *think* he doesn't."

"Did the foam padding help with the rattles in that damn thing?"

"Nope."

"That's the nicest-shittiest car I've ever known."

"Pisses me off just to think about it."

In the lull of our conversation, I saw him. Baby-Daddy. The crackhead I slept with on my last drunk night. Walking by the diner's window, whistling, and carrying a black-metal lunch box. Since the Homing Inn wasn't far away, I assumed he was walking home.

"Wait, Charlie. I'll be right back."

"What? Who's that? Lela, no!"

I was already outside, shouting to get Baby-Daddy's attention. God, he looked good!

He didn't recognize his "name" and turned around only when I shouted, "It's Tennessee!" Baby-Daddy stopped in his tracks and turned to walk back towards me.

"Hey, Tennessee! Haven't seen you in a long time, girl. What's up?"

"Well, I'm sober."

"Me, too. Five months."

"No shit? I'm seven. Seven and a half, actually. How's Snaggle-Tooth?"

"Who?"

"Oh, whatever his name was. You know, the guy that hung out with us when I lived there."

"Oh, those two are long gone. No clue what happened to them."

There seemed to be nothing else to say, but my temples were throbbing as I eyed him up and down. I imagined the beautiful tattoo on his muscular chest, which looked even more ripped now. "So you've been working?"

"Every day. Being clean and sober helps," he chuckled.

"Yeah, I guess." I found myself obsessed with looking at his body, remembering the power of the sex we had that last night. Funny how I didn't remember how horrible the rest of it was. "So, are you doing anything later? Want to hook up?"

Baby-Daddy's eyes widened. "Seriously? Hell-yeah, I want to hook up! You're smokin' hot, Tennessee."

"I could say the same."

"Then why don't you?"

A giggle, feeling proud to know I still had it in me to turn a man on. "You're smokin' hot and I want you. I want you *bad!*"

"Bad? Yeah, I can be bad," he teased. We stared at each other for a long, silent minute, me blatantly checking out his crotch and muscular legs... and him staring longingly at my now-more-obvious curves. He reached out to touch my waist. "You're not so skinny now, Tennessee. You look damn good."

"So, you're bad, and I'm good?"

He laughed. "Yep. Sounds like we'd be perfect together." He licked his lips and ran his finger along my jawline and across my lips. "Yeah... perfect."

I shook myself out of the trance of desire just long enough to make a plan, then reached into my pocket. "I tell ya what... take this," I said, handing him $42. "Go get us a room. The Blue Flamingo back down that way." I pointed south. "Before I got sober, I stayed there a few nights. In another lifetime, it seems. It's not so bad. It'll do for an hour or two."

"And you'll meet me there?"

"After I get away from my friend, who can't know *anything* about this. Nothing! So don't touch me again. Not 'til, uh, later. Let's just shake hands and you keep going the way you came. Eventually, you can turn around. But stay away from that window. Wait for me. Twenty minutes, max."

"Oh hell, how can I wait that long? I want to lay you out in this parking lot right now!"

"Good things come to those who wait, baby."

"I'll wait for what I know is a good thing."

A handshake, a wave goodbye. Then I turned on my heel and walked back to the diner, trying to keep a straight face. Charlie was watching my every move; I felt her eyes drilling into me and knew if I could look closer, I'd see the steam coming out of her ears. She'd either be mad as hell, jealous, or concerned. And I didn't want a lecture.

Each step confirmed that I'd keep my secret because I didn't want to mess up Charlie's sobriety. It didn't occur to me how much it could mess up my own.

<<<<<<<<<>>>>>>>>>

Baby-Daddy left the room-number message at the front desk. Surprise! It was the same room I'd stayed in when I was there. When I was first homeless... not so long ago. *You've come far, Lela. This... it's just a break for a roll in the hay. It's not like you're gonna relapse because of it!*

I knocked softly and heard a brusque "come in." Baby-Daddy lay naked on the bed, fresh from the shower, rubbing his erect penis. *Oh, God. This will be awesome. Be crazy-sexy, Lela, like you used to be. It's been too long.*

<<<<<<<<<>>>>>>>>>

When I unlocked my apartment door, the silent buzz/ring of the house-arrest unit in the bedroom sent a blue flash to the light of my ankle bracelet. The machine instantly disconnected, letting me know it had connected on the last ring of its five. *Whew! That was way too close, girl. Why the hell did you stay with him so long? You knew you had a deadline!*

A pause to gather my thoughts. *I stayed because it was damn-good to be myself again. I needed the sex, and I needed the risk. How glorious to be wanted again!*

But the evening brought an inevitable crash of Guilt and Remorse. I sobbed, yearning for Jenny, for Dude, for peace, for a kernel of self-respect. I didn't find a scrap of justification for doing what I did, only Shame by the bushel and Hate for myself in a torrent of crashing waves.

Why, Lela? Why? What the hell were you thinking? And now, of course, you crave alcohol. Are you also going to say it's "just a thing" to buy a six of beer? A bottle of wine? Go out for another date, to another bar, and throw down drink after drink? What the HELL were you thinking?

After an hour of self-bashing, my cell phone rang. Aloud, I screamed, "I don't want to talk to *anybody!* Who would want to talk to a loser like me, anyway?" I didn't even look at the phone to see who was calling. "Screw 'em! Screw 'em all!"

I twitched and fidgeted for another hour, unable to focus on TV or anything online, lost in the bittersweet joy of beating myself up. At last, I sat down with my journal and wrote page after page of my inner thoughts, examining my motivations and the consequences of doing what I did.

It wasn't pretty; I'd really screwed myself up.

I wrote out a prayer, a "confession," of sorts, to Dude, followed by a promise to do better tomorrow. Jenny had taught me that's all I needed to do. Her quote, "Positive things can come from horrible things," repeated in my head. When I set the journal aside, I was ready for things to return to normal.

I assumed it would be instantaneous, but I was wrong. Especially that night.

With my stomach finally able to handle food, I sat on the sofa with a bowl of cereal and noticed my phone flashing — a voice mail. I pushed the PLAY button.

Hey baby... your favorite husband Stuart here. [soft laughter] I've been missing you terribly over the past few days, and I worry that you may still be unemployed for whatever reason. If you need money, I can help – all you have to do is call. My handy-dandy counterfeiter has a fresh bunch of twenties that look great. The best-ever, really. So you can get groceries, or pay your rent... whatever you need. I mean, seriously. I don't want my baby to go hungry!

Then again, I've noticed you're starting to fill out a little. You look great, sweetheart. But, of course, you were always so hot, so beautiful – inside and out. I wish I could be with you, lay you out of a bed of roses like we did that time in Jacksonville...

remember that? Ahhh, such a ferocious lover you are! Sure you don't want to see me? If nothing else, just for a romantic night? [laughter] Or maybe you'd call it revenge sex.

I wish you could love me again, Lela-baby. [sigh]. And I wish you'd call, and please, darling, call if you need money. I'll be nice. In fact, I wish we'd call off this divorce bullshit. You're sober, and I'm sober... we could be great together, and I promise not to call the cops on you ever again. I know that's what broke us up. Damn cops!

Oh! Maybe a few twenties will fill up the tank in your new Jetta. Nice car, sweetie. But you should have called ME! You know I can get good deals on used cars with my connections. Hell, I would've even bought it for you... no car payments. Never forget how well I took care of you. You'll never find another who loves you more.

My stomach turned; waves of nausea hit as I felt on the verge of throwing up.

No tears would come, so I sat numb, my cereal now a soggy mess. *How does he know about my new car? I've been so careful!* I still suspected it might have been Stuart coming out of the apartment complex that day when I picked Damon up from the airport. *But if he'd seen me then, the sonofabitch would've asked who was with me. So how does he know about my car! Is he watching every move I make?*

A shiver traveled down my spine. *Why won't he leave me alone?! Why can't I just live in peace?*

It took a few minutes to correct my thinking, stiffen my upper lip, and move forward. I gave myself an internal lecture: *Just be ultra-careful, Lela. Be aware of your surroundings at all times. And don't let him know about your new job. Take a circuitous route, pull into a random office building and get out, THEN drive the rest of the way to Ellie Cherry.*

My thoughts turned to what I would wear on my first day of work. *Monday! Monday!* I couldn't wait to get back in the saddle and show my worth as an advertising writer. Determined to excel, finally.

EXCEL SOBER.

I loved the line so much; I immediately typed and printed a "sign" to post on the fridge. *You'll be okay, Lela Fox. Stay sober, and all will be well. You will excel. And screw Stuart! He can't hold you back.*

<<<<<<<>>>>>>

NO FAIRY TALES HERE
CHAPTER 10

I pulled into the POWERLESS parking lot on Saturday just after 11:30, right on time for the "meeting before the meeting." Several of my friends milled about, talking trash and smoking cigarettes. Best of all, Charlie was there. "How's it hanging, girl? Has the Serenity Sisters house burned down yet?"

"I wish! It sucks as much as it did the last time I talked to you."

"I wish you could get the hell out of there, my friend."

"They still won't give me enough hours at work. Can't afford to leave. There's an opening for a full-time CSR, though, and I'm kissing the manager's ass hoping to get it. Hell, I'd even get benefits! Paid vacation and everything!"

"I got a job myself. I haven't told you yet."

"Great, Lela," she said, but in a faraway voice. I knew Charlie wanted me to do well, but she'd dropped hints of bitterness about my "fancy" college degree and "rich person" salary. We were on different ends of the spectrum when it came to employment and I didn't want her to resent me, but it seemed she did. Guilt stopped me from saying anything further about my soon-to-be job.

Charlie's top-ponytail swung around with her head. "Hey! There's your boyfriend!" she said. I followed her gaze to see the wide-shouldered guy who I'd caught looking at me several times.

"Boyfriend, my ass! I don't even know his name!"

"I'll fix that right now." She grabbed the inside of my elbow and began dragging me toward the bigger crowd close to the club's entrance.

"Stop! Quit! No!" I wrestled with her until noticing other people watching us... then reasoned that to go willingly would draw less attention. I feared she would get face-to-face with him and introduce me, but she swung me in front of her at the last minute and pushed me forward. Suddenly, *I* was the one face-to-face with Mr. Shoulders.

Charlie, please! Don't do this! She held me in place with a grip I wasn't willing to break. I felt my face on fire, then his breath on my cheek.

"Hello there," he said. *Wow. Such a low, low voice! Is there something lower than baritone? Bass? Sub-bass? Jeez, he sounds like the mid-Earth, like a midnight radio host or something.*

He must have seen the shock on my face and immediately raised the tone in a quick squeaky sing-song voice. "Hello there!" I cracked up laughing. He sounded like a girl full of testosterone.

I muttered, "Hello." Nervous laughter. "Sorry, but my friend pushed me over here and I didn't mean to..." I couldn't finish the sentence; I didn't even know what I was trying to say.

"Didn't mean to what?"

Shit. Just talk to him or you'll look even dumber. "So where'd you get such a low voice?"

He laughed from deep in his belly. "Walmart in Boca Raton. In the fishing department."

Too nervous to laugh by then, I nodded. "That's a good one. Let me guess – I'm not the first to ask you that."

"Right."

"So you're in radio?"

"Only when I turn it up and jam."

I laughed. "You're quick. And you're messing with me, mister. Do you ever give a straight answer?"

He studied me for a few beats; I felt his eyes burned through the skin of my face. "So, what if I asked where you got that curly hair?"

"I'd say... my personal assistant bought it at Saks Fifth Avenue."

"Oh, I found a *smart* lady!"

"That's smart*ass* lady to you. And you didn't find me."

"I've found you now." His grin glowed with sincerity. It seemed he'd closed out the world to look only at me.

Too embarrassed to keep up the banter, I lowered my head. *Surely your face is the color of a fire engine. Flirting was so much easier when you were drinking.*

A hand appeared in my line of vision, extended for a handshake. "Hi. I'm Bear."

I looked up to that warm smile, nestled within a tanned face and surrounded by silky salt-and-pepper hair. *Bear? What kind of name is that? But whatever... he's even better-looking up close. Too good-looking for YOU. Forget it. Damn you, Charlie, why did you push me over here?!* A weak croak of "Nice to meet you" was all I could muster.

"So, Ms. Curly, do you have a name?"

"Oh, didn't I say?"

"Nope."

"Lela."

"Hi, Lela. I have a niece named Lela."

"Yeah, everybody does. But I have no nephew named Bear. How'd you get a name like that?"

He chuckled, deep in his throat. "Sometimes a Grizzly Bear... sometimes a teddy bear."

Puh-lease! He doesn't look like an asshole, but that sure sounded like it. Then he flashed the smile again, a grin that had "trustful, honest nice guy" stenciled all over it. *No way he's faking THAT smile. A nice-looking nice guy? Those don't exist in AA.*

"I've seen you around, but only lately. Do you live around here?"

"Well, kinda. But I've been coming here since I got sober."

"And how long ago was that?"

"Seven months."

His head went back with a jerk. "Oh, hell. I'm in trouble!" Laughter.

My eyebrows became one. I had no idea what he was talking about. "In trouble for what?"

He shook his head as if shaking water from his ears. "Ever heard the term thirteen-stepping?" His laugh was as deep as his voice and twice as friendly.

"Never heard of it."

"See... you're still a newcomer. I don't want to mess up your sobriety."

"How could you do that?" My confusion was pure.

He blew a burst of air from his lungs then sucked it back in as a chuckle. "Never mind." I saw him look around, and wondered what I'd said wrong. Then someone across the parking lot shouted his name, and Bear shouted back. "Yo, Steve! Come to rescue me!"

I snapped a look at his face, now tinged with pink. Confused, I asked, "Rescue you from what?" I thought I knew, but playing dumb could never hurt, I thought.

Bear squirmed; his whole body seemed to waver as if he was trying to make himself small. "Rescue me from a beautiful, naïve newcomer."

"Naïve!? But I'm not!"

The man's buddy arrived, slapping him on the shoulder and reaching in for a handshake. "What's up, Scary Bear?"

"Lela, meet Sleazy Steve. Steve, meet Lela."

The man named Steve looked me up and down without trying to hide his visual assault. I stopped him in his sleazy tracks. "Oh, no, Sleazy Steve. Keep your eyes to yourself. That's rude and disgusting!"

A brilliant smile beamed from Bear's face. "Don't mess with a naïve newcomer, Steve, especially one who calls you on your shit!" Sleazy Steve rolled his eyes as Bear's drilled his into mine. "Way to go, Lela. You'll do alright around here."

"I don't take any shit from AA people. Half of them are crazy, and the other half are sociopaths."

Bear laughed hysterically and reached to poke Sleazy Steve in the ribs. "That's your exit line, buddy. Leave the pretty lady alone."

I snapped at Bear. "I don't need your protect–"

He was quick to interrupt. "No, you don't need my protection, obviously! Good for you, Ms. Lela Newcomer."

"Fox."

"What?"

"Don't call me a newcomer like it's a label. I'm Lela Fox."

"And a feisty fox, I see."

"I guess so."

"I like feisty."

"I like big shoulders."

"I have those."

"Yes, you do. Two of them."

We continued the tit-for-tat banter for a while, me teasing him about having a little polar bear in him, too, with his "snow-capped" hair. He was my age and remembered Yogi Bear when I called him that name. We laughed as each other's playful jabs until, suddenly, we were alone in the parking lot. "We're missing the meeting," I said.

"Here's an idea: we could go have coffee instead?" Bear said it so fast that I almost didn't catch it was an invitation. Then his face turned crimson.

I put on a Southern Belle accent, knowing I did an excellent Scarlet O'Hara when I tried. "Well, shame on you, Mr. Scary Bear... invitin' me t' coffee when a naïve newcomer like little ol' me can't afford t' miss a meetin' any day of th' week!" I fanned myself, sans fan, of course, and pursed my lips. *Oh, Lela, you bad, bad girl. Flirting your ass off when you should be in a meeting, especially when you should be in there finding a sponsor!*

Our eyes met. *Wow! There's a vibration happening with this guy.* Then I heard a *pssst* sound coming from the doorway. Charlie. I shouldn't have acted put-out, but I did. "What now, Charlie? Another crisis?"

"She's here!"

"Who?"

"That woman!"

Bear had turned away and wandered six feet to the left. I looked back at Charlie, realizing – maybe – who she was talking about. "Do you mean that 'maybe sponsor,' Oakley? The one you call 'the new Jenny?'"

"Yeah! Oakley. That's her name."

"And what kind of name is that?"

Charlie huffed as if frustrated with me. "Maybe the name of a good sponsor for you, dumbass. Come on in! There's an empty seat beside her! I'll show you."

I turned to face the man called Bear, who was rubbing his temples. "Are you okay?"

He raised his brows and smiled, then cocked his head to look at me convincingly. "Yeah! Yeah, I'm fine!"

"I gotta go. There's a lady I need to see in there. Oakley. Do you know her?"

"Yes! Oakley is great."

"Well, I need a new sponsor, and I thought–"

"She'd be an awesome sponsor for you!"

"Really?"

"Really!"

"Okay... see you again?"

"I live here."

"Ha, ha. Bye!"

Charlie grabbed my arm, and once again, I struggled against her, but it didn't stop her at all. She pulled me to the left. I saw the empty seat beside Oakley and took it.

She smiled at me when I sat down, and patted my leg, like a mother. Sure of her good intentions, the action still felt a bit too invasive, or maybe the word is "forward." After all, I didn't know her well.

It was another rousing meeting; the topic was forgiveness, and my mind leveled on Stuart. *Can I ever forgive him for his cruelty? Or does the fact that I still consider it "cruelty" the reason I won't forgive him?*

The topic required deep examination, and, once again, I thought about asking my shrink for a recommendation for a talk therapist. Having both a sponsor and a therapist would speed my recovery; I was sure about that, and I felt an overwhelming need to be 100 percent honest with somebody. The thoughts bouncing in my head were making me crazy.

I held hands with Oakley at the closing prayer, practicing what I would say to entice her to be my sponsor. *Do I have to entice somebody like that? Jenny was so in-my-face about it; appointed herself, in fact. I know I have to ask, but is it like a "sales presentation" or a benefit-oriented speech, letting her know I'm willing to learn?*

I decided that letting her know I respected her and was "yearning to learn," as they said, would be a simple but effective sales job. The question itself: "Will you be my sponsor?" still seemed so hard to ask. I feared she would say no... *then* what would I do?

After my behavior with Baby-Daddy, I thought maybe I was still too crazy for a sponsor to deal with. Or maybe all my work so far was too Jenny-oriented and, therefore, wrong in some way. So maybe the lack of confidence I felt at that moment was warranted. Maybe I'd amount to nothing.

When the prayer ended, I turned to Oakley and blurted a full paragraph without stopping for a breath. With each word, her smile broadened, and by the time I got to the key question, she was chuckling. "I'd *love* to be your sponsor, Lela! I've heard you share in meetings... enough to know you want to grow, no matter how scattered you are. And you *are* scattered!"

"A lot more than you know, I'm afraid."

"Let's take care of that together. What do you say?"

"I'd love to do just that, Oakley. But I first have to tell you that my original sponsor fired me, as they say. Or maybe I fired her. Or whatever happened. Her name was Jenny Jenkins."

"Jenny? I know her well. Had a good program at one time, but she's never come back after falling off the wagon. So sad."

I spoke in a faraway voice. "Definitely sad..."

"I'm sorry, Lela. That must have been a bad ending."

I burst into tears without knowing they were building in my heart. Feeling even more betrayed by Jenny, more used, and more confused, I said, "She... she..." I couldn't complete the sentence; maybe I didn't even know how to sum up the bevy of emotions I felt.

"Come here, girl. You need a good, long hug. I have lots of padding, so just sink in. As my momma used to say, 'let me pet you.'"

I snapped a look at her and smiled through the tears still dripping from my eyes. "Wow! My mother says the same thing! 'Let me pet you.' So I bet we have a lot of things in common."

"Could be. But still, come here for a hug. Cry about Jenny. You need to, it seems."

I wiped my tears, flicked the liquid off of my fingers onto the wooden floor. "I hate to cry in public, Oakley."

"Don't worry about that *here!* You're in an AA club, girl. The damn place is *full* of tears."

I hugged her and held on for dear life; she was right about the amount of comfortable padding her body offered. After we broke the hug, she put her hands on my shoulders and peered up at my face from her low height. "I must tell you first thing, though: I'm a take-no-shit, hard-ass sponsor. You will call me every night. No exceptions. Even if you just leave a message, you will call. And we'll meet once a week, usually before or after a meeting. My homegroup is here, the 5:30. Can you make that meeting every day?"

"Uh, timing may be a problem for the next few weeks. I have, uh, curfews, I guess you could call them. I could tell you, but it's a looong story."

"House arrest?"

"You knew that quick?" The embarrassment was second to being impressed with her instant understanding. And her tone was the opposite of accusatory or judge-y.

"Not my first rodeo, Lela."

"None of us are Puritans."

Her snorting laugh blew through the nearly empty room. "That is a very true statement. Just imagine a room full of those bonnets!" I laughed, too, but Oakley went back to business in a snap. "So then we can meet at *your* place. Study sessions, work, work, work. No rest for the wicked."

As I wiped my tears, she rattled off a flurry of details about her life circumstances. She was an RN at Bethesda Hospital, recently divorced (a friendly breakup), had a twenty-year-old son, and an oddball "imaginary Higher Power."

Her words sent a rush of joy through my heart. *I can keep Dude! She won't try to change that!* I still feared being pushed into religion in AA, and my jaw clenched just thinking about it.

I told her the basics of where my head was, a summary of my whacked-out thoughts and Bi-Polar diagnosis. "But I'm not near as sober as I want to be. Jenny taught me a lot, if any of it was true."

"She wouldn't have steered you off-track, surely!"

"But she was even going to meetings during the relapse! And making *me* go with her! If that's not a lie, I don't know what is!"

"No, no. Going to a meeting is never a lie."

"But why go when you're drinking?"

"Because once you've been sober, you can never be a successful drunk again. The more you know about sobriety, the more powerful the Guilt. And that part sucks. Trust me – I know."

"You, too?"

"Yes. You'll learn my rollercoaster journey. There are no fairy tales in this room."

"I always thought my path would be like a fairy tale. But shit keeps happening! *Bad* shit."

"Perspective – that's what it's about. We'll talk. You may not agree with me, but I tell you what I think, anyway. And I won't take any sass from you. Trust me on that. Being my sponsee is work – hard work. No pussies allowed."

"I'm ready."

"Me, too. See you later, kid. I'm off to see the wizard."

Nightly phone calls and weekly study sessions, a self-described hard-ass sponsor – exactly what I need.

Oakley's phrase, "There are no fairy tales in these rooms," comforted me as I repeated it in my mind – not just on that day, but for twenty years beyond. It taught me that I wasn't the only one who struggled, and that I shouldn't expect everything to turn out peachy-keen.

Early on, when I screwed up, as I had with Baby-Daddy, the phrase gave me hope that I could still move forward, no matter how faltering my steps. I didn't have to go back to Point A because I missed a spot at point D or E. Or Z.

Once I knew I didn't have to do things perfectly, I relaxed enough to begin the true healing process. I began to forgive myself bit by bit. It's taken a looooong time; I'm still working on it, in fact. A lifetime of self-hate can't be easily eradicated.

Each millimeter that disappears begins with face-to-face honesty with myself. Painful honesty.

And as Oakley predicted, the rest of my sober life was far from a fairy tale. The rollercoaster lasted for another seventeen years until coming to a slow roll at age sixty.

The bad decisions continued, the self-destruction continued, the chaos continued… but that's getting ahead of the story. I guess that's why there are still more books to write.

<<<<<<<>>>>>>

FIRST DAY, WORST DAY
CHAPTER II

Sunday night, I set my alarm for 6:00 AM, planning carefully for my first day of work. But I awoke early, at 5:11, and turned off the alarm. A zombie-walk to the coffeemaker and a check of the morning news. The lead story highlighted a local tennis star who'd won Wimbledon, Venus Williams. She and her sister hailed from Palm Beach Gardens, just a few miles from my new office.

I'd laid out my clothes – I hoped fashionable enough for the avant-garde Ellie Cherry and casual enough for the creative department. First-day-jitters had me speeding on the drive up I-95, but, as planned, I passed the exit and pulled into an office complex on Palm Beach Garden's main drag. Determined to stay incognito and fool Stuart Weinstein and his goons, I pledged to play the same trick every day.

Briefcase in hand, I entered the main-tower door, sat on a foyer bench for precisely eight minutes, then went back to the Jetta wearing a scarf to hide my face. Then I circled the block, just in case, before taking the ramp and zooming one exit south. Five minutes later, I pulled into the parking lot of Ellie Cherry and Associates.

I sat in the car for a series of deep breaths, psyching myself up for making a good impression from the start. I looked in the rearview mirror and repeated the speech my dad gave me every chance he got: the famous encouragement speech. Starting at age twelve-or-so, he'd look me square in the eye and carefully enunciate the same three sentences that I said out loud that day. "Lela Fox... you are beautiful. You are invincible. You are irreplaceable."

Deep breath. Ready. *Go get 'em, tiger.*

<<<<<<<<<<>>>>>>>>>>

Prudence ushered me into my office, looking down her nose at me and commenting viciously about the size of the box I brought in with me. Feeling the need to explain, I said, "I try to personalize my office, surround myself with creative things so *I* can be more creative. I guess you'd say my desk becomes a shrine of sorts. It's half superstition, but I think of the silly collection as my inspiration."

Her expression was flat; her reply absent. Prudence continued the all-business attitude and the room vibrated with tension. She turned and stuck a crooked index finger at me. "Rule: do NOT stock up on office supplies for your desk. Take only ONE pen at a time, for example. Do you understand?" Her eyes were wide, challenging me to disagree, it seemed.

There were more Prudence-rules about office supplies. "Take only ONE notepad, ONE stick of staples, and no more than ten paper clips. You need no more than that, and I keep close tabs on the inventory. Take heed, Ms. Fox: I know who uses the combination on the cabinet and how often they open it."

I cringed as she spoke. *Oh, that hurts! I'll have to sit on my hands to keep my office supply fetish at bay! I'll salivate at that cabinet, and I need twenty of everything!* I guess she saw my face screw up and asked, "Is there a problem, Ms. Fox?"

"First, please call me Lela. We work together now, right? Or should I be calling you something other than Prudence?"

"Prudence is fine. You wouldn't be able to pronounce my last name, anyway."

Of course, that comment made me even more curious about her last name, assuming it would be equally snotty and a mouthful of bitchy. As I began the question, she again wagged her finger at me. "Don't ask, don't tell."

Her tone was like a slap in the face by my authoritarian second-grade teacher. I shrugged, trying to appear unfazed. "Okay then."

A pause; neither of us had moved since entering the office. *Does she have rules about entering and exiting, too?* "Well, thank you, Prudence, for the supplies and the cabinet combination. I'll guard it with my life."

"You best do that. Morning status meeting at 9:30 in the conference room. Bring a notepad. You'll get your weekly assignments there. And remember, you are on a week by week contract."

"Sorry, but that's not correct. The contract runs for the full two months, not a week at a time."

"Week by week. Trust me."

Eyeing her sideways, catching her accusatory meaning, I said, "But you'll find my work exemplary, I guarantee it, so I'll be a full-time employee in no time!"

"We'll see." Such a bitchy tone the woman had! Then, as if marching, she turned on her heel and passed my doorway in two strides, taking a ninety-degree left turn into the hall.

I sat; the chair was nice and comfy, but like most offices, the walls were bare. I'd have to fix that, I knew. No way I could work in a dull, windowless room filled with echoes and sharp edges.

What the hell? I might as well get started. This 10 x 10 room will scream "Lela's Full-of-Fun Office!" when I'm finished. So I began unpacking; my flamingo desk clock was first out. The time: 9:11. *There's eleven again! What does that one mean? That I'm supposed to be here?*

<<<<<<<<<<>>>>>>>>>>

I was the first to arrive in the conference room, meeting the Creative Director one-on-one. Cole Connors sat at the head of the table and welcomed me as if greeting a long-lost friend. "All 32 of us will attend this morning, plus Ellie and Prudence, and our team is a kickass and high-spirited group. You'll find creative energy here, sprinkled with creative freedom from *most* clients."

"Sounds fantastic, Cole. Glad to be here." *Oops! Don't speak AA at work.*

"You'll love this job." His white teeth gleamed against a glowing tanned face; his skin surprisingly bright for an older man.

Dressed like a laid-back tourist, he wore a vibrant orange and blue tropical-print shirt, untucked, over worn jeans. Leather sandals, and leopard-print reading glasses perched atop his balding head. But the prize was his smile, the very definition of "beaming."

In his late 50s, I guessed, his white eyebrows were a curly forest above bright, alert eyes. I hoped his mind was as open as his mouth when he laughed, and his laughter had been nearly constant in the first few minutes of the meeting.

Cole introduced me to each person, one at a time, and encouraged a round of applause at the end of the process. Judging only by looks and outfits, Cole was right in describing a laid-back, ultra-creative team. My mind saw scenarios of being cheered for my creative style; I worked best when free to be silly, bouncing off the walls while devising out-of-the-box ideas.

Then Cole called the meeting to order and opened the flaps on a whiteboard with the two headings: "Projects In Progress" and "On the Horizon." The flaps listed active clients, and I silently screamed with excitement. The list, only the highlights:

All the Jack Nicklaus golf clubs across the world

Embassy Suites and two other hotel chains

The Florida Tourism Agency

Bausch & Lomb Vision

Wilson Sporting Goods

Carnival Cruise Lines

Three different drug rehab centers (Perfect choice for me!)

A half-dozen real estate developments, all high-end

Although I'd seen the list on the agency's website, I marveled again at the reality of working with these big-time, big-budget clients. Oh, what fun I could have! And the prestige! *I will kick some serious ass here... win more Addy awards and flaunt them in Miller McKeown's face! I've hit the copywriter's lottery!*

My heart beat double-time, eyeing the thirty-plus upcoming projects and wondering which of the wonderful choices would be assigned to me.

Neither Prudence nor Ellie Cherry spoke during the meeting; it was all Cole. But I glanced at the bosses who listened carefully. Isabella the poodle, cuddled against Ellie's shoulder as she stroked its fur rhythmically, mesmerized me for a while. Then Prudence rubbed Purell sanitizing lotion on her hands for the third time since the meeting began. *What is so dirty in here, Prudence?*

Cole stopped at the third entry of the "Projects in Progress" list and pointed at me. "Lela, you'll take this over from Lori. She's swamped."

Lori shouted from the end of the table, "Yay for the new copywriter! Maybe I can actually see my kids sometime before Christmas. Glad you're here, Lela."

"Glad to be here." *Oops again. Don't speak AA! Wait... maybe normal people say that, too.*

I didn't have time to ponder the comment long; Cole added six more projects to my list. I assumed the deadlines were the end of the week and wondered if I could keep work at that pace. It had been a long time since I'd worked for somebody else; when I free-lanced in other Lifetimes, I was the one who set the deadlines and ran the show. This would be a whole new scene.

The meeting ended with a ceremony: Cole presented awards, what he called "Cherries," and made a point to explain them to me: "Shout-outs to staff members who did something kickass last week, some to the creative staff, some to the account execs. We even gave one to Ellie once," he said. Everybody laughed.

The "Cherry" was just a cheap glass stone with the agency's cherry-and-stem logo. Though available at any craft store, the stones were obvious treasures to the staff. All four people who earned them grinned ear to ear, and shouts of congratulations surrounded the room. Then a suave-looking tall woman, Deidre, received a "Super Cherry" from Cole. An account executive who'd landed a new client. She made a short speech from the head of the table.

By that time, I'd relaxed, feeling more confident that I could fit in and grow with the agency. When Cole dismissed the group, he pointed to the chair beside him. "Here, Lela. I'll get you started. I assume Prudence gave you a stack of paperwork, too."

"Not really. I'm on contract here for the first two months. So no withholding forms or any of that."

"Why just a contract?" I told him the story of what my video portfolio lacked, and he laughed loudly, slapping his knee. "I'm going to like you, Lela. We need resourceful people."

I blushed, promising I wouldn't let him down. "I'm eager to start writing. The client list is phenomenal, with fun and challenging projects of all sizes. I'm ready to sink my teeth into some killer ideas."

"I'll be honest about something, though. One of our most, uh, troublesome clients is on your list. I have to spread the hard stuff around – I'm sure you understand. Creative freedom isn't a possibility with the assholes at Calvin Inns, and sometimes the folks at Bausch & Lomb get weird. I'll drop by to give you some history later."

<<<<<<<<<<>>>>>>>>>>

Three people, including Cole, asked me to have lunch with them, but I had to turn them all down; I'd scheduled a phone conference with my divorce lawyer.

Attorney Bethany Reynolds had received an offer from Stuart's lawyer, according to her message, and I was anxious to hear it. I hoped for at least $10,000, enough to pay off my credit cards and put a little away for rainy days. It *had* to be better than his first offer: zero dollars, period. No repayment for what he'd swindled from me or for the pain and suffering he'd caused in our short-but-traumatic marriage.

Screw that; I'll just wait him out. When he wants the divorce bad enough, he'll cough up the money.

After two minutes of elevator music, Bethany picked up. I noticed the time; 12:11. She said in haste, "There's an offer on the table, and I think it's a good one."

"Hit me with it."

Rustling papers. "I'll read the key sentence only, if that's acceptable."

"Please."

"The complainant hereby offers a total sum of $15,000 to the defendant Lela Lynn Fox, payable in a lump sum upon settlement of his mother's estate."

"Whaaat?! *That's bullshit!*"

In an uppity voice, she snapped, "But it's better than–"

"Yeah, better than *nothing*, but I have no intention of waiting that long!"

"How *old* is his mother?"

"No clue, but the old bitty is too mean to die! And she hates Stuart so much that I doubt he'll inherit a dime! It's a pie-in-the-sky promise that means nothing."

"It means he has no money of his own."

I paused to think about that, knowing she was right. "Then he'll just have to find it. Bethany, he's been calling and stalking me since I left!"

"I'm sorry, Lela, but that has nothing to do with these negotiations."

"It does for *me!*"

"It seems your emotions are mixed with business, Lela. The fact that your husband is not such a nice guy doesn't affect the validity of the offer."

"Yes, it does, because he's lying. I won't see a dime if it's done that way. I want money, and I want it now."

"Lela, I don't advise that."

"I have no other choice! Do you know how much money he stole from me?! I'm barely making minimum payments on those cards – *that's* how bad I need the cash."

"You can't get money from a turnip."

"Dammit! I *knew* you'd repeat that cliché."

"But it's true. If Mr. Weinstein had a dime to give, he would have offered it already. Because later in the document, his lawyer asks for immediate actions, immediate declaration of divorce."

"Hell will freeze over first."

"You *have* to answer the offer, Lela. Within thirty days."

"I didn't answer his previous offer."

"And he could've gone before the judge, and the divorce would have been granted in your absence. The fact that he made a second offer is a bonus. Take the offer, Lela. It's this or nothing."

"I'm not falling for his bullshit, Bethany. Tell his damn lawyer to go to hell and good riddance."

"You're risking your future."

"Every time I leave the apartment, I'm risking my *life!* He's evil enough to kill me, don't you see? I'm *scared* of the sonofabitch."

"You're making a big mistake with these tactics, Lela."

"You're a fool to advise me to believe a compulsive liar."

"It's a legal document! We can check death records monthly to see if his mother has passed, and Florida's probate court filings are faxed to our office each week, to another partner you haven't met. I *promise* we can monitor this and get your settlement when the time comes."

"Sorry, I'm not falling for it. No can do."

Bethany sighed. "You're refusing to negotiate?"

"I'm refusing to even *consider* it."

"Then I must withdraw as your attorney of record. On grounds of your refusal to negotiate."

I gasped, re-thinking everything. "Wait! You can't do that!"

"Oh-yes-I-can! And I *do*. Good day, Ms. Fox. I'll send my final bill at the end of the week."

She hung up, just that fast.

The silence on the line pounded like a jackhammer. I kept the phone to my ear until a constant double-buzz began. Feeling like I was in a faraway land, my arm extended to place the handset in its cradle. I missed the slot, not just once, but twice. My hand was beyond merely shaking; it *jerked,* and a barrage of tears ejected from my eyes. Projectile tears that skipped my face and landed on my desk with a series of plops.

I had to scream silently so my new co-workers couldn't hear a crazy woman bellow FUUUUUUCK!

My heart, beating double-time, had sunk to my feet. Hearing Bethany's message about a settlement has made me hopeful for the first time in months. I'd laid out a plan for paying off the credit cards, my timeline carefully scripted on a purple paisley-margined notepad, stashed in the "long-term" file.

Dammit!

<<<<<<<>>>>>>

THE SENSITIVE IDIOT

CHAPTER 12

My job was challenging, especially the twenty-word-maximum "email blast" campaigns to encourage tee-time reservations on slow days. It took nearly three hours to whittle the words down, and the copy ran three words over, but the client approved it with no changes. *Ca-Ching!*

All the projects, even the small ones, were prestigious, and the way Prudence organized the input sheets from the account manager gave little room for misunderstanding. I left each day feeling like I'd done a damn-good job; I didn't get praise, but I didn't get complaints, either.

The best part was that clients didn't nitpick and request multiple rewrites. I hated that shit.

On the Wednesday before I was to get my house-arrest anklet off, I dashed to POWERLESS for the 5:30 meeting. I would see Oakley; by then, we'd had four study sessions and spent a gazillion hours on the phone. She knew me and my story from beginning to end.

Just as Jenny had, Oakley said, "You're a tough nut to crack, Lela Fox," but I still didn't know why they thought so. In my mind, I was like clay in a potter's hands, eager to be sculped into something beautiful and useful.

My main problems, according to a smart Oakley, were pride and closed-mindedness about my Higher Power. "But I don't want anything even *close* to religious, Oakley. It gives me the creeps," I explained.

85

"But you can't run from people who lean that way. It's to your detriment."

Wanting a complete change in the subject, I asked, "What do you know about Bear? Is it teddy bear or Grizzly bear or scary bear?"

She looked at me accusingly; I guess surprised at the sudden turn in the conversation. But she answered. "Bear is a nice guy. Twelve years sober, I think. Totally unaware of how good-looking he is." Then Oakley choked in a deep blast of breath, understanding why I'd asked. "No! Not you! Lela, you're not ready for a relationship! You know that, surely!"

"But he's a nice guy with a strong program, just like you said."

"That doesn't make *you* ready."

"We've been talking at meetings, and the before and after. We've talked several times, in fact, and he's been nothing but a gentleman. He seems to, uh, favor me."

"Favor you?"

"Is that too Southern of a phrase for you, Oakley?" She shrugged. "It means he seems to like me better than the others, makes a point to talk to me, and talks until I say goodbye. The next step is a date invitation. I feel it coming."

Oakley's face was flat. "You're not going to listen to me about this, are you?"

"I'm not saying I'll marry him, Oakley! What's wrong with a cup of coffee with a friend?"

"Because it turns into more than that."

"I won't sleep with him, either."

"Let me guess: you said that about Baby-Daddy, too."

I cringed. Oakley had been very concerned about that stunt of mine, no matter how much I tried to downplay it. "No! Not the same at all. Baby-Daddy was just a snap decision. A *stupid* snap decision, but there was no pre-meditation and more Remorse than you can imagine."

"You're pretty needy, still. And Bear doesn't have what you need."

"I guess I'll find out at the coffee shop."

<<<<<<<<<<<>>>>>>>>>>>

I felt bad to leave an hour early from work – they were ultra-picky about attendance – but I had no choice. It's not like the probation bitch would stay late for my benefit.

"You're free from probation and house arrest, Ms. Fox. And I assume you received the letter where I went to bat for you. Usually, just one absence from a home-check means immediate arrest."

"I would say I owe you one, but to be honest, I don't want to owe you a *damn* thing. I never want to see you again."

The probation manager, or whatever her title was, the same woman who put the damn bracelet on in the first place, threw her head back to laugh. "That's beautifully honest. I checked with your sponsor, per twelve-step allowance rules, and I'm thrilled you're still sober. I hope the home confinement helped in that way."

"'Home confinement,' as you call it, helped *nothing*. And my ex is still stalking me, calling me all the time. As I told you last time, *he's* the one who should've been wearing this damn jewelry."

Her lips pursed. "I just follow orders, Ms. Fox."

I flipped my hand to dismiss her. "Whatever!"

"You're free to go," then she stated the date and time. December 11, 4:11 PM. *Damn! Elevens again!*

"I won't be back," I promised.

"I hope not."

On the way home, I sang in the car, as loud as I could, every word of *Free Bird.*

<<<<<<<<<>>>>>>>>

I flew home for Christmas, spending way too much money on an airline ticket. And I cried almost the whole time I was there, sincerely touched by each greeting and each nice thing said. Karen and I hugged for more than a minute; we both ended up crying happy tears. I'd missed everybody so much! Mom had made my favorite Rice Krispy treats, "just for you," she'd said.

Daddy had stashed a gift for me, "not allowed" by our ban on presents for adults.

He led me to the guest room and pushed a package in my hand, wrapped so badly that I cracked up laughing. "Just open it!" he insisted. I did.

"Oh, Daddy!" He didn't give money away – *ever!* But there it was in my hand: three hundred-dollar-bills, folded in thirds.

"Toward your credit card balance, okay? You must lose sleep with all that debt, and my sweet, sober daughter should sleep like a baby."

"Daddy, I can't take this! The last time you gave me money was…" I couldn't even remember.

"The last time, you were sixteen and even *told* me you used it to buy beer."

Laughing through my words, I said, "That won't happen now, but still, Daddy, it's too much!"

"No, it's not *enough*, dear. But there are conditions." I cringed, ready for a lecture about how I managed my money. But it wasn't a lecture. He whispered, "You can't tell your mother."

"Daddy! Keeping secrets! That makes it even worse!"

"Hush. Put it in your pocket. I'll deny ever giving it to you." After a while, I kissed his cheek, my tears squeezing between us. "But use it only to pay your Visa."

"I will, Daddy, I promise. Thank you for trusting me. It means a lot."

"Thank *you* for being trustworthy."

"Let's have a 'thank you argument.' Because I *know* I'm more thankful than you are."

"No way in hell, little girl. You are my hero. Just stay sober."

When Daddy opened the door for me, Jennifer and Karen were in the hall, both with quizzical faces. Karen blurted, "What are you two doing in there? Having sex?"

I laughed… Jennifer huffed with impatience and rolled her eyes… Daddy made a silly face. We each had our roles.

After dinner, I called Bo, and we passed the phone around the circle. I still heard the hesitation in his voice when talking to me, like a distance I couldn't close. Tears rolled. Afterward, for the first time, I told somebody how distraught I was about Bo still not forgiving me. Of course, I chose Karen.

"Time, Lela. It will just take *time*. I can't say I'm 100 percent comfortable yet, either, to tell you the truth. Worried. Careful. Because what if something I might say send you off the deep end?"

"Even you? There's a distance? A hesitation?"

"Even me. Sorry, though. I really didn't know I felt that way until you said Bo was also hesitant. When I put myself in his shoes, it makes perfect sense."

"I'm just want to rebuild the relationship ASAP. I screwed him up being a drunk mother, and I want to fix it *right now!*"

"You can't. Just stay sober and keep trying."

I hung my head. Part of the sourness in my gut was continuing Shame, part Resentment, and part simple exasperation. I knew Karen was right; I'd just have to wait. But I didn't know how long I could stand it.

Karen said, "Hey – I heard something that might help. The quote was: 'Patience is a form of action.' Pretty good, huh?"

"Good as in 'trying to run in quicksand' is good. But I have no choice, Karen. I've just got to keep trying and wait. And wait more."

Can you stay sober while you wait? Do you understand that to drink is not just to die, but it would also kill your relationship with Bo?

Tears seemed to be the only way to deal with my pain. I asked Karen to give me a minute before I joined her back in the living room.

<<<<<<<<<<>>>>>>>>>>

"I had a wonderful Christmas! Thanks for asking. I flew home, and everybody was there except for my son. That part was a bummer, but everything else proved awesome. Did *you* go home? You're from Cape Cod, right?"

Bear grimaced. "I'm not exactly welcome at home in Cape Cod. At least not yet."

"You mean because of your drunken past? Isn't fourteen years enough to convince them of your new, sober life!? Damn! What does it take?"

Another grimace. "I did some pretty shitty things, Lela. Pawned the family jewels, crap like that."

"But if you don't go back to visit, you can't show them how you've changed."

"It's not as simple as that. My father is, uh, difficult."

"Difficult?" *Oh. That.* I sat back, realizing again that not everybody had a supportive family like I had. Talking about it had pissed a lot of people off already, as a matter of fact. But the concept of having bad parents was so foreign to me, I forgot to be sensitive about it. I zipped my lip, not wanting to piss Bear off – not that day.

"Oh, sorry." I fidgeted with the sugar container, not knowing what to say. "It's, uh, I forget how lucky I am to have such a great family. Over the holiday, I was bitching about them not trusting *me* yet, with less than a year under my belt."

"But going strong, I hear."

"You *hear?* From *who?*"

"You don't know?"

"No idea what you're talking about."

"Well, I, uh, asked permission to take you for coffee."

"Permission!? What the hell? Oh, damn... from Oakley." My heart sunk as much as it sang with satisfaction that she'd said yes to Bear.

"Yeah. It was the proper thing to do. Like I said the first time, I don't want to mess up your sobriety."

In a flash, my gratitude for being there disappeared. *How DARE my sponsor try to control me? How DARE this man try to get in through the back door? What does he think I am? An idiot?*

My blood pressure began to rise; anger reddened my face. "What *is* it about you people!? Like having coffee with a man could make me *drink?* Who would be that–"

"A *lot* of women would be that sensitive. Or fragile, or whatever you want to call it."

"Well it pisses me off!" *Oops! That was louder than I wanted it to be.* I looked around the diner, happy to see nobody staring at me.

"Yep, you're still feisty."

"No, just *smart.* Smarter than the average alcoholic, stronger than the average woman, and independent as hell. Mix *that* with a shitload of new-found confidence and determination."

"Then why do you cry so much?"

Shocked by his question, I paused, sat back in the diner booth, and studied his face. "What did she tell you? Everything? Isn't there some anonymity around here?"

"Surely she didn't tell me everything. It's just–"

Livid, I spewed loud enough for all diners to hear. "Forget it! I'm outta here! I won't be managed like a damn robot, like a...child!" In a huff, I threw up my hands in frustration. "Sponsors suck! I'm in a cult, somehow. This is ridiculous!" I didn't leave, as I'd planned, but my rant continued; I was mad as hell but trying not to lash out at Bear himself. It wasn't his fault.

He sat without reacting, sipping his coffee and staring out the window. At last, I took a breath.

In that brief pause, Bear sputtered, "You and me, dinner tonight? Joe's Crab Shack? I'll feed you lobster."

Flabbergasted, I could only laugh. "What? Just like that? While I'm mad as hell and after all that blubbering? You must be as crazy as I am!"

"I'm not eight months sober, Lela. You're allowed. And please, don't be mad at Oakley. She's tough on sponsees. And a big-big believer in the 'no relationships for a year' rule."

"But it's not a relationship! It's a date!"

Bear smiled. "A date! So you'll go! Fantastic!"

It took a minute or two, but my heart rate slowly returned to normal as I contemplated the surprising change in conversation. "You're still asking? Despite what Oakley said?"

"Why not?"

"But why did you sit here and listen to me cussing and spitting venom? One helluva rant. And now I'm embarrassed."

"I listened because you needed to rant. Don't worry – you'll probably get one from me some time. Alkies aren't known for lack of emotion. And I'm just as Bi-Polar as you are."

"She told you *that*?"

"Hey, it's okay! I told her about me *first*."

A minute or two passed before I spoke again, and I had a lot to ponder during that time. Eventually, I relaxed and asked for a coffee refill. "What'd ya say we start this all over again?"

"We will tonight. I'll pick you up?"

"Oakley would say to meet you there, to keep my car with me."

"You have nothing to fear, but I'll accept that. Say at seven o'clock?"

"I'll be there."

<<<<<<<<<<>>>>>>>>>>

The food was great, the service excellent, and I had the lobster at Bear's insistence. He chose from the "lighter side" menu, and when the dessert cart came around, an odd look spread on his face. Splotches of red, like a giant's birthmarks, dotted his forehead and cheeks while staring at the yummy pies and cakes. In a faraway voice, he asked if I'd like dessert.

"I'm stuffed. But thank you." The cart rolled away, and his sigh was full-body. Bear's discomfort was 100 percent obvious, and I was determined to know why. I quizzed him. I couldn't help it – it was like he had an aversion to eating. Or maybe he was allergic to dessert. But something was up, and I had to know what.

He explained, "I have another addiction."

His answer confused me at first. I racked my brain, thinking of other addictions in the world. Counting on my fingers, I went through sex, shopping, gambling, and – *oh, I get it.* "Food?" He nodded, cocking his head with his eyes shut. I marveled, "But you don't *look* overweight! Not at all! You're just a big g–"

"A big *eater*. Not a big *guy*. Weight has nothing to do with it, which most people don't understand. But I've lost quite a bit, unaware, because of my diet plan. No flour, no sugar, no dairy, very few carbs, no red meat. For over a year now."

"Wow. So how much have you lost?"

"I don't own scales, so I have no idea. Just buy new clothes every month or two."

"That's why you didn't eat the cheddar biscuits?"

"Yep."

"Did you mind that I ate them?"

"Can't say I 'didn't mind,'" He gestured air quotes, "But it's not my place to manage *your* diet. I'm getting better at eating out, better at dealing with all of it. I go to Overeaters Anonymous about twice a week."

"They have those?"

Bear laughed. "Oh yes... there are a twelve-step programs for everything but breathing."

My eyes darted around the room as I thought about his problem. *How horrible to be addicted to something you can't completely do without! With alcohol, it's yay or nay – easy if you think of it that way. But...food? Poor guy.*

I thought of Karen's bout with bulimia way back when, and her struggles with body image every day since, and wondered if Bear had the same issues. But I dared not ask.

He pushed all the dishes and miscellany to the back of the table and reached toward me with both hands. "Here, hold my hands. Let's pray."

"Here? Hell, no!"

"Silently, Lela."

"But I cry when I pray. I try not to, but a wave of connection pulsates through my body and tears flow."

"That's fine with me."

"Not with me."

"Give me your hands, anyway, nitwit. Think about whatever you want to think about."

Our forearms on the table, we held hands, and Bear lowered his head. I looked around, trying hard not to "speak" to Dude but despite the fight against it, I overflowed with gratitude. Chills went down my spine.

Despite my fight to stay in control, my throat began to close and the sting of tears burned behind my eyes. *Stop, Lela. Don't! It's our first date, and he already thinks you cry too much! Stop! Think about something else! Anything else! Dude! Go away! Later, please!*

When Bear raised his head, my eyes were full of tears, but none had escaped. "You're crying," he said.

Half-angry, I replied in a snap. "No, I'm not!" Just that tiny movement, just moving my mouth to speak, squeezed one tear from the corner of my eye. I laughed; the timing was too perfect. A few more tears fell as I laughed, but I caught them with one layer of cloth napkin before they dripped down my face. Bear laughed during this scene, too, though I was sure it was for different reasons.

The main thing was he didn't freak out when I cried. Every man in my life up to that point had gone haywire when I "turned on the waterworks," as asshole Miller once said. I believed that men didn't know shit about how to deal with a woman's emotions. Maybe they think the reason for the woman's tears is somehow their fault and/or their problem to fix, or that it means they won't get laid. *Whatever!*

My crying had always been like an alarm bell that made men want to run away from me, and run fast. But Bear didn't run. Didn't even flash that "Oh, shit!" look. Didn't flinch. He just smiled.

"I think it's great that you feel so deeply, Lela. No reason to deny it or hide it. It's said somewhere that there's no shame in expressing your authentic feelings, no matter what."

"Please don't bring up Shame," I snapped.

Taken aback, he spoke quickly. "I know you're a crier because Oakley told me."

"That damn Oakley!"

"Tear Bucket Jim? Your dad calls you that, right?"

I couldn't help but smile. Daddy's nickname for me had been lifelong, though it probably started with his frustration about a kid who was waaaay too sensitive. "Still, it's not cool to cry in public, Bear. I feel like an idiot."

"You're not an idiot."

"*I* think I am! Jeez! People think a crying woman is a crazy woman. But I did! And on a first date! That's being an idiot!"

"Okay... a sensitive, beautiful idiot." He raised his coffee cup for a toast.

Just as I opened my mouth to object to being called beautiful, my phone rang. I dove in the big, black hole of my purse to dig it out, thinking it might be Bo or somebody with an emergency.

But it wasn't Bo. And it wasn't an emergency. It was Stuart.

Without considering where I was or who I was with, I growled. Like a *loud* angry hyena. With no intention to answer, I threw the phone back into my purse – and missed. It bounced off the bench cushion of the booth and tumbled to the floor. Honestly, I hoped it had broken.

"What, Lela? What's wrong?" His sub-bass voice, full of concern, seemed to accentuate my anger.

But alas, the tears began in earnest and I spilled the story I hated to tell. Bear's eyebrows joined in one straight line throughout the fifteen-minute explanation, and, as most people did, he suggested I call the police.

"That's a whole 'nother story."

"Tell me the whole 'nother story."

"Oh... is that a Southern phrase? Sorry." He didn't answer, just kept up the look that drilled through my brain and into my central nervous system. I was tingling – upset, but somehow calm and trusting of the guy across from me.

What's the problem with telling him? It's not like he's some AA loser who will judge you for going to jail. Ha! And it seems like he really wants to know, so spill the beans, Lela. You're in a safe place.

I took a deep breath. "Okay, the short version." Trying to downplay it, I told him of the drama in court when I told the judge Stuart wouldn't stop harassing me. "The judge said it was a difficult case because he believed *both* of us. The asshole."

"Judges can definitely be assholes," Bear chuckled.

"Well, he said we must be separated, and because I was the one with the domestic abuse charge, I was the one thrown in jail."

"That's terrible!"

"It gets worse. There was some kind of clerical error, and the judge's damn sentence of three days became two weeks! And two weeks without my psych meds. It really screwed me up."

I added details here and there but didn't cry until I told him that the spot between my toes had bled because of the jail flip-flops. Then everything came thundering back. My hands shook in jerks, and my stuffed belly curdled.

Don't lose the lobster, Lela! The alliterative thought brought a chuckle, small but enough to break the tension and uncomfortable focus on me, me, me.

"You've had it rough, girl, and still stayed sober. Do you realize how *amazing* that is? Do you know how *strong* you are?"

"I didn't have a lot of choice in the matter. To drink is to die, right?"

"Drinking is always a choice, but you haven't made that choice. That's why Oakley says you have a strong program... why you're a winner."

"She said that?"

"Exactly that."

"Wow. She tells me I'm resistant, too prideful, too judgemental, too *everything*. And a tough nut to crack."

"That's what sponsors are supposed to say."

The third time the waiter checked on us, I suggested we leave, but Bear grabbed my hands across the table again. "I have to say a little prayer."

I sighed, impatient and not wanting to cry anymore.

He prayed out loud this time, his voice thankfully quiet. "God... please forgive me for not telling Lela she has black streaks all over her face. But she's beautiful even with the streaks, so thank you."

"Dammit, Bear!" I jerked my hands away to grab a napkin, dunk it in my leftover water, and dab under my eyes.

"A beautiful, sensitive, troubled, idiot woman who cries at hard things *and* soft things. Just what I ordered!"

"Stop!"

"You're right – I ordered the salmon."

I love the silliness of this man! He's so much like me it's kinda spooky. Bear looked at his watch. "It's 9:11. Best two hours I've had in weeks."

"Eleven again! I'll tell you about it some time."

"*Next* time. So we can we go to dinner again?"

And his grin! Silly and serious rolled into one! So endearing. I like him. A lot. Maybe a WHOLE lot.

Vulnerable enough to be coy, I answered, "If you insist."

<<<<<<<>>>>>>

A NEW LOOK AT LUST
CHAPTER 13

Bear and I had made a pact at the end of our second date: no flirting at the POWERLESS club. We would sit on opposite sides of the huge room and be on our own in the parking-lot meetings before and after the scheduled meeting.

As I explained, "Two reasons for this: I don't want your friends to give you shit about thirteen-stepping, and my friends don't need to know that I'm diluting my focus on sobriety."

Plus, it was about setting boundaries. Bear was crazy about me, made it obvious whenever he could, and it felt a little too... um, invasive. When I asked, "We're not middle-schoolers, right? We don't need to touch each other constantly?" he hung his head.

"Repeat, my dear Koala Bear, you know my stance on being paired up in the first place. I'm not ready for a steady – and that's not just Oakley talking, it's me, too."

I talked a good game, but I admit – it was a front. Bear made me feel so special, so loved and important. Knowing I could see him that day got me out of bed in the morning. Though scared of how I'd "become" in a close relationship, I'd dreamed of dipping my toe in the water because I trusted Bear.

But with Oakley's insistence, I lied about how much I liked him. I wanted him to think I was 100 percent independent and would stay that way. "Faking disinterest" was new, and challenging, because it felt like blatant dishonesty. So I let my fear take center stage, insisting I wasn't ready.

Bear grimaced, as he had the first time I told him we wouldn't be an item. He said, "Yeah... I know you're not ready for a steady, as you say. And again, I'll say I hope you're ready soon. There's so much I don't know about you yet, and I'm intrigued as a man can ever be!"

I reddened with embarrassment. How much longer could I play hard to get? I was just as intrigued with him; butterflies filled my stomach, even seeing him from a distance. But I played a cautious, prudish, stand-offish version of a Lela Fox I didn't quite understand yet. *Which Lela am I?*

I didn't reply to his "hope you'll be ready soon" comment, and that helped make my point, I think. Bear took a puff from his mini-cigar and turned for a casual wave at another alkie who passed by. But I remained curious about his instant agreement with my "no flirting at meetings" suggestion and wanted clarification. "But just for curiosity, do public displays of affection bother you?"

"No, no, no! But maybe not at a meeting... out of respect for our singleness of purpose." I simply nodded, then flipped my spent cigarette toward the sandpile we used as an ashtray. Then he grinned, "Otherwise, I'd public-display all over you, dammit! You are... so..." He trailed off, then cleared his throat. "You are of utmost importance to me, as they say. I'd like to make you glow with happiness, treat you like a queen–"

"Listen, Bear. The truth: I still have a lot of issues to work out. I won't burden you with all my baggage."

"But I'm an excellent and ultra-gentle baggage handler. In my younger days, I worked at the airport."

"No shit?"

The grin broadened. "Naw. I'm kidding" I play-punched Bear, giving him shit for teasing me. As we walked into the double doors to the meeting room, he said, "Remember, Lela, we're both alkies – and both of us come with baggage. I'm not one to judge." He tossed his mini-cigar in the sand pile. "No judgement at all."

Yeah, right. If you only knew. I hadn't even told him I'd been thrice-married and wondered how I'd ever tell a boyfriend that I'd slept with more people than *he* had. Oakley said I should never say those things out loud, but I'd feel like a big liar if I didn't infer it somehow.

Maybe you still feel so much Shame that you'll NEVER be able to have sex again.

I sat on the far side, "in the ell," as we called it, usually filled with women near my age. Perched happily in the center was my friend Charlie; she'd *finally* moved out of the halfway house. On her knees in the chair, she was so obviously the leader of her three roomies, who sat with her, hanging on her every word.

Charlie's top-mounted ponytail wagged as she preached to her choir. I couldn't hear her words; I didn't need to. She was setting the world on fire. *Good for you, Charlie! Sober and sane.* Then I swallowed hard, wondering if I could say the same about myself.

But, as my mind wandered during the preamble and readings, I flashed back to what Bear told me. He said something like, "Lela, you're not a run-of-the-mill newcomer. Underneath, you have your shit together. I see a woman who is damn-determined to live the AA way." The phrase echoed in my brain.

Bear gave me confidence. He said I inspired him... and that my idealism made him feel like he'd become lazy over the years. *An old-timer inspired by a newcomer? That's almost backward – but he said that's part of how AA works.* And several times, Bear had told me he was *proud* of me! I was, like, wow!

Those words meant the world to me, still unsure that I was doing it right. *But why does he think you're so smart, Lela? That word he used... sapiosexual? Being attracted to smart people? If you'd let him, Bear could feed your ego straight to bed.*

My mind snapped back to reality when I heard the reverberating low-bass voice of Bear. He rarely shared, but the meeting topic was grief, and a string of people had spoken in small bits. My sweet Bear's super-sexy, soap-opera voice boomed through the big room and seemed to bounce off the walls of the L-shaped section where I sat. He talked about his even-worse-than-dysfunctional relationship with his dad, a sore subject and something he didn't share with me much. But at that meeting, Bear said it was grief, pure and simple, like losing his father when he was still alive.

The more he talked, the more his voice cracked, then a tear escaped from the outside corner of his eye. I found my throat closing up, too, trying to hold back tears. His vulnerability tore my heart out, and I wanted to run over and hug him, squeeze him tight.

Bear, you are so beautifully and intricately human. Sharing such things, either one-on-one or with the group, make me feel so close to you... maybe close enough to share my own vulnerability. But to cry in front of

99

a room of your peers, you must be two things: sincerely hurt and searching for ease, and incredibly confident in yourself and those who surround you. Funny how an AA meeting filled with losers is still a "safe place to talk about hard things."

I looked down so no one could see the tears that threatened to fall, and I listened as many more people shared their grief – not only about those who died, but about the loss of relationships, bridges burned, and opportunities lost. Heartbreak was the common them; I left feeling sad and depressed, not even up for the "meeting after the meeting."

Goddamn disease! I hate alcoholism!

I waved a quick goodbye to Bear as he mouthed the words "call me" and gestured the same.

No radio on the ride home. Deep in thought, I contemplated my sobriety and how lucky I was. And I marveled at Oakley's compliment from the day before: "Lela," she had said, "You have overcome so much – you've been mistreated and betrayed, and you've screwed *yourself* out of much more than that. Yet you don't complain. You're not a whiner. That, my friend, is what sobriety has done for you."

Her comments gave me hope that I could push through the bullshit to come and still stay sober. She said I'd "matured," because – and I quote – "You've stopped making excuses and started making changes." I felt damn-good about my progress and lived and breathed by way of Oakley's bragging on me.

The most surprising thing: the Shame that drove me all my life had begun to ease, little by little, as I learned what Oakley said was the key to my sobriety: "In order to love who you are," she said, "You can't hate the experiences that shaped you."

It seemed Oakley had a quote or an answer to everything. The woman had her shit together in a way I envied, though I doubted I could ever be so serene – ever. Still, I tried to remember how far I'd come, not just how far I had to go.

<<<<<<<<<>>>>>>>>

The night of the grief meeting, I took three hours of "me time." I took time to journal, pouring out the garbage and working through the things eating at me.

After a long bubble bath, I called Bear. We talked about the meeting and I told him how much his sharing had touched me. Obviously, he needed to talk more about his dad, and he did. His voice broke several more times, which made me cry, too.

I offered what I hoped would be a solution. "What about God? Have you told him all this?"

"You don't understand much about my particular God."

"So tell me."

He sighed. "It's a looong story."

"I have a looong time to listen."

After a few beats of silence, he began by describing his religious training as a child in a Catholic church with services spoken in Latin. Like me, he found the Christian hypocrites unnerving, and doubted everything about the Jesus part in particular. Mary, he said, was perhaps a saint, but nothing to "hang your hat on."

We discussed that specific shared belief (or is it *dis*belief?) for a good while, even laughing some. But overall, it was a somber and serious conversation.

Never saying the exact words, it became obvious that his Higher Power was a fairly traditional God, just without "the son" by his side.

"Heaven and Hell? Do you believe?" I asked.

"Definitely. And Purgatory for those who need a second chance."

"Not for babies?"

"No. Babies are pure. I think they go straight to Heaven. We're all God's children. God's miracles, in fact."

"What about baptism?"

"I was baptized, confirmed, too, both in my childhood church. But I don't think God loves me any more or any less because of it."

"I believe the same." With a chuckle, I shared my story of trying church as a way to cure my alcoholism. "I got baptized when I was about 25, and I honestly thought the heavens would suddenly open up... that I'd become a different person."

"*That* only comes with a spiritual experience, dear. The kind Dr. Bob says is absolutely required to get sober."

"I had one of those, too... a spiritual experience, I mean. In fact, maybe *two* of them."

"Do tell..."

I caught my breath, nearly choking. "It's too weird. My Higher Power is of the 'build-it-yourself' variety. He is NOT the Baptist's God, or the Catholic's God, or–"

"Is it a God of any sort?"

"*My* God."

"Then it's not weird. Hit me with it."

He listened carefully as I told my story, from the flash-vision of "Dude," my cousin Lewis wearing torn jeans and smoking a cigarette, to the many times I'd been "overtaken" by the power of Dude. "I cry just thinking about him, Bear. Dude is *so* deep in my heart."

"That sounds wonderful. And if it keeps you sober, I don't care if your Higher Power is Mickey Mouse."

I chuckled. "Yeah, Jenny used to call her Higher Power a Pop-Tart. But I think it was more like a Mother Nature thing. Earthy, just like Jenny."

"Okay, now I have to know who Jenny is."

"Who Jenny *was*."

"Keep talking, dear. I want to know allllll about you."

We talked for nearly two hours. It was an eye-opening 50/50 sharing of our innermost feelings and beliefs. The only thing I left out is how I still struggled in believing that I was worthy of much at all. I shared only morsels of the Shame within me.

Bear kept bragging on how confident I was, and I didn't want to tell him I was the polar opposite.

His honesty, showing his vulnerabilities and innermost fears, sent my heart aflutter; I felt like I knew him intimately. *Uh, oh… intimately – watch how you even MENTION that word, Lela! You're certainly not ready for that!*

Just minutes later, his tone softened, and he whispered, "Can I come over?"

Hesitating, I answered, "It's late, Bear."

"Just barely late. I want to hold you… and… what the hell… I want you to hold me, too. I feel so close to you right now, Lela, and I like the sensation. Let me come over just for an hour. I have to work tomorrow, too."

Oh, God! He wants to make love. I can't! I'm not ready! How could I possibly? I stumbled through a wishy-washy answer that only leaned toward no, and, suddenly, Bear said, "I'll be there in fifteen minutes."

<<<<<<<<<>>>>>>>>>

Cuddling on the sofa, we held each other tight, continuing to share our innermost pain and fears. The topics spanned from continued talk of God, to family relationships, to the meaning of life with an ultra-personal twist.

I shivered with excitement to hear the philosophies of a sober person who was sane and stable in their sobriety. My admiration and respect for Bear had doubled in a matter of three hours.

And we held each other as it clutching life preservers.

The holding became cuddling, which led to kissing, then deeper kissing. I felt a bevy of emotions – from fear to lust and back again a dozen times.

I didn't tell him how nervous I was until he scooped me up and carried me to the bedroom. His cooing and assurances were heartfelt, and I kicked myself for feeling so nervous, fighting the urge to tell him I was "very experienced."

I still thought I should say something but heard Oakley's voice in the back of my mind, speaking louder than the catcalls of "all the men and women" who'd been in my bed.

Halfway into it, he commented: "You definitely know what you're doing, baby." Bear thought it was a compliment, of course, but I burst into tears and everything stopped with a screech.

He didn't push me, didn't ask for an explanation... he just let me cry. I laid my head in the perfect spot big men have – the crook between shoulder and chest. I cried with Shame and embarrassment, pulling the covers up to my chin. My tears dropped on his skin; only once did he chuckle, saying the rolling of my tears tickled his armpit.

Still, I cried.

We both fell asleep in that position. I woke at sunrise. The apartment seemed so quiet, despite a soft snore from Bear's not-so-small nose. I gingerly crawled to the end of the bed without rousing him, put the coffee on, and felt the buzz of anxiety begin its trip through my body. It started at my toes and slowly burned as it rose to my eyes, where it spilled over into tears I didn't try to catch or wipe away.

I tried to reason with myself: *Lela, it's not like you got drunk and slept with the first guy who caught your eye. It's not like he's drunk and only wanting to get in your pants. There's FEELING here.*

Maybe that was the problem; I couldn't force myself to trust the enormous feelings from his end – feelings he made obvious as hell with kind looks and a gentle touch. Feelings and actions so unselfish that he comforted me despite the timing of my outburst, which happened at the worst-possible time for him. He'd been on the verge.

Can you really let someone care for you? Can you trust it? SHOULD you trust it? What if it's another infamous Lela Fox mistake, and you know this seals the deal? And the way your mind works, it means the deal is sealed forever – good, bad, or ugly.

Then I thought... if I was really a slut, as I feared, I wouldn't question whether sex was okay or not. Maybe I'd play-act the refusal, but my true feelings were far different. Not just "real" feelings, but from deep in my heart. Not just from lust or need, but from a practical need to protect myself from myself.

I had a long talk with Dude as I sat on the sofa, and after another cup of coffee, I made my decision. I strutted down the hall to wake Bear wearing nothing but a smile.

Sober sex was weird, so purposeful and tame by comparison. Scary, maybe, and a bit awkward. But not shameful.

Not shameful at all.

>   Whew! What a swirl of feelings on that monumental day. Dazed and confused... but I felt loved, even cherished. Cherished? *Me?* As flabbergasted as I was about Bear's signs of love and kindness toward me, I was beyond flabbergasted about the way I'd taken this huge step without beating myself up or feeling like I'd "sold out."

>   The lovemaking was not at all like I imagined it would be. I felt alive and complete for the first time in years... certainly for the first time since June 29, the day of my last drink. The sex wasn't dirty or like a performance. It was a giving; a giving of the whole of me. And it felt honest.

>   Sex in the years that followed was just as carefully thought-out and just as honest. I thought I'd successfully killed the Shame Monster, at least when it came to making love, but Shame wasn't done with me yet; there was too much of it after so many years of practice.

>   Bear and I became a true pair after that night. But I was still a bit uncomfortable to be so adored, and I pushed him away anytime I felt things were getting too serious.

>   It would become an issue in a very Lela-esque way, time after time.

A DARK AND STORMY NIGHT
CHAPTER 14

The Monday morning status meeting at Ellie Cherry & Associates had become ho-hum; I'd fallen into a steady rhythm since I'd passed the test of my two-month contract. In fact, I'd been on the official payroll for five months, going on six.

During that time, I'd only received only two Cherry awards, which was disconcerting to me. I thought I deserved more. After all, Lela Fox had been the winner of *all* awards *everywhere, all the time* in her previous life, and the so-so accolades pissed me off. The Palm Beach Addy awards were coming up, though, and I hoped to rack up. Funny, it was the Addy's anniversary year – celebrating 111 years. The eleven thing bombarded me daily.

But even without a bushel of awards at Ellie Cherry, everybody seemed happy with my work. I'd had no complaints, and the occasional "atta-boy" from Cole kept me motivated. So I believed I was in the right place, career-wise, and things were smooth as a gentle brook in my personal life.

Spiritually, I rocked. It'd been months of continuous growth, so much so that Dude had become a constant companion in my mind. I didn't always cry when we connected; the relationship had become easy and a part of my everyday life. Prayers were still as casual as talking to my best pal, which also described how I felt about Dude: he was my buddy. My friendly adviser.

I still "saw" him most every time I prayed, and the expressions on his face told me if my thinking was good or bad, according to his judgement. I wanted to please him, desperately so, and I worked hard to keep his expression peaceful and happy.

With Oakley's help and the tons of advice from Bear, I learned how to live in honesty and with kindness in my heart. So my Dude smiled 95 percent of the time.

So maybe it was Dude agreeing with my career progress... or the aura of the Ellie Cherry building, but the eleven thing continued. No matter the cause, elevens fed my sense of satisfaction with my position in life and work.

Every time I looked at the clock, it was eleven-something or something-eleven. And many times, my wallet held exactly eleven bucks. Once, eleven pennies, too. My milk always seemed to list the eleventh day of the month as its expiration date. Even the job number for my big TV production for Bausch & Lomb was 11111.

I'd come to see the elevens as Dude giving me a sign that "all was well," and I'd started thanking him out loud each time his message came through.

A few weeks prior, those thank you's got me in hot water. In Deidre's office with Ellie and Prudence, at the moment my boss emphasized a key fact that I should've written down and circled, Deidre's fancy clock chimed eleven. I said, "Thanks, Dude" in the silence, and they looked at me like I was a Looney Tunes. There was no viable explanation, so I simply said, "Never mind," but I saw their eyes roll... I saw them mistrust me.

Of course, in my magic magnifying mind, that meant I would be fired immediately after the meeting, released for koo-koo issues, and I got nervous. But the next time I glanced at Deidre's clock, it read 11:11. This time I *wrote* "Thanks, Dude" on my notepad, along with a smiley face.

<<<<<<<<<<>>>>>>>>>

The day Bo's graduation invitation came in the mail, I booked my flight to Nashville. Every time I thought about how far away he was, though, I cried. Despite three years' time to come to terms with it, I still hadn't healed from losing custody of him. *But you KNOW you couldn't have taken care of him when you were drinking! And you are SO LUCKY that his dad wanted to, even in Bo's oh-so-sassy teen years.*

I had never imagined pain that deep, or the level of disappointment in myself could drive me so much further into alcoholism. I still believed it was a turning point in my life and my disease.

Memories of the day Andy told me they were moving flooded back as if it had happened yesterday. Oh, how hard I'd cried! How much I hated myself! And how drunk I got... for weeks and weeks afterward.

I came face-to-face with my alcoholism as my teenaged son set up a perfect room in a perfect home with Andy and his perfect wife Ella in a perfect new community hundreds of miles away. And no amount of sobriety and acceptance could ease the pain I still felt.

I would be there for his special day, no doubt, and I'd bring the whole fam-damily with me. Dozens of phone calls later, I everybody was in. Mom and Dad would caravan with Karen and John from Jackson City, plus Jennifer and her new husband Thayer would travel from Rockville. The ceremony was Friday night; the cheapest flight was at – yep, 9:11 AM.

At the Monday meeting before my trip, I announced I'd be gone on Friday and requested a four-day workload instead of five. For reasons I didn't understand, the room silenced immediately, and Cole looked at me with an open mouth. Surprised? Angry? I didn't know what he was thinking.

My eyes darted around the room, met by grimaces and open-mouthed looks of astonishment mixed with... *is that disgust?*

I asked, "What? Hey, y'all, it's my son's high school graduation! I *won't* miss that!" No expressions changed as their eyes seared my skin.

Prudence, who rarely spoke at those meetings, croaked "Lela, you must..." then cleared her throat and straightened up primly in her chair. "See me after the meeting, please."

"Sure, Prudence." I reasoned it had something to do with the deadline for two specific projects that Cole had listed for Friday. *No problem. Surely he can move them or get another writer to finish, or I can just try to get them done early. Why is everybody being so weird about it?*

As if on cue, Isabella, who'd grown out of puppyhood but remained small enough to fit in a small purse, yipped from her perch on Ellie's lap. Thankfully, laughter from the group broke the tension. *But why the tension? What the hell is going on?*

<<<<<<<<<>>>>>>>>>

Prudence's office felt cold, like a museum of organizational techniques; her pens and pencils aligned just-so, project bags carefully placed in wall pockets, also perfectly in line. Nothing personal adorned her desk, not even a photograph, and she had color-coded her otherwise all-business black-and-white calendar. Notes were also color-coded and written in neat and perfect architect's block lettering.

I marveled that anyone could be so anal. *You're a little OCD yourself, and so is Damon, but she's spooky-extreme. Persnickety Prudence needs a therapist, or maybe just to get laid.*

The largest object on her desk: a gallon jug of Purell hand sanitizer, complete with an oversized pump. She'd already pumped it twice by the time she pulled a monstrous binder from the too-neat bookcase. "Lela. There is a problem. A serious problem."

My eyes grew wide; I had no idea what she was talking about. "What problem? Did I do something wrong?"

"Did you ever!" I cocked my head, trying to think what I could have done to gain the disdain of Hitler. She dropped the bomb: "Requests for days off must come two weeks prior to the release, Lela. It's in the employment contract in black and white. A heading, in fact."

"Oh." *Has it been so long since you've worked for somebody else that you forgot shit like that? I know she's picky about being on time, but it's just ONE day! And a Friday, which is pretty casual around here.*

Muttering, I said, "I guess, uh, I didn't even think about it. Maybe because I've been self-employed for so long, ya know?" *Admit that it's been years since you've worked for yourself, Lela. You didn't think of it because you're too much into your own life to think about the needs of others!*

I'd had problems with rules all my life, especially through rehab, but I assumed adult professionals would prove more flexible. Humans allowing other humans to have normal human needs. I said as much to Prudence.

Her answer was snippy and perfectly enunciated. "Being yourself is contrary to our policies." It sounded so ridiculous that I laughed. An open mouth, slap-your-knee laugh.

"What could *possibly* be funny? This is a serious infraction, Ms. Fox!"

"So we're back to 'Ms. Fox' again, huh? I guess I should've just called in sick."

Prudence gasped and jerked herself to full sitting height. "That is an *outrageous* attitude! This is your *job*, not your personal life. We hired you to *work* every day, every week, nine until five. And we pay you well, Ms. Fox. *You owe us your loyalty.*"

I paused, thinking how inhumane her comment had been. "Sorry. I'm way more loyal to my son." I stood to go. There was no reason to take this kind of shit from such an uppity bitch. "Prudence, I will handle it differently next time."

"You realize that 'next time' may be your last?"

"What? *Two* strikes and you're out?"

"Exactly. This is a chargeable offense."

"You're writing me up?" The buzz between my ears began, softly at first, then rising to a scream when I realized part of what Prudence had said was correct. I was an employee. They pay me well. I broke the rules.

"Ellie will want to speak with you, too."

"More of this.... admonishment! I only need to be told once, okay?"

"Evidently not."

"Whatever, Prudence!" I sighed. "Write me up. This is ridiculous. How can I be creative when I'm being micro-managed by you and your anal-retentive rules? Huh? Answer me that!"

Prudence didn't reply; her face reddened, and I saw her jaw clench. She stood, pushing up with her fingers on the desk. "You are excused, Ms. Fox."

"Excused? Like, my *absence* is excused?"

"Absolutely not!"

"Okay, okay! Chill out. Don't have a stroke here in the office. Might be messy."

Her jaw clenched tighter as I turned toward the door. Then I stopped just before the hall, spun around, and blew her a kiss.

Sober or not, don't mess with Lela Fox. Dare to treat me like a child, and I'll kill you with kindness. Piss you off just for fun. So back off, Hitler.

"Have a blessed day," I cooed like a bird, then stomped back to the creative department, closed my office door, and called Oakley. She had no sympathy for me, either. In fact, she gave me more shit than Prudence had.

What is wrong with you, Lela? Are you just an asshole at heart? I wonder what Bear will say. Have I really screwed up, or do I just work at the wrong place?

I looked at the clock, hoping for an eleven, counted the bills in my wallet... nothing. "I need you, Dude," I said aloud. No reply, not even a tingle in my spine. My heart sunk as I realized the problem was mine, and I was on my own.

Okay, you slob, brace yourself and come to terms with the facts. You screwed up. An honest mistake, maybe, but you broke a rule, just as Oakley said. And you have to pay the price.

"Sobriety sucks!" The fact that nobody heard me made the concept even more ominous.

<<<<<<<<<<>>>>>>>>>

The rental car had a Tennessee plate, which made me smile. I met Mom and Dad at the hotel in Nashville around four; my sisters and their hubs had been in the lobby when I came in, and we'd talked trash for a half-hour. Seeing everybody again made my heart swell, so grateful for their love and support that tears came without warning.

Seeing Bo walk across the stage would be bittersweet, not just because he'd be crowned an official adult, but also because I disagreed with his choices for the future.

After Bo's dad, Andy, cheated on his wife and moved in with the hussy mistress, my sweet son had decided to stay with his recently-ex-stepmother Ella and commute to some bullshit community college.

I felt he was putting his life on hold for a pissant divorcée in mourning. Even worse, I knew Ella depended on my kid Bo for emotional comfort and handyman tasks! Bo had told me.

I had big-time issues with her for demanding that Bo be her caretaker. If I thought too long and kept Dude's opinion out of it, I could envision my hands around her throat, choking the life from her red-headed ass.

She'd been so good to him for seven years, supporting him and encouraging his success in all areas... then this. *What is she thinking? How DARE she use my child for her own adult needs?!*

I pondered this on the drive to Parnell High School. An hour later, my family and I stood by a fence on the football field – front row – and watched kids in robes *rush* across the stage. The principal had knowingly sped the process, seeing the coal-black cloud moving our way.

The wind picked up in the F's of alphabetic names. A doozy of a storm was coming our way, no doubt. It was like watching a scary movie, seeing the bad guy creeping up behind the fence in cut-away screenshots. Doom was upon us and the crowd's whispers turned to alarmed screeches as the last student walked.

The kids threw their caps in the air, then the bottom fell out of the sky.

A bolt of thunder arrived simultaneously with a streak of lightning bright enough to cause squints. A storm challenging the apocalypse at a crowded high school football field, among a crowd of 500, each of us a prime target for a lightning strike. I heard Mom say a prayer as Daddy put his protective arm around her.

The second shot of lightning ended in a deafening *"CRACK!"* from the front of the school. One tree, gone. Who or what would be next?

We ran like hell, becoming separated by the frantic crowd and Bo fled with the graduates to parts unknown. I worried about Karen, knowing her pace was slow, but felt assured Jennifer and Thayer would be fine.

Worry for myself began when my suede pumps sunk into the sodden earth, and I realized I couldn't remember where I parked in relation to the "shortcut" I'd taken. *White car, Tennessee plates. Shit! Everybody will have Tennessee plates! Is it this way or more to the left?* People were running ahead of me and others passed in a dead run, left and right. I'd removed my shoes and stubbed my toe when stepping onto the asphalt. Then I stopped. *No need to rush. I'm drenched already and hopelessly lost.*

Karen and John had ridden with me. Walking with my head down, I heard Karen shout my name from a few yards behind. "John knows where we parked!" *Of course he does! John knows everything... all the time. How else could the scattered Karen function?*

I dug for my keys, rain dripping off my face and hair and into my purse. All four of us were panting from the exertion, and the first thirty seconds in the car were silent except for our gasps for air. "Wow! What about that?! I've never seen such a..." Karen couldn't finish the sentence.

I added, "And to see it coming in such... so black and white. Spooky as hell. Mother Nature must be completely pissed off!"

Ever the practical John said, "But the problem isn't over. The party at Ella's is outdoors, right? I'm sure the tent has blown away. Maybe I can chase it down, find it somewhere in the neighborhood. Do you think Andy will help?"

I answered with a sigh. "I have no clue what Bo's dad will do, nor what Ella will do when she sees his new harlot-girlfriend. Bo says they haven't met yet. What a night it will be!"

<<<<<<<<<>>>>>>>>

"Good to see you, Lela. Welcome. The kids are still out in the rain, whooping it up, I'm sure. Some storm, huh?" Ella's tone was high-pitched; she must have been nervous as hell. I'm sure the mixed-family party didn't sit well with her.

My family, her family, Andy's family... all mixed together and headed by Andy's mother and Bo's grandmother, Grandma Joy. As always, Joy played the fake socialite, acting happy to see everybody, when, in reality, she hated them all, and especially me.

I was just grateful that his ex-stepfather, my ex Miller McKeown, wasn't there.

Grandma Joy's ooey-gooey fakery made me proud of my mother's genuine demeanor, though 100 percent conservative and exactly what she considered "appropriate." Again, people commented on how opposite my Mom and Dad were... my father, the gregarious teaser, and Mom, the Southern Belle.

I met Andy at the punch bowl by happenstance and put my plan in motion without hesitating. "Andy, I'm sober. Nine months and counting. I have my shit together and, maybe-just-maybe, everybody will start trusting me again. Bo's not ready yet, I don't think, but he'll get there."

"So what's up with the necklace?"

"What necklace?"

"Yours, dumbass. Is that your new cult symbol?"

I'd been shopping at the Recovery Store, chock-full of AA trinkets. "Oh... this." I touched my pendant, a round disc in amethyst and sterling. "It's the AA triangle. Unity, recovery, and service. One day at a time, of course." I smiled, quite proud of my new jewelry and my strong ties to Alcoholics Anonymous.

"Like I said, a cult."

"No, Andy! Not at all! You're judging something you don't know about."

"I've known people... AA is a cult and makes an alcoholic drink *more!* So don't come around me bragging about your sobriety. I don't buy it – not one bit."

Numb, I said nothing more until I felt a presence beside me. As I turned my head, Andy said, "Lela, meet Joann, my wife." *Oh, my God! What an ugly woman! And they're MARRIED!*

This Joann woman's teeth were brown, and several ended in a point, rotten. Black hair, tinged with sickly gray, fell to her mid-back and outward, but it was so thin and damaged that she looked bald. Her scalp showed, covered with red-and-rust scabs that could have been psoriasis or gangrene or a weeping infection. Either way, she was a frightening mess, making me think of the Wicked Witch. *Yes, a witch. All she needs is a hat.*

Andy beamed, wrapping his arm around her shoulders as she looked up at him with creepy adoration. I shuddered; Andy noticed and asked, "What's the problem, Lela? Jealous?"

"Hell-no!"

"Then what?"

You have to say something. Some kind of bullshit... whatever. Speak up, Lela! "Uh, just wondering how Ella is handling this, I guess."

Joann put her hand on my arm. *No! Don't touch me!* "I really *can't* care what she thinks, Lela. She hates me, of course... thinks I ruined her life, but what can I do? This day is for Bo. His entire family should be here, and we should all get along."

"I agree, 100 percent. Andy and I have always had a calm and respectful relationship..." I ignored Andy's snort in the background. "But some people are just more vindictive. I guess that's the word."

Andy raised his voice. "Vindictive is an understatement!" His eyes bulged out of his head, and I realized a shitload of stories about how Ella had wronged him were sure to come.

So the timing was perfect: five boys in graduation gowns burst through the front door and the crowd stood to applaud. Daddy put two fingers to his lips and let loose with one of his famous cat-call whistles from across the room. I rushed to hug Bo, proud mom that I was.

As Bo went down the line of his family, ex-family, and ex-step-family, Grandma Joy continued with shrieks of how proud she was of the smaarrrt boy. More fakery, more uncomfortable small talk. Wishing I could be anywhere but there, I had a long discussion with Dude to get me through. My fake smile looked genuine, according to Karen, who was clueless enough to not feel the tension.

During the evening, I noticed Bo sneaking out now and then with his girlfriend and the other guys, then coming in laughing way too loud. It struck me that he could be drinking, and I panicked. Scooting next to Karen, I asked. "You think Bo is drinking in the backyard?"

Thankfully, she didn't react dramatically; that would've sent me to the moon with worry and the inevitable Guilt. "He's out there kissing on that *girl* and you know it! Bo is a blue-eyed, blonde-headed hunk of a man! And isn't this his first girlfriend?"

"As far as I know."

"Maybe they're planning something for tonight, like a prom-night repeat. Quit worrying."

But I did worry. All night.

Bo came to our hotel on Saturday morning, and we all went out to breakfast. Except for his meek girlfriend, we were loud – a table from hell for the waitress. But I'd maneuvered the crowd, insisting that I sit next to Bo.

Throughout the meal, we poked fun at each other, and I glowed about his attitude toward me; he was welcoming, open, and happy... treating me beautifully different from his ways over the past nine months of sobriety. *Maybe he's ready to trust me again. Maybe he believes in me now! Oh, Dude, please! Let it be true!*

After his last pancake, he turned to me, leaning low to whisper in my ear. "Mom, do you need those decapacitating classes?"

My forehead showed deep burrows of confusion. "What are you talking about?"

"I mean... well, to get you back to normal after leaving the cult. I'll help you if you need me to."

Looking him directly in the eye, I opened my mouth to explain, but I was, literally, speechless. "You... don't... oh, Bo, it's..." To correct his vocabulary to "decompression classes" would make his belief in a cult even stronger... to say anything about *anything* would make everything worse.

I closed my eyes, encompassed in a black cloud of doom and emotional separation from my own son. Tears stung my eyes, but I refused to cry at the table, especially in front of Bo and his girlfriend. *What could be more embarrassing than a sobbing mother at breakfast?*

He repeated, "What, Mom? What can I do?"

I shook my head, tried to shake off nausea the last sixty seconds had brought. "I'm fine, Bo. Never mind."

"Are you sure?"

"Seriously! I'm fine!" Desperate to change the subject, I said, "Have a great weekend, son. I'm happy to meet your girlfriend – she's cute and sweet, and, most importantly, she giggles at you like she's supposed to."

"I think I'm in love."

I closed my eyes again, feeling faint. "There's plenty of time to figure all that out, son. One day at a time."

<<<<<<<>>>>>>

SIDELINE BUCKS
CHAPTER 15

Bear and I were at Longhorn Steakhouse when he offered the ingenious solution. We'd finished a grand dinner, and I'd thanked him three times for accommodating my primal need for a ribeye when he had to opt for the grilled chicken. Despite his diet, he denied me nothing when it came to food.

But that night was the third time I'd caught him staring at my plate and salivating, and it creeped me out. "Bear, if you want a bite, take it. Please. Otherwise, keep your eyes off my food. It's weird."

"Oh? Was I doing that?"

"You know you were. The whole thing makes me feel terrible!"

"No, don't let it make you feel bad in *any* way. My diet is not your diet."

I looked up through my eyelashes at him. "But I've been thinking... maybe I *am* doing wrong. Isn't eating in front of you the same as drinking in front of an alcoholic?"

"That depends on who the alcoholic is, dear. I mean, you wouldn't drink in front of somebody just out of detox, but this diet has been my thing for a long time and I'm cool with it. Haven't relapsed in over a year this time."

"But sometimes you watch me eat."

He sat back farther into the booth. "I don't mean to do it, but, yeah, watching that juicy steak swirled in butter slide between your clean, white teeth... it's so exciting!" He closed his eyes and smacked his lips.

"Stop! You're being a creep!"

"I am not!" he said, speaking through a chuckle.

I laughed, too, but I squirmed at the same time. The conversation made me uncomfortable, though I'd been the one to bring it up. Bear flashed the million-dollar smile. "Seriously, honey, I'm happy that you're free to eat. It's just that... I'm not."

I pushed for answers despite the discomfort; the topic had been bothering me, and it wasn't so easy to bring up. "Because it goes deeper than a diet for you, right? It's an *addiction*. So you're sure I don't tempt you?

"Not really."

"Not really... but not a full 'no?'"

With his index fingers pressed together and resting on his upper lip, he looked at the ceiling, thinking. "I don't guess I'll ever stop dreaming about fattening foods, but it has nothing to do with *you*. If I watch you, then I must watch everybody without knowing it.

"Still, I don't want to make you feel bad."

"No way you could do that!" He burst into a wide grin. "With you, it's quite the opposite! You make me feel *great!*" Bear grabbed my hand and brought it to his mouth to kiss. I'd yet to tell him how much I hated that... because I also loved it.

"Okay, Romeo. Just don't look at my food. No sideways glances, either."

"I promise." He held up three fingers, the symbol for Boy Scouts' honor.

Bear cleared his throat. Twice. "Since we're on touchy subjects, can I ask you something?" Then he waved his hand in front of his mouth as if trying to erase the words. "No, sorry. It's none of my business. Forget I said anything!" He sat back again, looking defeated.

"Stop that shit. Now you *have to* ask."

He muttered several beginnings of a sentence he couldn't finish, and I sat still, wondering what could be so hard to say. The buzz between my ears said it may be something important. As if telling a secret, he said, "I tried to not look, I really did."

"Dammit! Just say it!"

A long pause, during which my blood pressure started an alarming rise. "Okay. At your apartment the other day?" His urging expression caused me to nod. "I saw a big pile of your credit card bills and one with a huge, huge balance. That makes me worry."

In shock and 100 percent embarrassed, I snapped myself up to full sitting height, grabbed my napkin, and dabbed my lips, which didn't need dabbing. I fidgeted with the black cloth, folding it in triangles, folding again. I didn't speak for a full two minutes while Bear blubbered multiple apologies and assurances that he wasn't trying to get into my business.

He ended with a summary. "It's just, honey, I know you make a good salary, and I'd like to know if you're short on money."

I snapped my head toward him, raising one eyebrow. "That's *none* of your business, dammit! And you've really pissed me off." I tried to keep an even tone, but there was a growl deep within.

He was frantic. "Wait! No! Because I can help you!" He paused, then spoke out loud to himself. "But I've obviously pissed her off and now she's going to slap me and tell me to leave her the hell alone. She might even break up with me! Oh, if she only knew how sorry I was! If she just knew that my motivations are pure!"

"I don't need your help, Bear. I'm not, like, mad-mad at you, but I'm embarrassed as hell. *Nobody* knows those totals – not Damon, not Lola, not even my *mother!* Only Oakley. Definitely wreckage of the past... or, more specifically, the wreckage of Stuart."

"That sonofabitch put you in debt?"

"That's the biggest part of it. Then he robbed my apartment, and I had to buy a bunch of stuff as replacements. The debt keeps growing." I sighed. "It's out of control. Drives me batty."

"I can help you."

"*Hell* no! I won't take a dime! Look what you already give me! You take me to nice places, won't let me pay for anything! I should be–"

"I didn't mean that I'd give you money, silly."

Oh. Not realizing the anxiety encompassing my body until that moment, I took a deep breath to relax. Closing my eyes, I asked calmly, "Then *what?* What do you mean?"

Bear's volume rose two levels. "Now *I'm* pissed! First, that you think I'd be stupid enough to offer a headstrong, independent woman like Lela Fox a wad of cash! You would call that an insult, and that's *not at all* what I meant. Plus, I've heard of Stuart's counterfeit bills, so you'd thrown an even-bigger fit."

"True."

"What I offer is an opportunity to earn money on the side."

"Oh, that's better." Then my mind reeled. "No! It could be *worse!* What kind of sideline are you thinking ab–"

"Stop. Don't you know computers? Like how to do checkbooks on them... what's it called? That new money software?"

"Do you mean QuickBooks?"

"Yeah! That's the one. My company needs somebody to set up the program, and it's complicated for our multiple locations and contract salespeople. Plus, I know another lady, a wholesaler who needs somebody, and maybe another client for you. You could freelance."

My heart rate had returned to normal, and my mind churned with possibilities. "Actually... I *can* do that. I know a lot about QuickBooks. Did it for my sister's frame shop, payroll and everything, and a simpler setup for me. But I'm not an expert or anything. So I can't do something like a *real* computer pro would do, so–"

"Lori, that's the office manager at my company, told me the estimate from a QuickBooks installer, a professional guy. Two thousand bucks!"

"What?! That's ridiculous!"

"Then can you do it for seven hundred? I'll tell Lori the whole deal – that you're a friend and knowledgeable user but not an official computer geek.

"Tell me what you want the software to do and what reports you'll need."

"That's a Lori question. Let me talk to her, then you two can sit down and discuss details."

I pursed my lips... thinking of potential problems. "You realize I'd have to set up the payroll, too, and I'd find out how much you make. That would be too weird."

"Not weird, just go in there and change the number. Add several zeros and make it not taxable."

I smiled. "Be serious."

"That doesn't bother me, Lela. Besides, I'm on commission, right? My income varies so much you couldn't keep tabs on it."

He let me have silence to contemplate; in the end, I agreed whole-heartedly.

<<<<<<<<<<>>>>>>>>>>

A bright, sunny Saturday. "Hey, Lori! I'm here." She was a gracious woman, early 40s maybe, who set me up in an office at the yacht-sales office where Bear worked. The office was fancy, as appropriate for a yacht buyer, I suppose, but the rooms were empty and all sounds bounced off the Danish-Modern furniture, amplified three-fold.

I settled in, inserted the software disc and went to work, creating specific categories for each of the company's locations and subcategories for each type of expense. I set a template for reports and saved them in all the appropriate places, working efficiently for almost five hours. I hadn't finished by the time Lori had to leave – by four, she had said. I panicked.

"I'll have to come back next Saturday, Lori. I'm sorry." The delay wasn't really my fault; their needs were complicated. Overall, I was damn-proud of what I'd accomplished. But Lori's look of disappointment sucked all the pride from my gut.

Then she beamed a smile, disappointment replaced by hope. "Maybe tomorrow? Bear could come and let you in? I really need it this week, see?"

"I can do it. I'll call to make sure *he* can."

The next day, I met Bear at the door at noon. He unlocked it, and just a few steps inside, he reached under my arms and picked me up for a full-circle swirl. "I sure love my Lela!" he said.

Oh, shit! Did he say "love" as in "love-love?" No… that wouldn't be how he'd tell me if it was true. Surely not! His words freaked me out, because "love" wasn't the word I would use with him. At least not yet – I'd learned to pay attention to red flags after all I'd been through.

The food addiction was a big red flag, especially after two more instances of him eyeing my food. One night at TGI Fridays, his eyes ate my nachos for me. I got pissed, mostly for show, and offered to move to another table. But I had no way to win the "argument" except to not eat. And I refused to do that.

And I refused to follow him on the grilled chicken route; I didn't need to lose weight, anyway. If anything, I was still too thin.

As he swung me around the second time, I shouted in mid-air, "Put me down, babe. I must get busy!"

He lowered me gently and put his hands on both shoulders, looking deeply into my eyes. I thought, "Oh shit… here it comes." My butt cheeks squeezed together with anxiety. *Don't say it, Bear. Not yet. There are still too many unknowns.*

He kissed my forehead and pushed back, his hand still on my shoulders. "I have work to do, too, my love. Do you need help?"

"No, I'm still set up in the front office." *And since when do you call me "my love?" That's new. And stop it! That L-word scares me.*

"I have a lead on a pre-owned Boston Whaler in Miami, and a high-roller in Fort Lauderdale who wants it."

"Good! Go sell something! Do your yacht-broker thing, Mr. Big Bucks."

"If I can make the sale, we'll go out on the town!"

I laughed, but there would be no partying that night; that wasn't our thing. We went out to dinner a lot, but Bear and I were more the picnic-in-the-park type, long walks on the beach, playing trivia games at his place, reading recovery books to each other, and talking AA. After all those years in bars and taverns and pulling all-nighters, I loved our slow, intimate nights together.

Two hours later, I had finished setting up the office QuickBooks. Bear had only come in to distract me three times. I left a note for Lori (and an invoice!), setting up our training session for Monday night. Bear locked the door behind us and we walked on the sidewalk holding hands.

A great day to be grateful.

I programmed QuickBooks templates for several clients over the next six months and earned almost $4,000. These opportunities came from simple word of mouth, but it all began with Bear's first and second recommendations, and I felt grateful as hell.

He never took credit for my increasing success at this; wouldn't even accept my thanks. He just said, "I knew you could do it."

Bear was an enigma. He enjoyed taking care of me while encouraging me to take care of myself. I don't know how he did both; it still amazes me that Lela Fox, who believed she was a pile of shit her entire life, could also be a confident, self-sufficient woman.

I give credit to sobriety, of course, but also to Bear. Maybe he helped so much because he loved both sides of me and all 42 of my personalities. And he made sure I knew it.

<<<<<<<<>>>>>>>

IT'S FIESTA TIME
CHAPTER 16

About 75 percent of the QuickBooks money went straight to my Visa balance, but I was still deeply in debt. The Guilt about it ate at my stomach lining. Even though it was half Stuart's fault, I knew it was me who let it happen. In those days, I was too drunk and disoriented to stop it or put my foot down. So the balance grew exponentially as I watched with terrified eyes.

Then why are you buying shit on eBay now, Lela? Do you really think all that Fiesta Ware and antique dinnerware will make you rich?

It was in the early days of eBay, and on my lonely nights, I browsed for hours, at first looking for nothing in particular. Intrigued, I kept clicking back to the bright-colored 1940s antique Fiesta pieces, comparing prices and colors.

I bought four books about Fiesta's history and charts for piece-by-piece valuations, and spent two weeks studying before I placed my first bid. Soon, I became an eBay addict, and soon after that, became the proud owner of a shitload of fine Fiesta pieces.

The plates and teacups didn't excite me; I focused on the serving pieces: pitchers, platters, gravy boats, sugar bowls... those kinds of things.

Before long, there were sixty pieces in my collection, and, still, I kept buying. My dedication to using every extra cent to pay the credit balances had waned.

I displayed the Fiesta on my only nice piece of furniture, an antique cabinet with scoop-bin drawers above and below the massive top. The previous owner had restored it, stripping all the official value as an antique, but it was gorgeous.

The cabinet's colossal size made a bold statement; people noticed 100 percent of the time. Oakley offered me $400 for it, a lot of money back in the day, but I refused.

I sold the antique cabinet to begin Lifetime Number Nine, along with 200+ pieces of the Fiesta Ware I'd acquired during my perilous years as an eBay addict.

I stubbornly refused to sell any of it... until necessity became front-and-center. Now, I'm thrilled that I waited because I quadrupled Oakley's offer on the cabinet, and as I sold the Fiesta Ware to others (on eBay, of course), several pieces sold for seven or eight times my original investment. The money help finance my final Lifetime.

But as beautiful as the dinnerware was, it's to blame for a life-changing tragedy – one that required me to re-learn how to walk and talk and think and act.

Specifically, the culprit was a raincoat-yellow gravy boat. I sold that piece first, the only revenge I had. The highest bid was $415, a drop in the bucket compared to what it cost me otherwise.

<<<<<<<>>>>>>

BEWARE THE IDES OF MARCH
CHAPTER 17

"Lela! It's Lola. I'm glad you answered."

"I'm glad you called! We haven't talked all week, girl." I'd stayed in close touch with Lola, my ex-employee and professional enabler, as I called her. But she wasn't ex-anything by then. She was as close as a long-distance friend can be, challenging Mom for my phone time.

Lola had news, teasing me about what it was. "He said it out loud," she sang, her voice rising on the last syllable.

"*Who* said *what* out loud?"

"Damon."

"Damon said *what?* You're killing me!"

"In a crowd of people."

"What did he *say?!*"

Keeping the sing-song tone, Lola spilled the beans. "He told everybody he was in love with you and that the two of you would end up married. Then everybody started taking bets on it."

"*What?!* Dammit!"

"Lela, you best just accept it. He's in love and determined to win you over."

I sighed, feeling guilty for even being his friend, and angry that he still didn't understand how I felt.

"Then I'm not going to talk to him anymore. Ever. He obviously doesn't believe that I'm not girlfriend material."

"I still don't see why not."

"Because Damon is too damn *nice!* Too persnickety, too much of a caretaker, too worried about me. He's the type that would put his cape over the puddle so I wouldn't wet my feet, know what I mean? It creeps me out!"

"I still don't understand. Lela, everybody needs tender loving care!"

"I'm getting plenty of that from Bear. And loving every minute." I giggled.

"Yeah, Damon knows about your precious Bear."

Frustrated, I snapped, "Of *course* he knows! I've told him with no reservations! Because it doesn't matter, dammit! Damon and I are just *friends!*"

"He thinks he can talk you into marrying him."

I clenched my jaw. "Damon is not, and will never be, my boyfriend – and certainly not my husband!"

"When you get so mad about it, I wonder if you're fooling yourself... that you really do want him, but won't allow yourself to."

"No!"

"Then what are you going to do?"

I relaxed enough to sigh. "All I can do is talk to him *again*. Spell it out *again*: N-O, Damon!" I knew I had to do what I was trying to avoid, admitting it. "I'll just have to quit talking to him entirely, quit answering his calls."

Lola didn't reply. The silence lasted five seconds before I blurted, "I'm tired of talking about that! You're always pushing me, girl. I don't like it, and right now, my fuse is short."

"Okay, I'll change the subject. Any more good Fiesta Ware out there?"

"I don't want to talk about that, either."

Lola sighed. "You're being difficult."

"I guess I am."

Then she giggled. "Okay... I have good news."

"Spit it out."

"I bought my airline ticket!" Her sing-song voice had returned.

I cheered. "Yay! March fifteenth, Beware the Ides of March!"

"The what?"

"Shakespeare, Lola."

"Oh. Then no wonder I'm lost."

I ignored her, focusing on details. "What time do you get here?"

"Early! We'll have the full afternoon on Friday!"

"Don't back out, girl, because I had to move heaven and earth to get that day off."

Without pausing, Lola changed the subject. "Damon says you're even more beautiful sober."

"Quit talking about Damon!"

"I was talking about *you*. But I want to see your sober face. The last time I saw you..."

"At my wedding." I groaned, knowing what was coming next.

"Right. Sorry to put it this way, but you looked like shit. Like a drunk. Stuart looked like a zombie, too. Is he still leaving you alone?"

"Pretty much." Lola's silence afterward made it obvious she didn't believe me; I'd let too much slip. "But so far, he doesn't know where I work. I never go the same way twice."

"You poor girl, I wish–"

"I don't know why I'm telling you this, but I have to tell somebody. I'm going nuts!"

"What's going on, Miss Lela?"

"His messages have become more threatening. He's crazy-mad that I won't sign the divorce papers."

"Why hasn't he just gone to court alone? You don't *have* to be there."

"I don't know why he won't go, Lola. There must be a reason. Maybe he's in some kind of trouble. Hell, maybe he can't pay court costs with counterfeit money. Whatever, but it's time to change my phone number again."

"Again?"

"Yeah." A sigh. "I get tired of that part, but it's time. The last message he left was eerie. He said he'd hunt me down and beat the shit out of me."

"You're in danger, Lela! Again, *again* – call the damn police!"

"It might come to that... after this new threat. It was a direct warning, in fact, and his voice was sloppy. Like he was drunk, or so mad that he was foaming at the mouth. It's a visual I'm having a hard time getting out of my mind."

I let silence fall on the line, thinking she was probably right about calling the police... and that I probably wouldn't call. "I'll just change my number again, and I don't want to talk about that anymore, either."

"You're impossible!"

"No, I'm at peace and don't want to interrupt that peace with Stuart Weinstein's drama. Or *any* drama. So tell me what's up with you."

After arguing about my "denial of reality," she succumbed to my shift in topic and started talking... rambling, actually.

"Are you working full time yet?" I asked, interrupting.

"Nope. Still doing a zillion things by the job. But I'm making killer money right now and have about a dozen clients lined up for spring garden projects."

"Good. I know you love digging in the dirt!"

"What I really want to do is dig in the sand in West Palm Beach! The idols of March, right?"

I laughed. "*Ides. Ides* of March. It's a Roman calendar thing, my friend. Shakespeare, Julius Caesar. The day of his assassination, according to the–"

"Don't throw your fancy-dancy trivia crap on *me!* So that's why you're beating Bear at *Trivial Pursuit* every night, right?"

"Yeah, but he knows a lot of random things, too. Still, I usually win."

"So you think this relationship will last? At least until the Ides of March?"

"I see no reason why not." My mind whirled to the one reason that might make that statement untrue, but I left my doubts unsaid. "Lola, be warned: he's a big guy. A lumberjack of a guy. Goliath."

"Your words keep getting bigger."

"But he's getting smaller, I think."

"What? Why do you say that?"

"It's a long story. I'll tell you one day when I've had time to think it through. I may need your wise-girlfriend advice."

"Yours for the taking."

"Bye! I love you, Lola."

"You, too. Have a great night. Are you going out?"

"Bear's coming over in a bit. He's helping me arrange some things in my closet."

"Good to have a man around."

"You've got that right! My last two weren't handy at all. Bear is, indeed, a scary bear. And a cuddly teddy bear, then a Grizzly bear when need be. An all-around good bear."

Lola laughed. "Later, girl.

<<<<<<<<<>>>>>>>>

When Bear came over, he walked straight to the kitchen and opened the refrigerator. As always. For the tenth time, I asked, "Why do you do that?"

"Just curious," he answered, as always. But I knew the reason for his curiosity and rolled my eyes. It made my stomach turn sour.

I pushed him out of the kitchen toward the sofa. "Want to see my latest Fiesta purchases? Good stuff last week!"

"Sure." This was a constant when he came over... me showing off my latest Fiesta Ware finds. It may have been feigned excitement, for my benefit only, but he seemed to love the new green teapot, complete with a lid – a rare piece – and listened patiently as I pointed out its finer points.

A sugar/creamer set in turquoise was also rare, given only during a short promotion in 1940. I rattled on and on. Bless his heart... he placated me in so many ways. I sometimes worried if I was taking advantage of that.

With the handyman project complete, we sat on the sofa and tried to fight the beginnings of a make-out session. We lost, and lust won, as it had so many times.

<<<<<<<<>>>>>>>

MANIA TO MIRACLE
CHAPTER 18

Knee-deep in pre-shoot planning for the Bosch & Lomb television spot, job number 11111 in my continuing world of elevens, I confirmed final details with the producer. "The talent is booked, even the kids, and that was a bitch. Locations are confirmed, and we're scheduled balls-to-the-wall for Tuesday and Wednesday, crew call 6:00 AM. Everything cool on your end?"

"Rain date has changed to Friday. But we're half-and-half interior, so I don't see a problem."

"Me neither, but that's when problems come, right? When you don't see a problem?"

Deidre, the account executive for Bosch & Lomb, knocked on my door frame; I waved her in as I hung up with the producer. Deidre sat solemnly; instead of studying my new knick-knacks as she always did, she stared straight ahead and clicked her retractable ink pen – in and out and in and out. *Why is she so nervous? What's up? Deidre is usually pretty chill.*

"Good Morning, Deidre," I said, "Should I be *afraid* to ask what's wrong? Obviously, something is up, but I have good news to report. You can relax. I've just confirmed everything – *everything!* We're good to go for the shoot, scheduled down to the second. And I think you'll really be–"

"Lela, stop."

Not missing a beat, I asked, "Stop what? Talking? But I have a zillion details in my head and you need to know and I can't help but to–"

"Stop!"

I felt my stomach take a turn, twice. *This is not good news, whatever it is. Everything is so perfectly planned, Deidre. Please don't interfere, don't tell me something's amiss...it's too late!* I forced my brain to slow. "So then, *you* talk."

"You won't like it," Deidre said, not breaking eye contact. "Honestly, I don't like it either, but the client is always right."

I spoke during her tiny pause. "Screw clients! They're not always right *at all!* They don't know the mounds of wisdom we offer from a marketplace perspective, nor the benefits of being 100 percent different from the competition. It's up to us to guide them through the bevy of objections, push them out of their box. We know the market better than they do, as they pace in the top floor suite talking to their stockbrokers. I can do more than–"

"Dear God, Lela! Stop talking! Are you on some kind of upper or something?"

"Of course not! I'm just excited! I've been planning this for months, and it's ready to happen. A manic writer/producer is a good writer/producer – that's what *I* say." Deidre slumped in the chair and rolled her eyes, then started clicking the damn pen again. I took a deep breath and blew it out slow and audibly. "Okay, I'm calming down. Give me a minute."

Several deep breaths later, and a moment to fidget with my new Kid's Meal action figure, I had relaxed enough to fake it. "Okay. Hit me. What's the problem?"

"The CEO cut the last five scenes in the script. He thought the wink was too sexually explicit, and he hates the tag line."

I gasped, the blood draining from my face. "That's everything! This means starting all over again!" My blood pressure shot to the moon, sending a pounding whirr to my temples. I was frantic. Manic. Crazy as hell.

"Lela, I know it's bad, but..." Deidre sighed and looked at the ceiling while steam came out of my ears. "Here's what he wants instead."

I glanced at the hand-written paper. "Dear God! This script is a 'fill-in-the-blank-company' spot! As close to generic as possible and not one damn creative thing about it, Deidre. A monkey could write this! It's bullshit, pure and simple. I feel like I've been punched in the gut."

The feelings of shock begin to rise fast as reality sunk in, and the volume of my voice rose, too. I yelled, "What the *hell?* This is *crazy!* I can't *believe–*"

At first, Deidre seemed content to settle in and watch my meltdown, but that was before I lost control. Then her eyes became saucers. In a blind rage, I bellowed a roar that could've been heard in the front lobby. Saliva flew as I shouted, "Stupid fucking client! This is wrong! *Wrong!* The stupid sonofabitch has ruined the marketing plan for the goddamn *YEAR!* That's a good script, damn-good, and exactly what the company *needs!* Is he that stupid? A fucking WINK is too sexy?" What? So he not getting any at home? What a self-centered, pompous ASS!"

I'd drooled, and the last two words sent splashes of saliva across the desk – the very definition of spittin' mad.

Deidre wiped my errant saliva off her forearm with a look of surprise and disgust. Her tone was calm and controlled, which pissed me off even more. I opened my mouth to rant some more, but Deidre stopped me. "Lela, calm down, please! This is a professional workplace! And it's not like somebody died! You're overreacting–"

Her words, whatever they were, faded into the background as my anxiety screamed to the forefront. My hands had been clenched into fists, marking my palms with the curves of my fingernails. And I hadn't known I'd started crying, but the tears dripped onto the job folder. Plop-plop-plop, even faster than my heart rate. I stared at the drops for several seconds, until my peripheral vision closed in and sparkly dots floated in front of my eyes.

This crying will end my career, and I'll go blind. I don't know why that was my first thought; it made no sense. All I knew was I wanted to *not* feel what I was feeling.

So I became vicious.

"Get the hell out of my office! Get *out,* Deidre! Tell your client to rot in hell!" Then I collapsed into tears, put my head down on the desk and racked with sobs, wailing like a child. I looked up a few minutes after Deidre had left, noticing she'd closed the door behind her.

I looked around my office as if I didn't belong there. The time was 11:11; I watched the digits change. I took a deep breath and muttered a prayer, asking Dude to help me calm down. I blew my nose as the tears slowed, feeling safe enough to go out to smoke.

The hall was empty; nobody saw me leave through the back door, and nobody else was outside. I was alone and hoped I could gain some calm from the solitude. But racks of sobs shook me, and tingles jolted my body as if electrical current zapped every nerve. I couldn't stop crying.

It didn't occur to me that I was over-reacting. Not at all. Stress had built to a crescendo in planning the shoot, and I fell over the edge of the canyon. Gone. I forgot about anything that might be good in my world, even my sobriety, even my family, even Dude.

Blind with anger and frustration, and overcome with sadness.

Focused only on myself, I believed I was 100 percent right and that any writer/producer in my shoes would have the same reaction, cry the same amount, and, in fact, receive respect for such a strong belief in their work.

I smoked two cigarettes and stayed outside until the heat drove me in. I'd taken the box of Kleenex with me and threw a dozen tissues in my trash can as I sat at my desk.

Okay, deep breath, Lela. Forget that project – no rewrites today. I'll just cancel the production via email. Not cool, but I don't want to talk to *anybody*.

One of the Pru-ettes, unaware of my crisis, swung into my office and tossed four more job bags at my inbox. Though she was usually a faceless presence, she looked at me then did a double-take. "What happened to *you?*"

"Nothing. Why?"

"Your whole face is swollen! And what's up with your eyes? I can barely see them."

My answer: no words, just tears. I couldn't stop crying. The Pru-ette cocked her head; I suppose trying to decide if she should open herself to whatever drama had made me cry. She wasn't the friendly sort, on the side of Prudence with military style. So, clutching her remaining job bags, she backed out in baby steps and flashed a tiny wave before turning left in the hall.

No sympathy for Lela. Screw you. I don't need a damn thing from you unless you're the CEO of Bosch & Lomb – and then I'd bash your head against a brick wall until you bled to death.

That thought stopped me in my tracks. I had actually envisioned killing someone. At that moment, I realized I was too upset... that my emotions were completely out of control.

It scared me. And the fear brought more tears. And more. And more. I couldn't stop crying or calm my nerves. Maybe Bi-Polar out of control, but definitely not a cool way to be at work. Still, the tears flowed.

Over the next few hours, a series of "visitors" and "lectures" made me know Deidre had told the powers that be about my curious behavior. Ellie, bringing the damn dog of course, looked down her nose at me and spoke in the sharpest, bitchiest tone I'd ever heard from her – and she was bitchy on a *good* day. A Yankee admonishment to a Southern woman isn't pretty. Of course, it made me cry, and during my explanation, I hiccupped with sobs.

The same happened with Cole, the creative director, with Prudence, and the string of account managers who came to talk me down.

At noon, I decided to leave. I'd accomplished nothing except confirming then cancelling a months-in-the-making project that I'd poured my heart and soul into. I didn't tell anyone I was leaving; I just got in the Jetta and headed south.

When I exited at Delray Beach, a thought struck. Vodka tonic. Vodka-grapefruit. Even a nice, cold beer. *Can I? Will I? Who would know?*

I pulled into the parking lot of Crown Wine & Spirits, my foot shaking on the brake pedal. After thirty seconds, I put the car in PARK. *Think out the circumstances, as Jenny had said. And Oakley says to drink is to die. But just one drink? One of those little airline bottles I used to buy? One beer? Or should I go to a bar and not risk having leftovers? Yeah, I'll go to a bar instead.*

Pulling back onto Federal Highway, I drove south toward Boca Raton. *Pick an expensive bar. Maybe a guy will buy you a drink.* I passed two or three possibilities, nearly crashing into a Porsche as I changed lanes. Finally, I accelerated – hard – and began weaving in and out of traffic, revving my engine when people held me back in speed.

If you drive like this, you'll die. If you drink again, you'll die. What's the difference? Why not just go back to the railroad tracks where you came within an inch of jumping? Yeah – do it! Screw this! Screw everything!

I turned into a shopping center to turn around, and in the top loop of my screeching circle, my cell phone rang. Eerily, the tinkling ring tone was all I could hear, despite the screech of my tires and the road noise along the busy boulevard. I slammed on my brakes, ironically spinning to "park" perfectly straight in a marked parking place.

I dug in my purse for the flip phone and opened it. Oakley.

My savior/sponsor. How does she KNOW?

Tears ejected from my eyes as my lungs seemed to collapse. In a flash, my body changed from 100 percent tension-stiff to 100 percent exhausted-limp. So weak that I couldn't press the button to answer.

Sobs... such sobs! A grown woman crying like a baby, breathless, scared out of my wits. I saw me looking down at me from above... looking down on the damaged goods.

The phone rang one more time, but I had already decided not to answer. Oakley had delivered her message loud and clear, whatever it was. And the funny thing... she wasn't usually the one who called; I called *her.*

I sighed and looked again at the phone. The time now displayed on the front: 1:11, somehow glowing brighter than usual.

The timing of Oakley's call and the elevens that day still seem like a couldn't-be-true story, but it happened just like that.

Like a miracle.

I was meant to be saved from drinking that day. And fate stepped in to save me from killing myself; I had no power over those compulsions on my own.

The universe had decided, not me. Or maybe Dude had decided. Something, somebody, somehow saved my life.

As much as I despised the thought of being saved in the born-again Christian sense, a bizarre and exhilarating power "took me" on that day. Trust became a part of my being.

People in AA would call it turning my will and my life over to the care of Dude as I understood him, but it was more than that. Better than that.

Days later, after I'd had time to process the scene, I called it being hit in the head with a hammer and immediately falling in love with the hammer.

I'd only *thought* I had "worked the steps" and given my world to Dude, but I know now that the first time was just practice, just a baby step to keep an insane-but-sober alcoholic hopeful and teachable.

I became a new person in that parking lot, saved at nine months' sober. From that day forward, I began to believe that Dude was probably God.

I began an endless string of prayers throughout the day. I began to believe in myself, to love myself as a child of God. I became me.

The sober me, the grateful me.

<<<<<<<>>>>>>

BLACK, WHITE, AND GRAY
CHAPTER 19

Rattled and awed by the seeming miracle that happened in my rush to kill myself, I stayed parked in the shopping center as long as my swollen eyes could stand the sun's glare.

Mostly, I cried and screamed at the headliner of my car, and I must have said "thank you, thank you, thank you" a million times. Finally, I drove to the POWERLESS club in a daze, eager to tell Oakley what happened, and just as frightened to tell her. Everything in my head went hot to cold and back again several times.

I sat through two afternoon meetings before Oakley showed up; she saw my face and dragged me to the diner around the corner. She looked directly into my swollen eyes. "What happened to you? They said you'd gone AWOL – and that's a quote, for God's sake!"

"But first... why did you even call me? Your timing is part of the bizarre story."

"Doing what I *said* I would do: giving you the number of that shrink. You *have* to get back on your meds, Lela. But that's for later – first, tell me what happened. Why did you go AWOL?" Oakley's intense stare pushed me to answer quickly.

"I don't know how to explain it. I kinda freaked out. No, I *really* freaked out." I summarized what happened with my pet project and how it made me feel, trying to skim over the worst of my behavior. "That's when I just, uh, decided to leave. I have no reason, but it seemed like a good idea at the time. Then, after I talked myself out of stopping by the liquor store..." I heard Jenny gasp. "... and turned around for a dash to my favorite jump-in-front-of-the-train place, something happened."

"That's it? 'Something happened?' Tell me!"

"Something *phenomenal* happened." Oakley looked at me like my Momma does, with pure love. "And that's when you called. It snapped me back to reality with a shock wave behind it. And then the time was 1:11."

"No shit?"

"No shit. Suddenly, I feel so... maybe the word is 'small' instead of just regular 'humble.' Dude is *huge*, so much bigger and stronger than I ever thought possible. And now I have no doubts about him or me or sobriety or you or *anything*. No doubts at all."

Oakley cocked her head and squinted, watching me closely. "Seriously? No doubts? Doubt is your middle name."

"I've talked about doubts before?"

"Oh, my God! Yes! Every day! Many times a day! Some days I th–"

"I didn't know that I had doubts. Not really. But they're gone now. Kaput, outta here, goodbye. Oakley, it's like the ultimate *trust* has washed over me in waves, beautiful-beautiful waves. So damn weird. What happened to me?"

She munched a French fry. "No way to know. It can't be a bad thing. And I sure as hell hope it's what spurs you to get off the fence about truly living. Not just living the AA program, but *living* from the center of your soul. Only then can you get your shit together, Lela. Only then can you stop fighting – fighting everybody and everything, and especially *yourself*. You fight so much it wears me out! I don't mean to give you shit, but it's been a long time coming."

I stared at her without blinking, shocked at the turn of her tone. "So why have you continued to work with me if I was a hopeless case?"

"I didn't say hopeless. Nobody is hopeless if they're sober. But you're a true contradiction, and very frustrating to a sponsor. Lela, you think everything has two answers, and you drive yourself crazy going back and forth, covering both bases. Even with Bear – either he's your big-time boyfriend, or you're going to let what you call the 'crimson-red flag' make you end it. You can't go both ways. Think about how many things you do that way... keeping all your options open and working twice as hard."

Oakley made sense. That's exactly how I approached life, always giving myself an out. But I thought it was a good thing. Oakley's take made me think about Daddy's signature phrase: "Going around your elbow to get to your thumb." Or maybe it was another of his bits of wisdom: "Play both ends against the middle and end up with your head up your ass." Neither of those had made sense to me before that day.

My sponsor, now red-faced, had mumbled during the pause; words I didn't hear. I snapped back when she raised her voice. "Decide! Take a singular action! Are you going to stay sober or not? Or can you even stay *sane?!* You're defeating yourself by trying to cover *all* the bases *all* the time."

"That's not exactly untrue."

Oakley chuckled. "See? That's a great example – not saying it's true, not saying it's false." She poked my arm from across the table. "Girl, you fight with *everything!* But the truth is, most things are black and white, and your gray is going to run out. Then what will you do?"

"Not *everything* is black and white, Oakley. Think about it."

She shook her head, exasperated. "A lot of things are black and white – more than you think. What it comes down to is that you have to contend with gray, and up 'til now, that's when you fold, collapse into that incredible emotional state that sends you out of control. Like today... you just collapsed and lost control, right? Unfortunately, I've seen it before."

"But it's also the Bi-Polar shit. No meds, remember?"

"That's another black and white you avoid. There is no gray area about whether you should take medicine or not. So call the damn doctor! You're being stupid about that issue."

"So, I just give in?"

"Yes. Absolutely yes! The full 100 percent. But here's the deal: listen closely, Ms. Fox. You don't need a plan for every little dilemma, and you certainly don't need multiple plans! Sometimes you just need to breathe. Breathe! Trust! Let it all go. *Then* see what happens. Please... Lela, please don't think so damn much."

"But AA says 'Think, think, think.' It's on the wall!"

"Right. Three times is all you get. Quit thinking!"

I said nothing for several beats, replaying what she'd said.

And she's right! You're driving yourself crazy with a barrage of crazy thinking. But is there really another way? Oakley wouldn't tell you not to do something unless there was a solution. She knows what it is! You've said all this time you want what she has... she has peace of mind, and she's sitting there ready to tell you how to get it yourself – listen! Listen with wide-open ears!

"Oh, Oakley! I hear what you're saying loud and clear. And I'm ready, more ready than ever to do that. Can you teach me how?"

"Of course, but first be ready." Sweat had formed on her brow; I apologized for stressing her out. She dismissed my apology, saying she had been waiting for me to have some kind of breakthrough.

With a sudden "aha!" look, she said, "Let me quote you something *my* sponsor said to *me*..." She flipped to the back of her Big Book and removed a folded-up piece of paper, well-worn and scribbled front and back. She scanned the page. "It says: 'There's no rule that says you have to have everything figured out right now. Every step forward is progress.' That's gray, Lela. Just keep walking into the unknown, the gray, one step at a time."

"I like the quote."

"There are so many more here! I think I'll make you a copy. These kernels of wisdom keep me sober." She looked down at the paper again. "Aha! This one, too: 'Sometimes the smallest decisions are the most life-changing.' So – you, Lela Fox – make a damn decision! Today! Now! Make a decision to start choosing *one* direction on things and giving that your all. Quit wasting time chasing every possible answer. You're smart enough to make good decisions. Do you believe that?"

"Well, kinda. No – yeah, I'm smart enough."

"Tell me some smart choices you've made in the last little while."

"A lot of them."

"Be specific."

I huffed an impatient sigh. "Too many to list."

"And that means you're a good decision-maker. Accept that, *believe* that!"

I sat back in the booth and crossed my arms, looking at Oakley in a new light. *Or maybe you're looking at yourself in a new light. You DID just have some kind of spiritual experience, right? Don't you think that "wow" experience would change things for more than three hours? Wouldn't it make you see the world differently? Like, forever, don't you think?*

"I gotta go, Oakley. My brain is full."

"The 5:30 meeting isn't over yet. We could catch the end."

"I need to journal the hell out of this. Think about the gray-area stuff you said. And about making decisions, the whole 'suddenly-I-trust' thing. I'll call you tomorrow."

<<<<<<<<<>>>>>>>>

The next day, I went into Ellie Cherry and Associates with my head hung low, literally. Halfway to my office, I saw Cole's feet – right in front of me and blocking my way. With no way around him, I stopped and looked up.

Oh, no! What a face! A mix of disgust, fear, confusion, anger... worse than yesterday. I had planned out what to say, but those well-crafted words flew out of my memory the second I saw his frown.

"Lela! What the hell?"

"I'm sorry, Cole. I'm very, very sorry."

"Is there a reason? Or some way I can help?"

"No to both. I just... lost it."

"And disappeared." There was no question mark at the end of that sentence, and his tone was as flat as a coat of paint. The buzz between my ears began in a snap, and so loud! *Damn, Lela. He's pissed, but don't lose your cool again. It's not the end of the world.*

He said flatly, "Prudence wants to see you." *Oh, hell! It IS the end of the world.*

"Great."

"Lela, you left me in a bind. I had to do the re-write, re-casting, and re-scheduling myself, and there was hardly time in my day."

"You did it without me!"

"What the hell do you *think* I'd do?! I had no idea if you were *ever* coming back! You didn't even bother to call!"

"I was too embarrassed."

"You may just have embarrassed yourself out of a job. Ellie is pissed – more pissed than I've ever seen her, and I've known her a long time. She said she doesn't have time for your baby fits."

"Actually, it was more than a 'baby fit.' I apologize, Cole. I was stressed about getting everything just right, and then everything changed. I just couldn't handle it... and lost my cool."

"Maybe more than your cool, Lela. It may be that you've lost everything. I'm very disappointed in you. I thought you were a professional."

Ouch! That hurts! It was almost as bad as disappointing my Dad, the last thing I wanted to do.

"I *am* a professional, Cole! The only exception was two hours yesterday when I acted like a big baby. I'm back here today to prove myself worthy again. Worthy of your trust."

"Prove yourself might be a key word."

I furrowed my brow. "What do you mean?"

"Ask Prudence."

I breathed so deeply through my nose that I coughed as the air came out. "Okay, I'll see her now."

As I walked away, Cole shouted to my back, "And you're five minutes late!" *Oh, great. Now the nit-picky stuff comes. And I guess this is another write-up from Prudence. Two of two. Crap! I wish I could tell her what happened to me, about the, uh... do I still want to call it just a spiritual experience? A miracle? No. Of all people, Prudence wouldn't understand. It's only an AA thing. She'd think I was bat-shit crazy.*

I knocked on her door frame, and she waved me in; the phone was in her ear as she wrote so damn carefully on her desk pad. She's the one who had banned the use of speakerphones in the office, deeming the noise "disruptive." Prudence ruled the roost, no doubt about it.

The phone back in its cradle, Prudence leaned forward on her elbows and stared me down. Seconds passed as my head-buzz volume increased. I knew I was in big trouble, but this woman had a way of making me feel like a child being punished by a whip-wielding school principal.

Of course I'd screwed up, but she wanted me to suffer. Evidently, she got off on seeing me squirm – which I did, both literally and figuratively. Finally, she spoke. "Lela Fox." That was all, just my name. I didn't reply; saw no need.

After another long stare-down, she sat back and fumbled through her file cabinet adjacent to her tidy desk. She said nothing during her task, and the tension was building by the minute. My head-buzz became a shrill scream. In a sudden move, she slammed the file drawer shut and turned immediately toward me, leaning far over her desk and waving a piece of paper – a three-part form I recognized. She passed the form to me. "Your disciplinary write-up. Sign, please."

"You haven't filled out the top part. I'm not signing a blank form."

Prudence snatched the form from my hand and wrote – scribbling, which I didn't think she could do. She thrust it toward me again. "There. Sign and date."

Passing the form back, I guess I hesitated too long because she *snatched* it from my hand and tore at the perforations like a madman. One eyebrow was arched. I couldn't take it anymore and huffed at her. "Look, Prudence, you don't have to be so dramatic. I know you're mad, and I know what I did. And of course I know what I did was wrong. That's established. You don't have to treat me like a cretin."

"I haven't heard an apology, Ms. Fox. Not that it would matter..."

Even though a voice from Inner Earth was telling me to shut up, I began what would have been a long ramble if Prudence hadn't stopped me. She said, "I have a project for you. One that doesn't go through the normal channels. I am the account manager for this assignment, I guess you'd say."

"I don't underst–"

"I need a magazine story, double-spread with a fold-out, about the new Nicklaus course, The Bear's Paw in Japan. And I need it by Friday noon."

"Uh... okay..." This arrangement was highly irregular. There was a system – forms to fill out, in triplicate, with details about the job, and those forms went with every job, no matter how simple or small.

"I need a JDF form for details."

"There won't be a JDF. Not from me."

"But you designed the form! I *need* all that information to make sure I write the correct thing! Without it, I'm shooting in the dark."

"Like what kind of information do you need?"

"Everything! Like the name of the magazine and a sample copy, for one thing. An approximate word count – that comes from the publisher, and I'll need background info on the course design, past ads and brochures, details on the resort – how many restaurants, specifics on their services, and the number of rooms if a hotel is in the complex... I could go on. I need everything! How can I write about something I don't know a thing about?"

Her eyes had become wide during my list; half the time, she'd watched my fingers as I counted things off. I summed up the need-to-know input she would have to provide. "I mean, what's the point of the article? An invitation to an event? Announcement of the construction? What?"

"Just write it to make somebody want to go there."

I threw my head back, my chest exploding with a sarcastic chuckle. "Right. The questions are 'go where?' and 'why?' and 'what's in it for me?' I can't write it without that information. It's the account manager's job to supply all the background. Don't you *know* that?"

Prudence snapped, "Of *course* I know that!" Then she seemed to stop herself, straightening her lapels and clearing her throat. "I'll have to search for the information you need." The pause was long, and I noticed she wasn't jotting any notes in her old-fashioned shorthand.

"Prudence, have you ever served as an account manager on a project?"

"No." Then a snap back into the hard-ass bitch character that she was. "Once."

"Then why are you doing it this time?"

"Because everybody is busy." I knew who managed the Nicklaus account, Thomas Bowery, and I knew he wasn't busy. I'd met with him on Monday, and he bragged about having free time.

"That's not true, Prudence. Thomas isn't too busy."

She sat to full height, breathing deeply through her nose. Then she tossed her head back and shook out that perfectly coiffed hair. "I'm doing Thomas a favor. As if it's any of your business."

"Jeez! I'm not... it just seems so..."

She fanned her hand at me as if dismissing me altogether. "I need it by Friday."

At that moment, I remembered that the second write-up should mean I was fired. It just took two, she said, right? *Maybe the first one was too long ago... or Prudence wouldn't be giving you WORK, right? She'd be firing you.*

I pushed the idea from my mind, knowing that worry – that "black and white" – would get me in trouble. So I asked again, "When do I get the input information?"

"I'll shoot for this afternoon."

"I'll *need* it this afternoon for such a quick turnaround. I do have other projects in the works, too, you know."

"But not the Bausch and Lomb spot. No more TV projects for you, ever!"

Like a dagger through my heart, she'd given me the ad-writer's worse-possible punishment. I didn't care about being written up near as much as losing the opportunity to do prestigious work. "You don't have to go *that* far, Prudence. It's not like it will happen again."

"Once is too much."

Why are you trying to argue with a fence post, Lela? Give up and go to your desk. See what else you screwed up and who else is pissed at you. Apologize to Deidre and Bonny. And ask Thomas about this magazine spread job.

As I walked out, I said, "Bye, Prudence, my dear. Keep punishing me! It feels *great!*"

<<<<<<<<<<>>>>>>>>>

I called Bear as soon as I got home. "Sorry, babe, I have to cancel tonight. I have to work on a project. I think it's a test."

"How mad were they?"

I paused. What words would express "more than maximum mad?" I decided to lie, make Bear think I was okay. I didn't want him to worry, and maybe lying would help convince *myself* that all was well, too.

I signed off the call, making kissy noises as I always did. *Okay, now get to work, Lela Fox. Do your magic. Kick some copywriting ass.*

Determined to do my absolute best on the project, I Googled everything about the city and province in China, hitting travel sites about the culture and food, festivals, and celebrations. Four hours passed before I noticed the time. Late.

I zapped a frozen dinner, climbed into bed, and slept like a baby. I knew the quality of my work on this project was a black and white thing, a perfect or not thing, and I swore to make it perfect.

It didn't occur to me that "perfect creativity" was a misnomer – a gray area in everybody's life. Perfection wasn't an option when I wasn't the final judge.

And I knew I'd be judged. Deep in my soul, I knew something fishy was afoot at Ellie Cherry and Associates.

<<<<<<<>>>>>>

JUDGE AND JURY
CHAPTER 20

The next day was an early one; I entered the echo chamber of the empty Ellie Cherry building at 7:11, wanting some private time to work on the Nicklaus project. I'd done twice the amount of research I normally did, taking prolific notes, which I re-read and organized that morning.

With an open mind, like brainstorming with myself, I came up with several headline options. *This piece will be my best-ever work. Then I'll shove it down Prudence's throat. Whatever the arrangement with Thomas doesn't matter because I'll blow him away, too. Do it, Lela! Go get 'em, tiger.*

Nothing held me back; I pounded on the keyboard to flesh out an outline, then edited and edited and edited again. Approach-wise, Prudence had simply said, "Make them want to go there," so my tone was quite sales-oriented, but because of the ultra-wealthy target market, it couldn't be in-your-face sales. I walked the fine line... subtle, understated, but "make them want to go there" was at the core. Simple, right? For me, it should have been.

But I struggled and finally figured out that I was, literally, trying too hard. Still, I insisted this was black or white – perfect or not. Frustrated, I turned to focus on something else, hoping for new momentum later in the day.

As I turned, a Pru-ette popped into my office; I hadn't even realized it was past opening time. The clock read 9:11, which made me smile. Dude was confirming my path was correct.

Throwing bag bags at my inbox, the Pru-ette said, "Welcome back, Lela," in a tone more snotty than typical. *Fuck you, bitch. Go kiss Prudence's fat ass with a little more force.*

But she's left me something productive to do. See what new. I flipped through the job bags, and my heart sank with each flip – all brainless support pieces to campaigns that somebody else had written. Looking closer, I saw the deadlines were weeks away, too. The bottom of the barrel. Backwash. Busy work.

Yep, you're demoted. How are you going to re-prove yourself? And how long will it take? You're screwed, Lela Fox... but YOU are the cause. You screwed yourself.

For the next two days, I sweated over each keystroke for the Nicklaus project, editing, and perfecting and making every word count. I'd take a half-hour between each re-write, going back with new eyes.

On Friday, when the magazine story for "China's Premiere Golf Resort" was ready, I printed and packaged those perfect four pages of copy as per Prudence's rules, and hand-delivered them to her office, two hours early, in fact. She wasn't in; I sat on her chair and farted. With a second thought, I licked the dispenser pump on her gallon of Purell.

I didn't have much to do, really, so I piddled around before an extra-long lunch. Two o'clock – that's when Prudence walked into my office with her cheap perfume wafting. She didn't knock, I noticed, but maybe it was because of the heavy load of papers, folders, and job bags she held.

Before she sat in the chair that faced my desk, she heaved the pile of papers onto the chair beside it and plucked the top job bag from the pile. "I'm here about the Nicklaus China project, of course."

"Of course! I know you loved the copy! It's spot-on with lots of juicy details, don't you think?" I was eager to hear her brag on my work and knew it was worthy of the bragging.

"Well, there's a problem..." Prudence couldn't look me in the eye; her head tilted toward the ceiling.

"What?! What *kind* of problem?"

"You didn't follow instructions."

"The instructions came straight from your mouth, Prudence. Nothing was on paper as per your anal rules, which I find odd. So what 'instruction' did I not follow?"

"Well, it's more than that, Lela." I breathed in, holding it, and looked at her sideways. *It must be bad.* Prudence paused for a beat, then spoke fast. "Ellie hired a freelancer to write the same article, to compare it with yours, and we like hers better."

"What the *hell?*" My breath came out in a rush and I stood, leaning toward her. "What in the hell kind of trick was *that?* Pitting writer against writer? That's *bullshit!* And how could it be *better* when she doesn't even know the client. You're so full of it, Prudence! And tell Ellie I said the same damn thing!"

"We liked hers better because it was more editorial... not so sell-y."

"Your *only* instruction was – and I quote – 'make them want to go there.' That sure sounds like a sales thing to me! What the hell are you *doing?*" My breathing was ragged with rage, but I checked myself to keep it under control and sat in my chair, determined to keep my shit together. But my throat was squeezed shut. I squeaked, "Prudence, it almost seems like you're trying to get rid of me!"

In the ten seconds of silence that followed, Prudence inspected her manicure and cleared her throat several times. Finally, she spoke. "Well, let's say it this way... I'm not *trying* to get rid of you, as you say. It's been decided. You're fired." Then she looked at me with a snotty smile. "It's been nice working with you – I guess I should *at least* say that."

Time froze. My body froze. Then the buzz of mega-anxiety began in my head, vibrating my face and teeth. All I could see: the smug smile of Prudence as she gathered her armload of files.

What the hell? I just got fired??? Why? Because of my breakdown earlier this week? Could they really be this petty? Testing me on a project with the wrong instructions? Who is the freelance writer? Will she get my job? What do I do now? I'll never work in advertising again! Another bad recommendation, now two in a row! And I'm SOBER! This shit doesn't happen to sober people!

Prudence interrupted my erratic string of thoughts. "I'll need your office cleared by four o'clock. If a single staple or paper clip is missing, expect an invoice."

I sat in my chair, dumbfounded. Cole, the "best creative director ever," passed my office without looking at me, which had never happened before.

I guessed everybody knew; maybe they'd known for days. I sat completely stunned. And ashamed, because it was clear that my breakdown earlier in the week had caused it. *Nobody trusts crazy people, Lela. And you're bat-shit crazy. Admit it.*

I suppose another five minutes passed as I processed my new situation. I looked around, knowing I'd need four or five boxes to pack all the personal shit I'd brought with me and the new stuff I'd accumulated. The office didn't keep boxes around; Prudence didn't like the mess. So my only choice was to go to the liquor store for free boxes.

No, you could go to a storage place or U-Haul and pay for them. I thought about paying for something free and couldn't justify it. *Hell no, I'm not paying! Now I'm going to be broke again. Jobless and broke. Great. That'll put you on top of the world, especially with no meds. Why haven't you called that damn doctor yet?!*

I argued with myself for what seemed like an hour, finally feeling sane enough to drive to the liquor store. The closest one? I had no idea, which I thought was pretty cool. *You don't even notice them anymore.* So I just drove, looking on the right only because I was somewhat shaky behind the wheel.

Boxes in the car, I returned to the ad agency and slowly placed my Museum of the Weird into boxes. I reached high to remove the three-dimensional vowels from the wall, the beloved "ea" letters I deemed perfect for a writer's wall. I'd used huge nails to hang them, and the thought passed that I should patch the holes.

Hell no! Let the next sucker who moves in wonder what hung there. Screw 'em!

After four trips to the car with full boxes, I tucked the vowels under my arm and walked out the back door. I didn't say goodbye to anyone.

All I could think about: I need to tell Oakley. But I dreaded it, knowing she'd fuss at me in her non-fussing style. I felt bad enough on my own. I went to the POWERLESS club and didn't tell a soul. But when I saw Bear, I stiffened. *You'll* have *to tell him, Lela. You can't keep secrets like that.*

The irritating buzz in my head started again and lasted through our perfunctory greetings. With our "no flirting at meetings" pact, there was no hug, and I needed one so badly!

Despite my efforts to keep a calm demeanor, my bottom lip began quivering. Tears burned behind my eyes. And, being the observant Bear sweetheart I loved, he saw through my fakery. "What's wrong, babe?"

"I'll have to tell you later. We need to be alone."

"Now?"

"No! Please, no. I'm still processing it... deciding what it means."

"You look really worried. And sad. Are you okay?"

"Yeah. Let's just go to a meeting. But I want to sit with you this time."

"That'd be nice. Because... I have to tell you... when we sit apart, I end up not listening but just staring at you across the room, lost in a sexual fantasy."

"Stop."

"Unfortunately, it's the truth. Maybe it's time to let everybody know we're dating."

"Oakley says no."

"Oakley doesn't even like the fact that we *are* dating!"

"True. *But... what the hell? Why not?!* "Let's do it. Because right now, I need your big strong arms wrapped around me, and I need to make your shoulder wet with some pent-up tears."

"Let's go around the corner."

It wasn't any more private there, but at least we made an effort. Bear leaned his butt against the window glass and hugged me tightly and gently at the same time. He patted my head, telling me, "It's going to be fine. You're safe here with me," and shit like my Mom would say. Yet he didn't even know what happened!

Bear's kindness and care for me was unconditional, his support unquestioned. I wondered why I still harbored doubts about our future in moments like this – and there had been many moments like that.

I wiped my eyes on his sleeve and pulled back to get a Kleenex from my purse. He watched every move with a look so loving and caring that it made tears come again.

"I love you, Lela," he said.

For the second time that day, I froze. My body froze, my brain froze. I never thought he'd say it out loud, so I didn't feel bad about not being able to repeat it back to him. Instead, I said, "Let's go home."

"That's not the response I thought I'd get."

"Not the one I thought I'd give, either."

"Okay, we'll shelve that conversation for now. The next question: where is 'home?'"

I laughed. "Good question. I guess your place. I'll leave my car here. Mostly because I'm afraid I'll cry and not be able to see."

"I'm on the Harley... do you mind?"

"Maybe it'd be good having that vibration on my ass. And right now, I feel so weak and needy. I need a dose of Mother Nature, I think."

"So Father Time will take you to the beach for a walk. Is that cool?"

"Perfect."

<<<<<<<>>>>>>

LOLA LAUGHS LOUDER
CHAPTER 21

Frantic to find a job ASAP, I sent out 24 résumés over the weekend and thirty more through Wednesday of the following week. I'd broadened my search to include technical writing, ghostwriting for an architect, plus marketing management for several small companies... the list was long. And I didn't stop with the communications industry, either; I created a different résumé version and faxed it to every frame shop within twenty miles of home.

I shuddered to remember my last framing job with the alcoholic manager. *Roman-something... I can't even remember his last name. But his relapse was still your fault, still a humungous entry in your fourth step notebook. But you'll never be able to make amends, will you?*

The thoughts made me sad, and made me question whether I should even think about framing again. *But that experience can't hold you back! You've been in picture framing in one way or another since you were sixteen!*

Lola had called several times in the lead-up to her visit on the fifteenth. I double-booked that day, attending a Job Fair in the morning, then picking up Lola in the afternoon.

We'd decided to go straight to the beach and walk into the waves smoking little brown cigars – just as we'd done on a dozen girl's beach trips in the past. Tradition. Ridiculous, but a tradition. The same cigarillos that Bear smoked.

I'd talked to Mom and Dad each day during that unemployment period. For the past few months, I'd quit hiding the bad shit from them and yearned for their advice. Daddy preached about the Fox family work ethic, which he'd drilled into me from birth, and Mom just repeated twenty times per call: "You're smart... anybody would want to hire you."

Tears of gratitude flowed. *Lela, you are so blessed to have a supportive family. Revel in it. Lean on them, even when you mess up. They are there for you, cheering you on.*

Daddy asked, "So if Lola is a friend from the past, does that mean she drinks?"

Chuckling, I summarized Lola's odd habits. "Dad, she either drinks nothing at all – and will go for months stone-cold sober – then on a whim, she'll drink a whole damn bottle of Crown Royal in one sitting. The next day, she's back to being a non-drinker."

"Isn't that what they call a binge drinker?"

"No, Daddy. She's basically not a drinker. In fact, she was the one that took care of me *and the business* while my drinking was out of control. In the green house, remember? Lola was my enabler, as they call it."

"I think I was that, too."

"No way, Daddy-O. You gave me looks that let me know exactly how much I disappointed you, and – trust me – that's the opposite of enabling. I would crumble with those looks, cry about them for days. And neither of you covered for me or did my work when I was too drunk to do it. *That's* what an enabler is."

"We didn't do that."

"Of course not. What you *did* do is come running when I asked for help. And let me tell ya, Daddy, for that, I will be eternally grateful."

"I knew if I didn't come, my baby daughter would die... and you almost did."

"But because of you, I didn't."

"I love you, Lela – my sweet, sober-as-hell favorite baby daughter!"

"And I love *you!* I must admit: you're the best father I've ever had."

<<<<<<<<<>>>>>>>>

On the Ides of March, I got up to an early alarm and dressed in a suit fashionable and casual enough for Florida, yet austere enough for a CEO's nod of approval. I felt a boost of confidence, and, as luck would have it, it was a good hair day, literally. My curls fell naturally with no frizz; no gel needed. I both looked and felt damn-good. *Go get 'em, tiger.*

The day's timing was critical; I threw a swimsuit in my briefcase, planning to change in the car so Lola and I could jump to the beach without delay. *Changing in the car? Are you sure you want to do that, Lela?*

I hadn't been naked in public in almost ten months, not since I got sober. Granted, being behind the tinted glass of the Jetta wasn't officially "in public," but still... we'd be parallel-parked on a street with red lights and lots of traffic, so it counted. Or at least it counted enough to give me pause.

I was becoming like my mother, prude of the Southland.

The Job Fair was a disappointment, filled with timeshare companies needing shyster salespeople. Those people, taking advantage of gullible tourists, pissed me off, and locals judged them harshly. I could never sell a product I didn't believe in or a pallet of nuts and bolts, so I passed more than 75 percent of the booths without missing a step. A few jobs looked promising, but I got the hell out of Dodge quickly and headed for the airport.

<<<<<<<<<>>>>>>>>>

I sat at Gate 17, waiting for Lola's delayed plane to land. My brain was churning full-time but stopped with a screech when I saw her coming down the tube of the jetway. Wow! She looked great! I was still struck by the thickness of her long, glossy-black hair and her stunning Native American looks. *She's beautiful. And hasn't aged a day.*

I wondered what she would say about how I looked. If my appearance had changed as much as my attitude, she might not recognize me. But she saw me within a few steps.

Damn, what a smile! She is sincerely happy to see me! We're going to have so much fun! I stayed seated, wondering if I even remembered how to have fun. I took my sobriety seriously, maybe too seriously. I had a bevy of friends, but my definition of excitement was hanging with that group of women who discussed the ins and outs of sobriety and how it worked with human nature. Boring had become my middle name, I feared.

Can I still laugh and be silly? Lola and I have always been super foolish together, but I'd always been at least a little drunk. Can I do it sober? Will my serious-as-hell attitude and new focus on "appropriate" stop the fun in its tracks? I hope not. Come on, Lela, you have to relax at some point! Use your trust in a forever friendship with Lola to make it all open and comfortable.

She reached to hug me, and hung on tight. "Oh, Lela Fox! I'm so happy to see you! You look fabulous! Absolutely gorgeous!"

"Really?"

"I wouldn't lie. The only thing..." She scrutinized my face. "... you have a little lipstick on your teeth."

"Yeah, you bitch... you wouldn't lie." We laughed about it; the ease into instant friendship despite the miles and my sobriety was like oil on a Slip and Slide – smooth and easy. *Yes, I can laugh, even sober, and even with lipstick on my teeth. Hooray! Lola and Lela strike again! Watch out, Palm Beach!*

We locked arms and skipped, literally *skipped*, down the concourse, not caring what people thought about our ridiculous act. Two adult kids piled into my car, laughing hysterically.

But when Lola put her suitcase in my backseat, she freaked out. "What is all this *trash?* Lela, you have a nice car and you fill it with trash? It's up to the seat! You have to clean this out. I'll help you. I can't have my friend living like a homeless slob."

"It's not that bad!"

"It's *horrible!*"

"After the beach, I'll find a trash can or something. It's just junk mail and empty cigarette packs, nothing nasty. So drop it, okay? We're heading to the beach!"

"Where? Which beach?" Lola asked... as if she would know one from the other.

"It's a treat. We're going across the bridge to Palm Beach proper, where Bentleys and chauffeurs hang out, where the richy-rich live. There's a public beach that's usually deserted, probably because everybody has a private shoreline of their own."

"Cool. I'm wearing my swimsuit underneath my oh-so-Florida clothes." Passing through a palm-tree-lined boulevard, Lola's hand went to her heart. "It's breathtakingly beautiful here, Lela! I can't believe you see this every day, you lucky dog."

"I guess I get used to it, and take it for granted. But I do prefer palms to scrub pines... beaches to of mountains. Bet ya never thought a Tennessee girl would say that, huh?"

"I'll never leave my Smoky Mountains, but the beach... it's heaven."

"I've been floating on the water just before dusk, alone and toting my cheap float... just paddling out a little and floating. Thinking and trying to meditate. It's my peaceful place." Lola ooh'ed and aah'ed about having that luxury, then I chuckled. "But once, a damn pelican landed two feet from me, diving for a fish. I literally peed my pants, but you know what they say about pissing in the ocean."

She laughed, too. "Surprised you didn't poop your pants! I remember you doing that many times!"

My stomach fell to my feet. Shame. Regret, the kind Oakley said would eventually disappear, but it immediately chewed my stomach lining. "Lola, there's a lot of things I *used to* do that I don't do anymore.

"Well, I'd *hope* so! I remember one night you fell asleep on the toilet. That was hilarious."

Again, my gut churched, and my face reddened with Shame. "No, it's *not* hilarious, Lola. It makes me sick to my stomach. So please, no more war stories. I haven't quite forgiven myself, evidently."

"Oh... I'm so sorry! I didn't mean to make you feel bad! I swear! It's just..."

"Yeah, I'm different. Completely different."

"Again, I'm sorry."

What the hell, Lela! Don't be so serious, and don't make her feel bad. Lighten up! I put on a fake smile and raised my voice to a super-cheerful tone. "Up ahead is the Flagler bridge. Notice the abrupt curtain rise to a complete change in the environment. Even the air smells rich and proper."

"Proper? Uh, oh. Do we have to behave ourselves?"

After a beat of panic, thinking we best play it safe, I chuckled, "No, we don't have to behave. We'll never see these people again."

At the mouth of the bridge, where The Breakers' circular driveway spreads over a half-acre, Lola's mouth dropped open. "Oh, my God! It's a paradise!"

"Yeah, we'll drive Billionaire's row and see Mar-a-Largo before hitting the beach. And later, we *must* see Worth Avenue, home of some of the most hoity-toity designer stores in the nation. In fact, they call it the Rodeo Drive of the South. Tiffany's and all that shit, a bed store that sells $3,000 sheets, plus a sculpture garden that will blow you away."

"All sounds good. But... ta-da!" Lola dug in her purse to retrieve two plastic-wrapped cream-tipped brown cigars. "We're ready for the ocean! First things first!"

We parked at a meter, and I reached for my briefcase, stopping as I touched it. "Oh shit! I have my swimsuit... but no sandals, no coverup, not even a tank. Not even a towel!"

"No big deal."

"It's Florida, Lola. You can't walk barefoot in the hot sand!" She looked at me quizzically, and that's when I cracked up, knowing what I had to do. "I'll just wear my perfectly professional pumps; the heels will sink in the sand, but what the hell? And this jacket will work as a cover-up. I'm with *you*, right? So why do I worry about looking stupid?"

Lola could only laugh. And laugh. And laugh. She pulled off her tank to show an already-bronze torso. "You'll look like a prostitute, Lela. I'm the one who should be embarrassed... hanging out with a lady of the evening in the middle of the afternoon."

"Ha. Ha. Screw you."

"And you, too. Come on, get changed. Let's hit the water."

Ten hilarious minutes later, with my high heels full of sand, I kicked them off, and we walked knee-deep into the blue waters of the Gold Coast, cigarillos lit, and Groucho Marx accents at full volume. There were only two small groups on the shore, leaving us to be loud, obnoxious, and as silly as we wanted.

Lola had brought the other girls-trip staple: neon-green rubber alien ears that fit over our real ears, and she put them on, flashing the Dr. Spock two-finger split salute. Heads turned, double-takes. Our laughter was constant, telling corny jokes and flaunting our silliness.

For a long walk on the shore, I wore my suit jacket as a coverup, its plaid lapels and cuffs fighting with the floral print of my bikini. We fell together laughing, making a scene with every step. Soon, we came upon a fence to set off a private beach, but Lola wasn't daunted. She jumped over and dared me to do the same.

That's when the Dobermans started barking, racing to the fence like angry wolves and nipping at Lola's heels. I'd never seen her big, brown eyes pop so wide, and she moved faster than a speeding train, jumping the fence as if stepping over a tiny stick.

Despite the close call, all we could do is laugh. It was old times, sans vodka. Funny as hell for no reason other than being dumb and silly. So much fun! It's like I'd turned into a kid, or my quirky dad, within moments of seeing my old friend.

But our two hours of sun physically drained me. I suggested, "Let's walk down Worth Avenue, go to Tiffany's or one of those art galleries."

"You're going to wear your heels?"

"And my jacket."

Lola laughed. "You slut."

"And I'm wearing the green alien ears."

We both cracked up. I got "dressed," and when we reached the three-block-long Worth Avenue, I tried to keep a straight face, but the looks from the hooty-snooty-pootie-tooties were priceless. I laughed unapologetically.

A block later, we slipped into Tiffany's with a salesperson greeting us at the door, lathering but one syllable before he stopped short. I assumed his "Welc..." was supposed to be finished, "Welcome to Tiffany's," but the man's nose turned to the sky. As my dad would say, he looked like he smelled it but couldn't quite locate it.

Undaunted, we pretended to be wealthy and in search of engagement rings for each other. We put on thick Tennessee accents and played up Lola's casual dress against my prostitute costume. Three minutes into our act, we were asked to leave by the security guard, his bushy eyebrows becoming one straight line as he glared at us. When we continued to laugh, he removed his bully stick.

I gasped, then spit the words at him. "We were ready to leave, anyway, Mister Sir! This is the cheapest jewelry I've ever seen. No better than Walmart!" Lola pushed me out the door, and we giggled further down the avenue.

An art gallery owner also kicked us out as we studied an abstract, sharing a list of possibilities of its meaning, again in exaggerated redneck accents. We were "disturbing the peace," he said, though we were the only customers.

But the sculpture garden wasn't crowded, and we spent an hour mocking the poses of each human form. I hadn't laughed so much since I'd left home, hadn't felt bold enough to shock people or risk putting myself in a bad light. But with Lola, it seemed natural. And fun as hell.

"Oh, shit, Lela! It's four o'clock! Aren't we having dinner with Bear at six?"

"Oh, shit. And I bet the parking meter has run out, too."

Running down Worth Avenue in our costumes probably made more of a scene than our prior antics; I saw a few chauffeurs follow us with their watchful eyes.

The meter was expired, a ticket tucked under my windshield wiper. "Damn! And I've got to pay for it!"

"Most people don't, you know..."

"But I'm sober, Lola. And sober people pay for their mistakes."

She looked at me with a cocked head and furrowed brow. "Damn, girl... you *have* changed. A year ago, you'd have torn it into a million pieces."

"Yeah, well... sobriety is a whole 'nother story."

"Do I get to go to a meeting with you, too?"

"Sure, if you want. But you'll freak out. Some of my friends look like they sleep in the woods. Or haven't seen a dentist in their entire life. But those are the people I love the most. Basically, Lola, AA has saved my life. It sounds so trite, but it's true."

"Lela," she said, "I don't care if it was clown college that saved your life, I'm just glad you're alive and not with somebody like Stuart. Or Baby-Daddy. You rock, my friend. You have your shit together."

"But if you only knew how much I hide from you..."

"Really?"

"I stay in my head a lot."

"Is that something that will, uh, something you'll outgrow?"

"Oakley says maybe. She thinks I'm too hard on myself."

"I can see you doing that. You also had to be the best at everything."

"Until I was the worst at everything."

"But you still gave it your all. And do I get to meet Oakley, too?"

"Yes! We'll go to the Saturday noon meeting. She'll be there. So will Bear, probably. They're friends."

"Ooooh. Does your sponsor know you're sleeping with Bear?"

"Yes, but I hope Bear's lips stay sealed. He wants to shout and dance about our relationship. He's in love with me, and I'm not in love with him."

"You're not? Are you sure?"

"No, I'm not *sure,* but I get pretty weirded out when he tries to butt into 'me time.'"

"You're just a scare-dy cat."

"Maybe. But I'm determined to keep things loosey-goosey. After three marriages, I want to be single for a long while. Maybe forever." Lola's knowing look pissed me off, but I couldn't blame her for doubting me. My track record sucked.

<<<<<<<<<<>>>>>>>>>

As promised, I stopped at a dumpster to get rid of the trash in the back seat of the Jetta. Passing the POWERLESS club to show her my hang-out, I remembered that the strip club in the same parking lot had an oversized dumpster, and the place would be quiet in the afternoon.

We pulled in close, parking parallel. *Dammit! Too close!* I had to back up and try again so we could get the doors open.

Lola got out to help, making fun of me one more time for the heels-and-bikini prostitute outfit. "And the green ears complete the look, darling," she cooed. I guess our laughter was loud because a giant tattooed man opened the back door, screaming at us for "trespassing."

I spoke calmly. "Sir, it's just a dumpster, and just a little bit of trash."

"YOU'RE the trash! Look at you! I wouldn't even let one of my girls wear that getup. Who are you trying to fool?"

My mouth dropped open. "Is it that bad?"

I think I was asking Lola, but the giant bellowed back, "It's trashy as hell!"

That word started rolling laughter in my head... throwing away trash and he calls me trashy! I stood and laughed at him until he jumped down from the concrete stoop and reached toward my neck. Lola shouted, "Go!" and I dove into the open door of the Jetta. But my high heel caught on the bottom of the door frame when I slammed it, and it stayed there, half in and half out.

As I screeched out of the parking lot and onto Highway A-1-A, I started laughing. Hysterically. Which made Lola laugh just as loud and crazy.

Two miles later, we were both in tears with laughter, and I couldn't see well enough to drive. I pulled over to retrieve my shoe, which had been torn in the wind and managed by the door. Ruined.

"I guess I won't be wearing those anymore. Job interviews be damned!"

Lola couldn't answer, too busy trying to catch her breath.

<<<<<<<<<<>>>>>>>>>

On the way back to my apartment after having dinner with Bear, Lola rattled on and on about how "wonderful" and "good-looking" and "kind" he was. She'd been bowled over with the quality of my famous boyfriend.

"So you approve, huh?"

"Absolutely!"

"I thought you'd be fussing at me because it wasn't Damon Toomey."

"Oh. No, Lela. I get it. Damon's getting pretty weird. I've been hanging out with his friend Jesse – in fact, I just may be having a little romance of my own."

"Yay! Tell me you're leaving that asshole cowboy who thinks he owns you!"

"Mel treats me like shit."

"He always has. But do you listen to your friend Lela? Nooooooo."

"It's becoming clearer to me. And Jesse is the flip side of Mel. He works for the Post Office, too. In fact, Damon introduced us."

"Then he must be a nice guy."

"Still not as nice as Bear. He's top-shelf over Damon. Hang onto him."

"I plan to... if he can keep the lovey-dovey stuff in the closet. I'm not ready for a full lock-down commitment. Oakley definitely agrees on that point."

"And I meet Oakley tomorrow?"

"Absolutely. Bear may be at the meeting, too. But we don't act like we date at meetings, so don't get confused."

"Why?"

"Why do we pretend to not date at meetings?"

"Yes."

"Lots of reasons. AA people are... let's just say I don't want to give them anything to talk about."

This led to a discussion of the twelve steps, and Lola wanted to know how they worked in everyday life. So I spent the large part of Friday evening telling her about AA and how I tried to live with complete honesty in my life. She asked, "But little white lies are okay?"

"Actually, *anything* is okay. The rules are mine, defined by *me*, just based on AA principles. When I even think about lying, or faking my way through something, or denying my feelings, I get the heebie-jeebies. I'm afraid one misstep will send me to the liquor store."

"Do you still *want* to drink? I mean, like *crave* it?"

"I can trick myself into thinking it's a craving. But these days, I can go almost all day without thinking about alcohol even once."

"That's amazing progress!"

"One day at a time." We reached across the sofa to high-five. "The only struggles I have now, but full-time... there are three: Guilt, Shame, and Remorse." I laughed, knowing that summed up everything.

"What do you mean?" Her tone was serious.

"Let's keep it light, Lola, but what I mean is I still can't forgive myself for some of the things I've done. But I've overcome the first big step. I've been put in my place enough to know I'm not special. That was a hard fact to swallow at first. I thought I was so different, so unique... know what I mean?"

"I guess I'm not supposed to say that you *are* special."

"You are right. I'm just one of the cows, not even the leader of the herd. I've been through the same shit, on the same path as a million people before me. My story may be different from theirs, but it's also the same. All alcoholics think alike, pretty much."

"Lela, look at me." She pointed to her nose and opened those dark brown saucers wide. "What I want to say is I'm proud of you."

"You're not really allowed to say that, either." I chuckled. "I didn't do it. My Higher Power did."

"Dude?"

"The Dude indeed."

<<<<<<<<<<>>>>>>>>>>

Oakley was at the meeting and met Lola. My midwestern sponsor mostly freaked out about Lola's accent, much more southern than mine, and marveled at her thick, silky hair. The three of us hit up the diner for burgers and coffee afterward, and Oakley gave me the xeroxed sheet of quotes she kept in the back of her ever-present Big Book.

As I folded my copy, my eyes landed on the only passage written in red.

She never knew how strong she was until being strong was her only choice.

A lightbulb went off. The quote left me feeling weightless, powerful, and proud in just the right way.

For the rest of our time at the diner, in fact, for the rest of Lola's visit, I thought about how strong I was, all I'd endured, and how my strength and determination could push me the rest of the way through sobriety with new-found courage.

I knew my target: to remove all the Guilt, Shame, and Remorse still on my plate.

<<<<<<<<>>>>>>

PEACHY BLOWS

CHAPTER 22

"I have *direct* experience in what you need, Mike." The man nodded, sitting up straight in his chair and paying close attention to me. I felt confident at this job interview for a technical writer who was not technical.

The company was Barton Graphix, a large printing company that had developed software to automate orders for customized printed pieces. I was unsure of the concept until Mike offered samples, then I knew the job was perfect for me.

The first example: a full-color, bells-and-whistles booklet put out by the National Picture Framing Association, where a local frame shop could add a one-color imprint on the back panel, with their logo and location, as if the kickass promotional piece came from their little shop.

The other sample was an array of business cards for Florida State University – gold-embossed and full-color. They'd print a shitload of sheets with just the logo and campus location, or what he called "the blank," then each department would place an order for their own cards through a new brand of software, adding details of names, titles, and phone numbers.

Doing large print runs on the expensive part, followed by short runs on the cheap part, doubled the printing company's profits and halved the hassle of multiple orders.

The software, called Quadrix, was high technology in the early 2000s, and Barton Graphix needed somebody to write the user manual for those who would place the orders. So Mike Barton called it a "non-technical technical writer position."

Perfect for me.

Mike crooned, "I like your experience at Smyth Software, Lela. It sounds very similar to what we need you to do."

"Exactly the same, just on a smaller scale."

"But here's the, uh, big issue: this is a contract position. When it's done, it's done. No more work except intermittent training sessions. Will you be around for those?"

"I'll be around, Mike. And contract or not, I hope you understand how long this is going to take. Plus the training materials... PowerPoint slides, too, I imagine."

"If you can do that, it'd be a bonus."

"Consider yourself bonused." A sly grin slid across my face. "So tell me more about the 'intermittent training sessions.'"

Mike leaned further toward the desk, dislodging his comb-over. I wondered why a man with such thick black hair would need to part it so far over on the side; it looked like a tilted triangle hovering over his face.

With one eye exposed, he said, "I'd want you to lead the training sessions, along with Jeffrey, the sales manager. You'll meet him on your second interview."

"I get a second interview! Great!"

Mike chuckled, his beer belly pumping in and out, "I guess I said that, didn't I?"

"Thank you."

He cleared his throat and raked the hair chunk from his forehead, sending it back to its original position. "Training: we'll fly the big clients down here for a group presentation. Our conference room is high-tech and huge, and we throw quite a party. Barton's philosophy is to wine-and-dine and treat our clients well."

"That's good business."

"My point," Mike said as he pushed his tortoise-shell glasses up on his bulbous red nose, "Is we don't allow just anybody to interact with the clients. We need professionals. How do you feel about that?"

Though he had obviously surmised I was a good choice otherwise, with a guaranteed second interview, I knew my answer was vital. *Make it perfect, Lela. Put the bullshit meter on high.* I cleared my throat. "I'm certainly a professional, Mike, and 'clean up well,' as they say. My only downfall is I make jokes when I'm nervous." I laughed, hoping he'd do the same. He did.

"But these days, my nerves are made of steel. Honestly, I like to hob-nob, excellent at client relations. See, Mike... I may have been born in the creative department, but this isn't my first rodeo on the account team."

I looked down at my new shoes; it'd been a long time since I'd had to buy new dress pumps, and hoped I'd be wearing them again to hob-knob with Barton's clients. But I accidentally chuckled, thinking about how my last pair of shoes were ruined at the strip club. Of course – dammit – Mike asked what was funny.

Think fast, Lela. "Just thinking about a good approach to the manual and how well I know Microsoft Word. I won't need publishing software to do it. I can format it all, screenshots and the works, right inside of Word. That will make it very easy for your clients to open the attachment." Compatibility issues were touchy then – before .pdf format became a common standard.

"That's another bonus," he said. "Several people have come in here talking gibberish to me. Photoshop and PageMaker and Adobe this-and-that. Some kind of new-fangled 'desktop publishing' fad. You seem more of a writer than an artist."

"I am. And if it's not good content, it doesn't matter what it looks like. But I know how to make it look good, too."

Mike looked at me with an amused smile, but I could tell his mind was elsewhere. While his gears were turning fast, he stood and announced. "I'm going to get Jeffrey. If he agrees, and he will because I'll tell him to, you have the job. Can you wait?"

"Sure!"

When he left the room, I closed my eyes, reacting first with elation and relief. My mind screamed – not just "YAY!" but "GRATITUDE!! THANK YOU, DUDE!" The thankfulness brought me to tears, and I scrambled to wipe them before meeting the mysterious Jeffrey.

<<<<<<<<<<>>>>>>>>>>

"Oakley, it's the perfect job! I'll work at home to create the user manual, and I don't even have to print it there. Plus, I've checked the software out... I understand how to use it already!"

167

"That's great, kiddo," she said, "But it's just a contract position. How long will that last?"

"At least nine months, I'm thinking. And the money! Oh, my God! Sixty bucks an hour, forty hours a week! Do you know what that adds up to?"

"I bet you'll tell me to the penny."

"A total of $2,400 a week! Of course, it's self-employment, so I'll have to file business taxes, but I've done that before. No biggie."

"So you can pay off a big chunk of your debt," she said, pulling into the parking area of the public beach near Boca. "That must be a huge weight off your shoulders."

"Yep. Dude is good. No, Dude is *great!*"

"Okay, Miss Sunshine, get your raft. Maybe now you can afford one that doesn't leak." Oakley laughed. We got out of her Jeep just as three other vehicles, full of my friends from the AA club, pulled in to park.

We had a routine on Thursdays after the 5:30 meeting: hit the beach, create a flotilla of inflatables, and meditate. I'd found a semblance of peace in the water, floating weightlessly and thinking happy thoughts.

That day, I'd have even more happy thoughts. *I have a job! A GOOD job! Making a shitload of money and doing it at my own pace, without dealing with idiot coworkers or bosses or client changes!*

The only sadness in my heart: I'd told Mom and Dad I wouldn't be coming home for Easter that weekend; I felt I shouldn't leave when unemployed, but it turned out I could've gone. A missed opportunity. Though I talked to my parents and sisters often, a face-to-face had been rare in the past year. Easter was a big deal on the farm, and I always agreed to go to church with the family, despite my personal feelings about the hypocrisy in that damn chapel.

At one point, I'd planned to go to Nashville to hang out with Bo, too, but he said he'd be busy with "his family." That comment stung deep-down in the core of my soul. *Dammit, son! Am I not your family, too?* I couldn't bear to ask if "his family" was his dad or Ella's bible-thumping Church of God crew. Instead, I rushed to get off the phone before my throat completely closed with emotions I couldn't stop.

Bo's refusal to let me in his life hurt me more than anything ever had, bringing more heartbreak than I could bear. No amount of good sponsoring could abate the pain; Oakley had only told me to be patient. But my patience was quickly wearing thin.

My old roomie, Charlie, roused me from my thoughts. She grabbed my hand and pulled me toward the sand, screaming, "Let's go have fuuuuun!" I could always count on Charlie for a laugh and a positive attitude.

Soon, twelve women, ranging in age from early 20s to late 40s, were knee-deep in the gentle waves, climbing on some sort of a floating bed. Mine, a dollar-store special with a ridiculously narrow width, had a slow leak and a butt-ugly neon-peach design, so the girls called me "Peachy" at the beach. I liked the nickname, used frequently when I paddled shoreward to add air to my raft. "Blow, Peachy, blow," they'd chant.

It was great to have a group of sober friends. And now that I had a job and was soon to meditate with Dude, who fed my spirit, I felt my life glowed with 100 percent serenity. I believed everything was going to work out as peachy as my raft.

Laura, another early-40s friend, asked if I was spending Easter with my family. Salt in the wound. "No, Bear and I are having a picnic on this very beach. Because the restaurants are too crowded, right? I'm looking forward to it."

"So, you guys are a hot item? For sure now? I know you've been fighting it for a long time."

"I've been swayed by his charm," I chuckled. "There's not a bad thing about him. But my mom is concerned that his *multiple* addictions, to alcohol and food, will interfere."

"I call bullshit. It's not your mom's worry, it's *yours*." Laura squinted her eyes at me. "I don't get the food addiction thing because he's so slim. I mean, big and strong, but he's fit. Tight. And hot! So what's the beef?"

I laughed. First a chuckle, then a full-body guffaw. "Funny you should mention beef! He doesn't eat red meat."

"So do you, like, eat dessert in front of him and stuff? You're skinny enough to eat that."

"He says it doesn't bother him. A few times, I've caught him looking sheepish. And sometimes he watches me chew."

"Oh, gross!"

"He says his diet, weighing his food and all that, will soon start to taper off. But he'll never eat sugar, I'll guarantee that."

I'd been on my stomach and rose on my elbows, falling face-first into the water. Laura howled, "Peachy is sinking! She's out of hot air!"

Shouts of "She's full of shit and out of air!" and "A sinking peach from Tennessee!" and, my favorite, "Headline in the *Post:* 'Woman drowns while meditating.'"

I paddled to the shore, spitting water to more shouts, Oakley's the loudest: "Peachy blows!"

<<<<<<<<<>>>>>>>>

I came home sunburnt, exhausted, yet exhilarated. Floating on a happy cloud about my job... with a thousand ideas in my mind about how awesome the manual could be, I planned what to wear for the get-started meeting with Jeffrey on Monday morning.

After a shower to rinse the salt from my red skin, I picked up my cell phone and settled in to call my parents and friends to share the job news. The readout showed six missed calls, all from the same number. *Who could that be? Is it an emergency? Is it Barton Graphix or Jeffrey? Six times is no mistake.*

As careful as I'd been about keeping my new number private, I knew it couldn't be Stuart or anything sinister, and the number was too new for solicitors, so I pressed the CALL button to return-dial.

A man answered in a stern tone. "Hello? Who's calling? State your name."

"Uh, this is Lela Fox. Did you call me?"

"Ooooh, yeah! Lela – that's the name. Hold on. Somebody here needs to talk to you."

My blood pressure began a quick rise, and the buzz between my ears grew in volume. The phone must have been on MUTE because there was no sound at all. A dead line, void of air. *Should I hang up? This doesn't seem like a business call. And not Jeffery, not somebody with my résumé in-hand.*

A breathy Stuart sputtered, "Lela, don't hang up! I'm at a sober house with two weeks clean." Silence from my end. I didn't know what to say. He continued, "I want to see you. Maybe you can even be my sponsor."

More silence as I decided what my reply should be. Finally, I calmly mouthed the words carefully, "Fuck you. Don't ever call me again."

"But I'm clean and sober, Lela! So now we're both on the path to serenity. I want to walk there with you! Please, honey! God is good, and he's bringing us back together."

"Stuart, let me give you some advice..."

"I'll do whatever you say. *You've* managed to stay sober. But I'm sorry you lost your job. Don't worry, somebody will see your value. You have a lot to offer with your–"

"Eat shit and die." And I pressed the END button so hard that it hurt my index finger. Rage ran through me as my mood turned on a dime. I yelled at the empty apartment. "That sonofabitch! Why can't he just leave me alone! Doesn't he know I'm too smart to see somebody who tried to ruin my life? Somebody who thought it was funny to throw me in jail?!"

When I fell back onto the sofa, my thoughts changed. *If I hadn't gone to jail because of Stuart... if I hadn't gone to the psych ward because of his trick with the cops... if I hadn't been caught in so much trouble, I wouldn't be sober now. So I owe him a thank you, big time, because he started me on the right path. He may be an asshole, but I owe my new life to him. Thank you, Stuart. Don't eat shit and die, as I said. Instead, live sober. You deserve it.*

That was the moment I forgave Stuart Weinstein, and the weight of a thousand concrete trucks slid from my shoulders. I'd never *forget* what he did to me, but I needed to forgive him for the sake of my sobriety and serenity.

Over the next few years, there would be many more reasons to build a wall of hate and hide from Stuart; he continued to contact me with threats and pleas for reunions. And became even angrier when he found out that he could no longer upset me.

In the end, I pitied him.

Forgiveness is freedom; freedom from the hate that will eventually destroy me.

<<<<<<<>>>>>>>

EASTER BUNNY
CHAPTER 23

Friday's date with Bear hadn't gone well; he seemed out of sorts, and, for the first time in a long time, we hadn't made love. I'd almost gone home after our dinner out, but didn't want him to feel even worse... as if I could do something to make it better for him.

He seemed to be deep in his own head and wouldn't talk about whatever it was that bothered him. We played Trivial Pursuit again, but his heart wasn't in it and his "wild guesses," usually so bizarre that we rolled in laughter, were flat comments. "I have no idea," he said, time after time.

Accused of being a nag many times by other men, I resisted the urge to push for answers. I only asked what was wrong twice, but the whole thing made me nervous, made me think he was preparing to break up with me.

Inside my own head, I argued back and forth about what his reasoning for a breakup would be. Things had been hunky-dory on Thursday, and we'd had our usual Friday lunchtime phone call, – complete with hoochie-coochie whispers.

Finally, I shrugged it off and brought out a notepad to plan our Easter Sunday picnic.

"I'll bring the veggies and dip. But, of course, you won't want the dip. I kinda like chopping veggies, actually. And if there are leftovers, we'll throw them in the steamer for Monday's dinner. Does that sound good?"

"Sure." A faraway voice, uninterested.

"You're still poaching the salmon?"

"That's the plan."

"I love your salmon, baby. So savory and always perfectly cooked. I've never been able to find that sweet spot between too raw and too done." When he didn't comment, I began blabbing. "You just have a knack for it. And your spice mix! Awesome! It adds just the right amount of zing without overpowering the fish. How do you do it so beautifully every time, Bear? I'm–"

"Practice. That's all. Plus, growing up Catholic, fish was a weekly thing."

"But it will be Easter Sunday, not Fish Friday!"

"Whatever." He threw the dice... not a roll, a fling of disgust.

Silence. That's when I should have split; gone home to take a bubble bath or something. But I stayed, not knowing why. Maybe to purposely keep myself on edge, keep my jaw clenched, and let the buzz of anxiety sing in my ears – because that's exactly what happened.

We went to bed. At least the joke about laying down at 11:11 was said as normal, but even his prayer was short. And not so sweet. *What the hell is wrong with Bear?*

<<<<<<<<<>>>>>>>>>

We got up early to make it to the nine o'clock Saturday meeting, then parted ways. As I pulled out of his condo community's parking lot, I exhaled relief. I didn't realize how tense I'd been.

Now you have a Saturday to yourself, Lela. Spend it alone. Well... alone with Dude. That meant a bubble bath; my tub time had become a time for a direct connection to Dude, a time when I talked to him freely and received what seemed to be direct answers from him.

I knew better than to think Dude was actually talking to me, but since I saw him shaking his head "no" when I wanted to drink the champagne, I believed he spoke clear enough for me to watch oh-so-closely.

<<<<<<<<<>>>>>>>>>

Sunday morning, I woke grateful and full of energy. Humming as I worked, I'd cubed and/or sliced a variety of fresh fruits and vegetables for our picnic, excited about our plans for the day. Hopefully, Bear would be out of his sullen mood from Friday and our Easter picnic would be the romantic scene he'd suggested when it first came up.

At the stroke of noon, the doorbell rang. It was Bear.

In a freshly pressed shirt and brand-new navy shorts, he looked sharp. And the look on his face was priceless: like a little boy caught with his hand in the cookie jar.

His hands were behind his back, and he couldn't quite look me in the eye. I teased, "What did you do, young sir? Why is that sweet little pouty lip sticking out so far?" I giggled, thinking how cute and lovable my Bear was, and how lucky I was to have him.

With his right hand, he presented what he'd been hiding behind his back: an Easter basket he'd put together himself, a gift for me. It was an oversized woven-reed basket with pink grass, featuring a miniature pink stuffed bunny with white-silk ears, two packs of Reece's cups, a Snickers bar, and more, then sprinkled all over with Jolly Ranchers and Starburst candies.

"My sweet little Teddy Bear! You're so kind to do that! Come here, Mr. Easter Bunny, and let me love on you."

He entered but didn't move from the foyer, still holding one hand behind his back. I cocked my head and asked what was wrong but got nothing out of him, only more of the guilty, pouty stare. "Bear, come on! You're freaking me out – what's going on?"

"There's one more item for the Easter Basket," he said. And as I always did with his first comment, I marveled at how low and rich his voice was... and how it sent chills to my nether regions.

What else is behind his back? What could it be? My first thought: an engagement ring. He was acting funny enough for it to be something that big and important. *Are you ready, Lela Fox? What will you say? But wait... would he dare to propose when you're still officially married?*

Trying to make it easier for him, I put on a happy face and continued the tease. "Show me, Bear. What's the secret behind your back? Looks like you've been a busy Easter Bunny, huh?"

He slowly brought his hand forward, showing an extra-large chocolate bunny, the same kind the Easter Bunny brought when I was a kid. "Oh, you sweet man!" My words were like a dove coo, said sincerely. It was so sweet that he went to so much trouble just to make me smile.

I looked closer at the bunny, but it was pretty obvious. The head of the rabbit was gone. Eaten. "Uh... Bear? Did you–"

"Yes. I did." He closed his eyes, and the little-boy pout became a scared-man grimace. "I'm sorry, Lela! I just couldn't help myself! Your eating is driving me crazy! I can't do it anymore!"

Panic shifted my brain into high gear. "Take your head out of your hands, baby. Sit down and let's talk. Or lay down and put your head in my lap. I can see you're upset." But my panic had set in deep. My fear: this was the breakup. Just as soon as I'd decided the food addiction shouldn't keep us apart, he decided it should do just that.

"I'll sit. I'm too long for your sofa." Bear's eyes were open by then, open enough for me to see the watery tears balancing on his bottom eyelids.

"Bear, you're so upset! Tell me about it, baby! Let me help you feel better!"

"Not sure you can."

I huffed, "Of course I can! First, it's my *job* to take care of you... just as it's *your* job to take care of *me*. That's how it works, right?"

"Not always."

"What the hell? What's going on?" But I knew the answer.

"Lela. I just can't..."

"Can't what, Bear?" The buzz between my ears went from zero to sixty in two seconds flat.

"I can't watch you eat anymore. My nerves are shot."

"But sweetie, you're so close to branching out from your diet a little! That's what you said, right?"

"I'm not strong enough."

"No problem! I'll help you be strong."

Bear leaned forward, elbows on his knees and face buried in his hands. He spoke from within that cave, seemingly to himself, because I couldn't make it out. *Silence from you, dipshit. Let him work it out. But don't let him leave. You're too deep into this romance to let it go... you've invested too much to let him walk out on you.*

I sighed, and the breath wavered as a chill ran down my spine. *Wouldn't it be a real slap in the face to be rejected because you eat?! It's just food! Sustenance! It sucks that it's such a big deal for Bear. But you didn't do anything wrong! Still, don't let him break up with you! You're innocent!*

In a sudden move, he raised his head and snapped a look at me. "So have you or not?"

My sheepish answer... I hadn't heard the question: "Have I or have I not what?"

"Have you ever heard the phrase, 'If you go to the barbershop every day, sooner or later you're going to get a haircut.' Have you heard that?"

"Maybe, but I don't see what–"

"It's not YOU! Dammit! It's ME! If I keep eating at the same table with you, sooner or later I'll eat all the sugar and flour and red meat I crave. You will be the death of me, the end of my recovery. I can't let you tempt me anymore, Lela. This is the end of the road."

"You're breaking up with me?"

"And with the chocolate bunny."

"But, but... dammit, Bear!" Two tears escaped my left eye. "I guess I could say I'd join you on the diet but that would be–"

"You'd never do it. You don't *have to*. Besides, you'd miss your nachos too much."

"That was the last straw, huh?"

"There's been a *hundred* last straws."

"Why didn't you tell me how you were feeling? Maybe we could've worked it out!"

"I couldn't. We can't." Then he stood. "I love you, Lela Fox, but I've got to go."

He stood, towering over me. My legs were too weak to stand, I knew, so I let myself crumble within my own skin, falling against him. "But, Lela?"

"Yes, babe. Please stay. Please! I don't know what to do without you! Please!"

"I can't. I want to, but I can't. But I'll tell you this: I'll never forget you. And every time it's 1:11 or 11:11 or anything-11, I will think of you. Forever."

I was still sitting on the sofa with my mouth open in disbelief when I heard his car rev in the parking lot. And he pealed out, almost violently, then screeched forward.

He's running from you, Lela. You're no good for him. You're no good. Look what you've done! You let a nice guy, maybe a future husband, disappear into thin air. Love... lost. Effort... wasted. Heart... broken.

The taste of tears awoke me from the trance. In a whisper, I asked the ceiling, "What will I do without Bear? Is this a sign? Is something wrong with me? Like I didn't appreciate him enough? Didn't honor his needs enough?"

My mind kept talking, knowing I'd let him down. *Like a selfish piece of shit would do. So you're a piece of shit, Lela. Face it. You only THOUGHT you'd grown into a bubble of happy serenity. You just keep screwing up everything – everything! You're not worthy of a man like Bear, anyway. He's more sober and more kind than you'll EVER be!"*

<<<<<<<<<<>>>>>>>>>

"Daddy! I'm so glad you beat Mom to the phone! I need you, Dad, I just got dumped."

"Dumped? What does that mean?"

"Bear broke up with me."

"*Why?* You were the best girlfriend on earth! I was looking forward to meeting him."

The tears began, feeling safe with Daddy. "He ate my bunny!"

"Uh, what?

"He ate my bunny's head!"

"Dear... I can't understand what you're–"

"He said he couldn't stand to watch me eat! And he ate my chocolate! Daddy, he tried to be nice about it, but he told me nachos were the last straw! I just can't sit here and be–"

"Wait! Slow down, Tear Bucket Jim! He broke up with you because you ate nachos? Why would–"

"He has an eating disorder, Daddy! Remember? And he relapsed! Because of me! And ate the bunny."

The Daddy-snort. In my mind, I could see his stubby fingers squeezing his generous nose. "That's something I don't quite understand, darlin'. Addicted to *food?*"

"Just think about if you couldn't stop eating Mom's biscuits... couldn't think about anything else, no matter how hard you tried. And the more biscuits you ate, the more you wanted. Until you had to vomit them up. That's what food addiction is."

"So, like you with alcohol?"

"Exactly. Bear's been sober for fourteen years, but only free of the food addiction for two. But now... the bunny head probably set him into a full relapse. And he was so nice to bring me a basket, with all the things I like. And a little stuffed b-unnnn-nnny..." With every syllable, my voice rose an octave as my esophagus narrowed with oncoming sobs. "It's pink!" I squeaked.

I knew Daddy would never understand – not just the addiction part, but why I was so upset. But I also knew he would start mewing to me in hopes I'd feel better. And that's what he did, ending with: "I don't like anybody who makes my favorite youngest daughter cry."

"That's the thing! He's a nice guy! He said he loved me!"

"Well, he didn't love you *enough!* You need a boyfriend without so many problems."

"But everybody has problems, Daddy."

"I mean without *addiction* problems."

"But who else would understand me? I can't see being with someone not in the program. That's my whole *life* now. All my friends are AA friends, my life revolves around it."

"So is *that* healthy? Are you addicted to AA?"

The ridiculousness of that question stopped my tears... or maybe it was the truth behind that question. *AM I addicted to AA? Is that healthy? What is life like outside of the program? Could I be friends with people who drink – I mean drink normally?*

Then I thought about Lola, a normal drinker. Thinking deeper, I knew I could only be with her one-on-one, not with the whole crowd of us.

I thought of Jennifer and her wine, wondering if her consumption was normal drinking or not. I thought probably not. *But still, you're friends with your sister! Would it be horrible to sit with her as she sipped a glass? Surely you're strong enough for that!*

But would anybody except AA people understand you? Do they understand how your life revolves around doing the right thing? Getting energy from your Higher Power? Focusing on kindness, truth, compassion, acceptance, honesty, and all that shit? Do normal people focus on that? I think not.

Dad raised his volume. "Are you still there, Lela?"

"Yeah. Sorry. Lost in my own thoughts. Actually, Daddy, maybe I am too focused on AA, and I know I'm too focused on Bear right now because I'd rather talk to you about my new job!"

"New job! Tell me everything!"

I blabbed without stopping for at least five minutes, telling him the concept and all the work I'd already done in preparing a style format for the manual, ready to show at Monday's meeting. "Chapter headings, all caps, with two lines underneath – one thick purple one and a thin lime-green one. Subheads in italics, the font is basic Tahoma, and..." Blah, blah, blah. Thankfully, Daddy let me ramble. It was what I needed to ease the current trauma of being the ex-girlfriend of my dear Bear.

"Do you want to talk to your mother?"

"Is she busy?"

"Napping. But I'll wake her up."

"No, silly. You've had a big day. Easter with the family. Mom probably cooked for two days preparing for it."

"More like three days. But I sure wished *you* could've been here."

"Me, too, sweet Daddy. I love you from the bottom of your toes to the top of your wedged head."

"And I love *you* around and around and every which way. And in case nobody has told you yet today, you're perfect in every way. Trust me, I know what perfect is!" It was our traditional telephone closing. Kinda pukey, actually, if you didn't know my dad.

Though uplifted by talking to my father, I still wasn't ready for a "Happy Easter" call to Bo. Any more rejection would crush me, I knew. So I called Lola instead, and we talked for almost an hour. An hour! In fact, the conversation ended only because my phone battery died.

Lola had stifled giggles the whole time I was telling her about our breakup. She felt bad for me, but thought the circumstances were funny as hell. "He ate your bunny, and left you?" she asked several times, revolving to "He ate your bunny and left you!!!!" She couldn't understand why I didn't see the irony.

"Maybe one day I'll think it's funny, Lola, but not today."

I thought of calling Bear. I desperately wanted to hear his baritone-deep voice. I wanted to hear him skirt around the words, "I love you," as he'd done for months.

I wanted my head snuggled in the crook of his shoulder as I cried to plead my case. I wanted him to pet me like a kitten, and shush me with assurances that all would be well. I ached for him, and wanted everything back the way it was.

So I did what always worked when I needed to get out of my head: I wrote. I went back to my short story, halfway through a tale about a peeping tom named Tom and his prey, a showgirl called Flash. It was a nutshell of a romantic comedy with a surprise ending: Flash falls in love with the cop who catches Tom peeping.

The second after my phone flashed to indicate a full charge, it rang.

"Happy Easter, my love!" Damon.

I answered, "And happy Easter Sunday to you! Did you lead an egg hunt with your son?"

"No, he's with his mom. Bummer."

"I hear ya. Bo is with Ella's family, I think. Even worse. His ex-step-family, twice removed."

"*Removed* being the key word."

Tears rose in my eyes. "Yep. *Removed* is what sucks. I miss him. But, I swear, Damon. I'm scared to call him."

"That again?"

"Yep. Still the cold shoulder."

"Maybe this will make you feel better... I was thinking of coming down to celebrate your one-year sobriety anniversary. What'd 'ya say?"

"As always, your timing is incredible."

"Is that good or bad?"

"Let me ask: did you just talk to Lola?"

"As a matter of fact, I did."

"Figures."

"Again, is that good or bad?"

"You can't hide your intentions from me, Damon Toomey."

"I'm innocent! I left twenty minutes before it happened!" This was his standard funny line when someone accused him of doing something sneaky.

"Nice try. But what the hell... come on to West Palm. Oakley is planning a big to-do for the night. I'd love for you to be here. Your support for my sobriety has meant the world to me."

"I'll always be on your side, sista."

"Thanks, my bro."

Bear and I would meet again on Facebook twenty years later, joined by a group page called *I'm a Damn Democrat*. His very liberal political views match mine to a tee, and I found out how much I still

respect him. His beliefs about how to stumble through believing in America again also match mine.

He's smart and as witty as ever. The two of us spend hours on the phone, not just reminiscing, but discovering mutual interests we've found through our years apart.

Reconnecting with Bear seems like the prime example of life's inevitable karma. At one in the morning, we talk about athletes and hurricanes, motorcycles and mayhem, and – as always – the struggle of living happily sober.

And we talk about us. The then and the now. We text each other at 11:11 almost everyday, with two chances to do so. He's marveled at how many times elevens have continued to bombard him in his life, as they have in mine. "So I never, ever forgot about you, Lela," he says.

I look forward to our hour-long conversations; we never run out of things to talk about. And... who knows what will happen in the future? My mind is open.

<<<<<<<>>>>>>

THE COST OF A PAY-OFF
CHAPTER 24

Jeffrey Goins, the only paid employee of Quadrix, loved my ideas for the format and design of the user's manual. Though I'd been studying like a maniac, I asked a hundred questions about how the software worked, and several times he said something along the lines of, "You know more than I do!"

I replied, "I have to know exactly what the software does under every circumstance. As a 'simple salesman,' you don't."

"Simple salesman... you sneak!" Jeffrey was a hoot, the funniest guy I'd ever seen in a three-piece suit. Personable, even though he looked like an innocent, shy young boy. A strawberry blonde with see-through eyelashes, I pegged him to be about my age; he got my jokes about TV shows from the 70s ("Get outta my chair, Meathead!" from *All in the Family*, and the magical nose twitch from the hit show, *Bewitched*).

We had hit it off instantly, and it didn't take long for him to open up and fuss about Mike Barton's insistence on banker-like professionalism with clients. "I mean, look at this damn monkey suit! Who wears such garb these days? Especially in 95-degree heat?!"

"So you're usually a flip-flop kind of guy?"

"Flip-flops and a swimsuit... except when I wear my chef's apron over it. I'm one helluva chef. And we have lots of parties, casual and fun parties by the pool. You'll come to the next one?"

"Sure! Sounds like fun." But my stomach flopped. *A party with strangers who drink? How do I fake my way through THAT?*

"But, Lela... Mike said it twice. He's concerned you'll take advantage of the paid-by-the-hour thing. He asked me to tell you that an hour means an hour. Not exactly sure what he meant, but you get the gist."

"I have a deadline, and every hour must count. Plus, I don't cheat. Never have, even back when I could. And quite honestly, I'm sooo ready to get started. I don't have a, uh, distraction, anymore."

"What do you mean?"

"The sonofabitch broke up with me. This project will maintain my sanity, in addition to everything else."

"So I should say both 'I'm sorry,' 'Thank you,' and 'You're welcome' at the same time?"

I laughed. "Yes, it is all the above. Now you know I'm not normal."

"Normal is just a setting on the dryer," Jeffrey said, and I stopped in my tracks. Frozen.

Is he an alcoholic? Did he hear that at a meeting as I did? Do normal people say that? Should I react like I know something? He saw my reaction to his comment, evidently, and asked what had upset me. "I'm not upset, it's just that comment threw me a little. It's a good one. A setting on the dryer, indeed!"

"You too, huh?"

"Me too, what?"

"Friend of Bill W?"

Oh, hell! Do I say yes? It's like, at work! He seems so cool about it, though. Still, mixing work with personal things on the first day isn't a good idea. But you can't NOT say yes, right?

I took a deep breath and blew it out slowly. "Yep. I'm a friend of Bill's. And the only normal I have is on my dryer."

"It's true about all of us."

"Did you know about me, somehow, before the, uh, dryer comment?"

"Yes, a good guess, anyway."

"How?"

"You've got that new-sober glow."

"New? I've got almost a year!"

Jeffrey threw his head back to laugh. "A year! I have 23 years, almost 24."

"Wow. How did you do it?"

"Just like they say..."

"What is it they say?"

"I didn't drink, and I didn't die. That's how I did it."

"Where do you go to meetings?"

"Don't go much anymore."

"Really? And you can still stay sober?"

"You'll get there, too."

"Not now."

"No, *for sure* not yet. It happens around twenty years, I guess. It all becomes repeats."

"It's repeating already! First-step meetings, over and over and over. Drives me bonkers."

"Listen closely and every time, you'll hear something different."

"Damn, Jeffrey! You sound like my sponsor!"

"Good that you have one. And she'll probably say that we shouldn't discuss this dastardly disease during work hours."

"I agree with that. Because it's ... weird."

Jeffrey continued the casual banter, unphased. "You know we come from all over – and all shapes, sizes, colors, and breeds."

I laughed. "Breeds? So you're a dog now?"

"A St. Bernard, ready and willing to get you started on this monstrous project."

My smile broadened. I liked this guy... so easy-going and smooth. And since he didn't drink, I wouldn't have to worry about going to his parties as a sober person. *And I WILL go. I need to branch out from the folks at the AA club. Friendships with older sober people would be awesome.* I gathered my papers and readied myself to leave. "So should I just check in once a day? Maybe send you a half-chapter at a time or something?"

"That sounds like a plan. I can certainly tell Mike that you'll be honest with your timesheet."

"Guilt would eat me up otherwise. But with the tight deadline, I will *have to* work more than forty a week, especially at first. I've got to get everything nailed down before I rest."

"You're going to be a good one, Lela."

"A good what?"

"A good worker and a good alcoholic."

"There's such a thing as a good alcoholic?"

Jeffrey laughed. "Well, there are plenty of bad ones! Even bad *sober* ones. But put that *sober* word in quotes."

"My sponsor actually called me sober-minded, just still crazy as hell."

"Crazy helps."

"I'll remember that."

<<<<<<<<<>>>>>>>>>

I worked sixty hours the first week, not bothering to calculate the dollar amount. All I did was send my time sheet via email on Friday at noon, as instructed. Then I dove back into work, studying the ins and outs of the program from every angle. I scribbled a notepad full of notes (I'd reserved the pink ones for Quadrix) and didn't let up, damn-determined to organize the manual logically and efficiently.

At the next Monday's meeting, Jeffrey handed me a sealed envelope; I jumped, at first confused about what it could be. "Your pay, silly," Jeffrey said.

"Oh. I forgot. Hot-diggety dog!"

"It helps when you need to pay the rent."

We had a productive meeting with more funny banter, and I left with an even-better idea of getting Chapter One in the books. When I got home, I pulled the sealed envelope from my briefcase.

Aloud, to the gods of banking, perhaps, I said, "Be a lot. Be more than the rent. Be enough to make a big payment on my Visa." I gasped when I saw the amount, almost choking. *One weeks' pay?! A full $3,000? Holy shit!*

I decided to "clock out" for a few hours and celebrate – by writing checks to Visa, Best Buy, and MasterCard. On each check, I ended the amount with eleven cents; it just seemed the thing to do. Then I went to the bank with a deposit slip and a smile as broad as the number of zeros on that check.

The next week, I worked just a little over forty hours. My paycheck was $2,200, and I celebrated by writing more checks to my creditors. Week after week, I wrote big checks, paying the most to Visa, the account accruing interest the fastest.

Oakley had also been in debt when she first got sober, she said, though with smaller balances, and she taught me how to pay "the smart way." With her most helpful tone, she said, "You'll be solvent in no time with that kind of paycheck, dear Lela. I bet a ton of weight is slowly lifting from your shoulders."

"I feel free already!"

"Just don't let up. You're not rich until you're debt-free. And remember that paycheck goes away with every hour you work."

"That sounds completely wrong, doesn't it? The faster I work, the faster my money disappears."

"A project. It's only a one-time project. Keep that in mind, *please!* In a way, you're still unemployed."

But Oakley's advice rolled off my back like oil. I paid off Best Buy, then I paid off the MasterCard, and when I was within a thousand bucks of paying off the Visa, I bought an $800 camera with all the bells and whistles... a new, digital one. Brand-new technology in the day.

I didn't tell Oakley I bought it. In fact, I hid my camera when she came over and once had to lie about not charging anything new on my credit card. The guilt made each photo I took taste like rotten earth.

What's more, I'd worked every waking minute and hadn't been to a meeting in weeks. Again, I lied to Oakley about it. Twice.

The next week I bought a new outfit to wear to my one-year-sobriety party, including strappy little sandals priced at full retail. And a new purse to match. And earrings. Then I put the most expensive eggs in my grocery cart just to be feisty.

I couldn't even admit my wrongs to my very own Dude, and Oakley was pushing me to start making official amends ASAP, even while still working on what I called "the little things."

Maybe admitting the exact nature of my wrongs to myself would injure ME or others. Yep, that's the hold-up. I can hurt MYSELF by looking at what I'm doing wrong! And that would interfere with my sobriety!

<<<<<<<<<<>>>>>>>>>>

I drew a bubble bath after yet-another shopping trip where I'd pulled out the Visa, its balance edging up fast. Guilt abounded, but I couldn't seem to stop the spending.

As the bubbles popped and sank, I tried to imagine my worries doing the same. But the feeling of freedom didn't come; in fact, quite the opposite happened. My heart sunk with the bubbles, my old friend Shame rising in their place.

Why are you doing what you know to be wrong? And lying about it? Lying to Oakley! Lying to Mom! Your sins of omission are the opposite of the openness and honesty your program demands! So why? WHY?

Oakley had always said it was "all about gratitude," but that night, I realized gratitude was second to *honesty...* not just honesty with others, but also being honest with myself. Soon tears mixed with the tired bubbles of my bath and I prayed "for me," though I'd been taught not to do that. I prayed for restraint and the courage to tell the truth.

I feared Oakley would fire me when I told her I'd been defying her advice and lying straight to her face. *Aren't you more sober than that, Lela? Don't you know what could come of such easily excused, no-big-deal behavior?*

I knew I had to come clean, just as Daddy had made me tell the store manager that I stole candy when I was seven. I knew, without doubt, that I had to do an immediate tenth step and admit the wrong that would eat me up if I let it fester.

Otherwise, I couldn't give my all to Dude and Dude couldn't his all to me. I had to be honest.

After my bath, remembering a quote Oakley had given me, I unfolded the page of scribbled tidbits I kept in the back of my Big Book. And there it was.

Honesty is the only way to fight the inner demons.

I ran to my computer and typed the quote in large, bold letters, then used an AA magnet to post it on my fridge. Then I pulled out my prettiest journal and wrote non-stop for more than an hour.

Go get 'em, tiger.

<<<<<<<<>>>>>>>

ONE YEAR AND TWO DAYS
CHAPTER 25

After a meeting on Thursday night, a group of us hit up The Recovery Store on Clematis Street in the heart of West Palm's historic downtown. Smelling of incense and stocked with every imaginable item related to spirituality and twelve-step programs, the store was one of my favorite hang-outs in the few hours I wasn't working on the Quadrix manual.

My psych meds were doing their job; it'd been hell finding a doctor and paying for it with no insurance, but I was back on-target and stable. Mood-wise, serenity flows smother along a straight line.

That night, my friend Charlie was in search of a lighter with the NA logo, and I wanted a pinky ring with AA's triangle symbol. But for me, the real draw at this lust-worthy store was the selection of gorgeous journals, some fancy and some funky. Journaling had become my therapy, my way to process thoughts and finalize my goals in sobriety.

By then, my dedication to the program and emotional maturity were both on a fast track. I was still knee-deep in writing a fourth step inventory so thorough it would take a lifetime to make amends to everybody. But I welcomed the challenge of discovering my true self, and prayed that the discovery would ooze with freedom from the Guilt and Shame that threatened to destroy me.

My one-year anniversary was in two days, to be celebrated at the club's well-attended Sunday night speaker meeting. A group of twelve, Oakley leading the pack and Damon along for the ride, would overtake a local seafood place for a celebration dinner before a caravan to the club.

Damon and I had been in close touch, talking for hours on the phone, and I found myself warming to his charms and obvious concern for my well-being. He planned to take Friday off, booked for a flight arriving at 11:17 AM at the smaller-but-nicer Palm Beach airport.

He could stay through Tuesday, he said, though I told him I had a Monday meeting at Quadrix and needed to work six hours on Tuesday. It was as if I could see Damon's goofy smile when he said, "I'm a big boy and can find a way to occupy my time. We're in this together, right?"

I had to assume the "together" comment meant his upcoming visit, so I readily agreed. I'd come to depend on Damon, bouncing ideas off him – about work, my boss Jeffrey, and always about my spiritual growth. He seemed to understand Dude as I understood him and sent me encouraging greeting cards, signed "Dude."

<<<<<<<<<<>>>>>>>>>>

"Damon, meet my sponsor Oakley, and don't worry – she's no crazy Jenny. That scene won't happen again."

Damon took both of Oakley's hands in his. "You are a saint, a godsend to my dear Lela. I appreciate all you do for her, and I look forward to hanging out with you. Maybe, just maybe, you'll share some of your wisdom with me?" he teased.

Oakley's laugh was genuine. "Can I hug? I've heard so much about you, of course, and any friend of Lela's is a friend of mine. Believe it or not, she's become a good judge of character." They hugged, and Damon sneaked a kiss on her cheek, which made Oakley blush.

Damon boasted, "I've been on Lela's side for almost thirteen years. My character can pass the test."

"But there isn't a test with you, Damon. I can feel the good vibes Lela's described."

We'd found an open meeting at a church about eight miles south on A-1-A by the beach, a non-denominational chapel as charming as the South itself. Damon had never been to an AA meeting, and I found myself a bit anxious, maybe embarrassed, to be his escort. I feared he'd deem it a cult gathering.

The chants, the twelve of everything, the fancy language of the readings, and, of course, the oddball people in the room. It all suddenly seemed a grave embarrassment. "Alcoholics are generally weird," I tried to explain, "Especially in South Florida. Just keep an open mind."

"I don't care how weird they are, Lela. If an alcoholic is strong enough to be sober, he has my respect. I've seen *your* struggles, see how you've changed, and anybody who can turn their life around 180 degrees inspires me."

"Great attitude. Still, an open mind is required."

"And I want a peek at how you've been spending your time."

"But we have weird sayings, use weird language, and I guess the rules are weird, too."

"Then it suits my weird Lela perfectly."

"Har, har."

"Indeed."

We sat beside Oakley. A few of the POWERLESS regulars were there, too, making a new meeting adventure more comfortable. The process started as expected and I saw Damon's intense concentration... as if studying each of the chairman's words.

Later, at the points I thought I'd feel embarrassment in front of Damon, I found pride instead. The AA program was *me,* an entity inherent in my being, offering a sense of belonging I'd never had. *What's embarrassing about THAT, Lela? And Damon wants to know all of you – AA is a big part of who you are.*

Oakley shared about gratitude, summing her former pain and troubles as a drunk, then offering frothy appreciation for the ability to become a new person. "Sobriety is like a re-birth," she said, "The re-birth of myself and my happiness, certainly God-given. I guess nobody but an alkie would understand that, and I'm glad to be surrounded by those who understand my new way of thinking."

With an elbow to my rib, Oakley encouraged me to share, too. It was a small meeting and to stay silent would be a bit odd, so I spoke. I talked about my sponsor's insistence that I start my day with a gratitude list – five specific things with no repeats from the ten days before. "I thought it was stupid at first, and I thought it would be hard, but it taught me to love the little things in life. Like pretty paper and colored pencils, the money to fill my gas tank all the way up, the glory of a scrambled egg, and the awesome frying pan I got at the thrift store. Such small things are *huge* in my life now. It's all about gratitude, just like she says."

When I finished, Damon patted my leg. I turned to see his face full of joy, overflowing with care for me. It was at that moment that my fear of his love dissolved. How could I deny the adoration of a good man? *A man with my happiness as his top priority... why was I so against accepting Damon's love?*

But obviously, my face didn't show the glorious freedom I felt at the moment. Later, Damon said he saw terror in my eyes.

<<<<<<<<<>>>>>>>>

"Here's to Lela! One year and many more!" The toast came from my sweet friend Charlie, her top-of-the-head ponytail swinging in a circle. We were all stuffed; twelve alkies and one hungry man took full advantage of the all-you-can-eat seafood bar.

After the clink of water glasses and coffee cups, we laughed like hyenas leaving the restaurant. "Come on, we'll be late," Oakley said, pushing Damon and me toward my rattily Jetta. Not surprisingly, we were late for the meeting; the huge hall was Standing-Room-Only when we arrived.

The speaker was an Asian man, disowned by his traditional family as a drunk in San Francisco. His story was riveting, and I could tell Damon liked it, too.

When the speaker wrapped up his story, the chairman took the podium. "It's anniversary night!" he bellowed, and the crowd cheered. I noticed balloons tied to a few chairs and vases of flowers here and there, obviously belonging to the night's celebrants. I grimaced, having nothing to show for my hard years' work but a handful of cards in my purse.

A parade of grinning alcoholics rose and approached the podium as their names were called, some proudly displaying one-year chips, and one guy picking up a twenty-year token. I fidgeted, wondering when my turn would come until I saw Oakley's face, full of panic and fear. Moments later, the chairman announced the end of the parade, "That's it, guys! A total of 21 chips tonight, and I think that's a record."

I spoke up as Oakley's voice could only croak in protest. "There's one more!" The chairman peered to the back, looking at me with a surprised, almost-accusatory glare.

"There's nobody else on the list! Are you new or something?" I shot a look at Oakley, knowing a sponsor was always in charge of arranging the presentation of their sponsee's token. She seemed still unable to speak, mouth open but no sound coming out.

192

With her right hand on her heart, she pushed me forward with her left. "Go! Go on! I forgot."

My sponsor has forgotten me? How could she do that? This is MY NIGHT! Like being a bride, but even more important! How would a simple and easy thing not make it the top of her to-do list? She's failed me... embarrassed me! And in front of Damon!

I zigged and zagged to the front. The chairman asked my name and number of years sober, then turned to the microphone to announce me. As I stepped to the podium, I saw a sea of faces – a million faces – looking at me with pity. *The woman whose sponsor forgot her. The woman with no friends. The woman barging in on our party.*

Shame rose to redden my cheeks. I remember saying something waaaay too loud into the microphone but don't remember my words except that I mentioned Oakley. I hoped her name would restore my credibility, and I did feel the vibes in the room relax a bit.

From the back, Oakley had obviously found her voice and shouted, "Way to go, Lela!" which prompted the crowd to say the same. The buzz of anxiety between my ears disappeared and I bit the side of the coin, per tradition. *Saved by Oakley once again. Too little, too late maybe, but saved.*

Outside, with my group of friends surrounding me, Bear stepped into the circle and reached to touch my arm. His deep voice shocked me; I suppose because I hadn't heard it in so long. "Congratulations, Lela. I knew you'd make it."

Something stopped me from speaking; my vocal cords squeezed together and no sound could push through. I simply nodded, feeling the tension in the air as my typical between-the-ears buzz sounded the alarm.

Perhaps it was the instant rise in tension that made Damon step forward. "Is there a problem?" he asked.

Surprised by the animosity churning in my gut, I looked at Bear while talking to Damon. "No problem. Just an old friend with good wishes." Then Bear stepped out of the circle as quickly as he'd stepped in.

"Was that Bear?"

"Yes."

"Are you okay?"

"Not really. I don't know why I couldn't speak to him. I acted rude to him, and that's not what I wanted... that's not how I feel." I looked imploringly into Damon's eyes, now full of concern for me. I jerked, knowing what I wanted to do. As I turned, I said, "I've got to apologize. Be right back."

Scanning crowd, I then looked beyond it to see Bear on his motorcycle, buckling his helmet. My shout, "Wait!" couldn't be heard through the helmet's padding, I knew, so I ran forward, waving my arms. He glanced at me, then raced away.

I put my head down, feeling like a bitch... like I'd let go of him forever. And I didn't want that.

<<<<<<<<<<>>>>>>>>>

Damon and I went to the beach on Saturday, me floating on the "Big Peachy" raft and Damon on a rushed-purchase inflatable just as cheap. "But not as ugly," he made sure to point out.

We talked about a million things, sharing our deepest feelings and greatest joys, in that order. The third time I had to paddle to shore to re-inflate my raft, Damon suggested we get out of the water and "un-prune."

On the sand, as we lay side by side on our rafts, Damon reached to hold my hand. *That's weird. Why would he do that?* Then he raised on one elbow and quickly ran his finger across my cheek. His words were slow and whispered. "Lela Fox, I love you. I want us to be together."

I froze with my arm in mid-air. I couldn't move; I couldn't believe what I was hearing. He continued. "Move back to Rockville with me, get out of this sweaty weather and come home. Where your family is... where *I* am. And closer to Bo."

I don't know how long my silence lasted. More than a minute, I'm sure. A thousand thoughts filled my brain, a thousand possibilities, half exciting and half frightening. At last, I found words. I came to terms with a move to be with Damon surprisingly quickly. But the practical things were roadblocks. "But my *job*, Damon..."

"You're on contract, right? You can work from anywhere. And there's a direct flight every Monday to Ft. Lauderdale. I checked. It's a big-time discount fare, too. Rockville to Lauderdale – you'll love this: $111. So you can fly back anytime they need you. For training or whatever."

Again, a long silence. I assumed Damon could see my gears turning; he waited patiently for an answer. I felt sure Jeffrey would agree to me being a "remote employee" because that's what I was already, just nearby. *He'll talk Mike Barton into it. And since I'll pay for any expense caused by the distance, how could they argue?*

194

Realizing it might work, I panicked more. "But my friends! Oakley! How could I leave them?"

"Don't you think your old friends are still in Rockville? And I don't mean your old drinking buddies, either. Lola, Kay-Kay... and so many more. Plus, your sister Jennifer." You can move into my condo, Lela, and work from there. Save all your money, get the last bit of debt paid off."

I said nothing, guessing my facial expression was one of sheer terror. *This could all work. And don't you already love Damon, anyway? And yesterday... you realized you'd been fighting against a damn-good thing. Quit doing that! It doesn't make sense!*

Damon put his index finger under my chin, raising my head to look at him. "I just want you to be happy, Lela."

"But..." I didn't know what to say, feeling like I still had to challenge him. "It sounds like more happiness for *you* than me."

A grimace contorted Damon's face. "I admit I've had lots of time to think about this, and yes, it would make me the happiest man in the world. I'm in love with you, Lela, and I have been for a long time. I think you know that."

"Yeah..." I admitted, my words fading into the sound of the waves. After a beat, I admitted an even bigger truth, "I've resisted loving you for so long."

"I know." Damon looked away, studying the waves. When he turned back toward me, there were tears in his eyes. "Why resist? What's the holdup?"

"I've never thought about... uh, sex... with you. It'd be like sleeping with my broth–"

He cut me off and raised his voice. "Do NOT say I'm your brother! And there's *no way* you'd think that after two seconds in bed with me. I *love* you, Lela!"

I looked down at the soft sand, contemplating the very essence of my life in Florida and the possibilities I'd regain in Tennessee. "I miss home. I miss my son. And my parents." Tears began a river down my salt-encrusted face, tingling on their way to my jaw.

"Be with me. You know it's in the cards, surely by now. *I* knew it the moment I met you."

"Oh, Damon, you are so sweet, so kind. But still too nice of a guy for a crazy bitch like me. Why would you–"

"Baby, you're so beautifully easy to love. I will take care of you, whether you need it or not. You'll never want for anything."

I giggled, nervous. "Don't overpromise, Damon. I feel like I'm in a damn romance movie. And you might be surprised by how much I demand from a partner. Three different husbands couldn't handle me, so what makes you think you're different?"

"Three *drunken* husbands. You're sober now, and everything – I mean everything – has changed. You're free to choose who you should share your life with, Lela, and I'm just saying it should be me."

Again, I laughed. "Damn, you're cute! And I believe you. But..."

"But what? Tell me. I'm listening."

"I'm just not sure I love you."

"Give it a minute."

"A *minute?*" My chuckle grew to a full guffaw. "It's a different kind of love, Damon. One I don't recognize."

"Maybe because it's *sober* love? The kind that's real and raw and not based on lust or using people?"

My tears began anew. "I've told Lola that I'd always love you. Said it many times."

"I know you love me. At least enough to take a chance. And it could be the chance of a lifetime, Lela. You've been burned so many times, I don't blame you for being cautious. I don't blame you for being bitter. But it's *me* you're talking to, not somebody only looking out for themselves."

I felt a rack of sobs coming. Damon was so right: I was overly cautious. And bitter. And afraid to take a chance. I was on the verge of being ready with Bear when he left. And my fear of the unknown was looming, so big I could taste it.

In my little life of recovery, I'd shut myself off to the possibility of a relationship with anybody at all, even resisting Bear until it was too late.

Why not Damon? He loves you, Lela. He's ALWAYS loved you. Why are you afraid of the only good man you know? Red flags don't exist here, so why are you fighting it?

Damon's arms surrounded me as I cried. He held me patiently, resting his chin on the top of my head and murmuring assurances. He didn't push me to answer, to believe him, or to stop with the emotional overflow. He wasn't doing *any* of the things I feared a man would do.

<<<<<<<<<<>>>>>>>>>>

When I came back home after the Monday meeting with Jeffrey at Quadrix, Damon was on the sofa, shirtless and smoking a cigarette. His look was a hopeful question mark; he knew I'd asked about a work-from-Tennessee arrangement.

"Well?" Damon stood, reaching for my shoulders. He held me at arm's length, searching my face for an answer.

I had planned to play a game, to tease him that it wasn't possible, but my joy exploded and I blabbed, "He said yes! I can work from Tennessee or Timbuktu, he said!"

If Damon answered, or cheered, I can't remember... I just remember a feeling of complete and utter elation, a sharing I'd never felt. His lips didn't leave mine as he picked me up and carried me to the bedroom; we made love for what seemed like hours. So gentle, then so intense, then back to gentle again.

He was an inspired, exuberant lover, and 100 percent correct that my fears about "brotherly" sex with him would instantly disappear. I craved him, wanting more and more and more. He denied me nothing.

<<<<<<<<<>>>>>>>>

I gave my keys to Damon and went to work. He'd asked for a run-down of the historic downtown district, and I was happy to tell him of the cool places, especially the coffee shop with outdoor tables perfect for people watching.

He came back around 4:00 with wrapped packages. "For you," he said. The tags both said "The Recovery Store," and that thrilled me.

"How did you know this was my favorite store?"

"I listen."

The first gift brought a happy scream – a super-sized burgundy coffee cup that said: DENIAL: IT'S NOT JUST A RIVER IN EGYPT. The second package, a smaller one, was a beautiful pair of sterling and amethyst earrings with a tiny AA logo dangling below. "Damon! Thank you! You're so sweet!"

"I meant to shop before your anniversary celebration. That's the purpose of these, so... happy year-two of sobriety!"

We went out to dinner. "Only the best lobster and filet mignon for my lady!" he proclaimed, and my thoughts immediately turned to Bear. Fear. Guilt. I guess Damon saw the pain on my face and changed his tune to the extreme opposite. "No! Scraps and leftovers for this Lousy Lela woman! That's obviously what she wants."

Slowly, my mood adjusted.

The waiter came for our drink order, and we chatted through the delay. But Damon was nervous and avoiding the topic, I knew; he must surely fear what Oakley's reaction had been to my news of the move to Tennessee. My new-found boyfriend fidgeted with his napkin and re-arranged the silverware a half-dozen times.

"Should I keep you waiting longer?"

"Waiting for what?"

"Ha! Like you don't know what I mean! What Oakley said..." I heard him gasp, but no words came out. He knew Oakley's approval of our relationship was the critical factor in my decision, and the guide for his. If she objected, he would go home and settle for thrice-weekly phone calls, he'd said.

"She had a fit, but I talked her around."

"Really? Yay!" After a pause, his true exuberance broke through. He raised his arms and shouted, "And the crowd goes wild!" One of his favorite lines.

"I think she purposely made me talk her into giving approval. She wants me to be sure."

"And *are* you sure?"

"Honestly, Damon..." I stopped, wondering how much to say. Or not say. Damon's face fell as if his entire body had been deflated in one whoosh.

"I'm not *completely, 100 percent* sure, but I don't think a big decision like this would ever be 100 percent. I'm just being honest. And I'm scared. Forgive me if I'm not chomping at the bit to hurry."

"Your lease is up in six weeks. That means we *have* to hurry."

"It doesn't take six weeks to plan a move, Damon! But I know where I can get as many boxes as I'd *ever* need – from work, the ones for reams of paper. They stack them ten-high in a corner of the press room."

"Then you can get started?"

"A little at a time."

"But it's all planned out! I've booked the moving van, rented the towing bar, signed the contract."

My temper flared. "What the hell? You did all that without my input? Without asking me anything?!"

Baffled, he asked, "Why not?"

"Because..." I didn't have an immediate answer for him, but I knew why. *It's simple, Lela. It's because YOU are usually the one in charge, Ms. OCD planner! Can't you let somebody else take control for a change?* Dropping the surprised look, I said, "I just thought, uh, that I'd do it. I like to take care of myself."

"Lucky that you don't have to do that anymore."

My stomach fell. "That makes me lucky? Sounds like that makes me dependent."

"What's wrong with being dependent! It's Damon Toomey in charge, my dear! What more could you want? Now you can relax. You don't *always* have to be at the helm. Besides, I've had a lot of time to plan this. Like... a year." His hiccup of a laugh that followed the comment was heartwarming.

Treading softly, I asked, "But what if I *want* to be at the helm? In charge of my own shit?"

"This isn't shit. And details are my thing."

"Mine, too–"

He talked over my objection. "I'll call around for the best rates on storage units when I get back to Rockville. There's a place about three miles away that..." I zoned him out. *Damon, the micro-manager, comes out of the woodwork. When I was drinking,I needed somebody to take care of me, but I don't need that now! I'm not so sure this is going to–*

"Don't you think so, too, baby?"

"Think what?"

"You weren't listening, were you?"

"Lost in another world. Sorry."

"Don't worry. I have it handled. You'll find out later and be pleased."

"What if I'm *not* pleased?"

"You *will* be. Never fear, my dear! Damon is here!"

<<<<<<<<>>>>>>

A SURPRISING FIND
CHAPTER 26

The next Monday at the weekly meeting with Jeffrey, I presented another completed chapter. "Here's chapter nine, so I'm finished with the order entry section. Six more chapters to go, then the booklet for the warehouse. Then it's done!"

"Damn-fine job, Lela! Everything is coming together for Quadrix. I sold the system to three more clients last week, and I've already scheduled four training sessions. Here's the official confirmation of the dates, but you may already know."

"I knew. And my boyfriend has already booked my flights."

"What? Wow. Some organized boyfriend, huh?"

"Well... I didn't *ask* him to book the flights. He just took control, like the control freak he is."

Jeffrey laughed and slapped his knee. "*Exactly* like an alcoholic!"

"But he's not an alcoholic. Just a control freak. It's beginning to drive me bonkers, to tell you the truth."

"Maybe he just knows you're busy and is trying to help."

After a pause, I agreed. "Could be, and there wasn't a ton of choices in flight times or whatever, but still..."

"Still what?"

"It's just... creepy. Too much in-my-face."

"Relax and let somebody else be responsible for once, woman! If I was mean, I'd accuse *you* of being a control freak! Look how you've proved it with the way you've handled this project. From beginning to end. There's been no supervision required. And you run a tight ship."

"Yeah, but it's my ship to run."

Jefferey shrugged. I had tried to roll with it, to let the discomfort of Damon's "management" of me slide, but it'd been eating my lunch. I didn't know how to tell him that I could take care of myself and I'd *prefer* to do exactly that. I didn't want to sound mean or unappreciative of his loving care for me, and, in fact, I welcomed him saving me time... but I felt stuck.

It was as if Damon was my mother, arranging my life for me.

Then again, one of the many things I loved about Damon was his love of detail; he had a true talent for planning. And he used different colored papers for different projects like I did, which I thought was precious. He certainly kept things in order; the only curious thing was why his condo remained a mess. Anal organization amid sloppy clutter.

"So, Jeffrey, I hope to have one more chapter ready before I move. Then another, say, three months for completion. That leaves ten days for review and corrections."

"Perfect! You're awesome, Lela Fox... in case nobody has told you that yet today."

I blushed. "Thanks, Jeffrey. You're much of the reason I strive for such perfection... because you brag on me all the time."

"It's deserved." He sat back in the chair, closing his padfolio. The meeting was over; each week, they got shorter and shorter.

I took ten or so packing boxes home from work that day, as many as would fit in my car. Damon had been overjoyed that the boxes would all be the same size; made loading the truck more manageable, he said.

I started on the manual's next chapter and stopped work in time to barely make the 5:30 meeting. Monday was the scheduled night for my sponsor meeting, but Oakley, in a rush and breathing hard, said she had to cancel. "Something has come up. We'll fix it next week, maybe meet twice. I have certain things I want to go over before you leave."

Disappointed to skip our always-inspiring meeting for the week, I decided it may have been in the cards and meant I should start packing. I had the boxes, after all.

I started in the left-side bedroom closet with a sigh. Many boxes were still unpacked from my move the year before, but I did as Damon asked and emptied them to re-pack in the uniform boxes from work. I worked for hours, finding things I'd forgotten about – things from previous Lifetimes. Trinkets, fun décor items, my sewing box, and a shitload of office supplies. (Yay! More note pads!)

At ten PM, I opened the last yet-unpacked box. Curiously, it was unmarked. And heavy. The sealing tape was half-rotten; it opened without a cutter. With a gasp, I spoke to the ceiling, my hand on my heart. "Oh, my God! It's my portfolio! And all the tapes, discs, extra samples... it was all there!"

But... there were photos of it burning in his mother's fireplace! I saw the binder in flames! Surely I didn't imagine those photos! I opened the leather binder – everything was intact. On the back, a three-inch-square singed and sooty spot where the leather had bubbled a bit. No other damage, no destruction. *What the hell?*

Again, I spoke aloud. "Dude? Did you do this? Is this, uh, some kind of miracle or something? What does it meeeeean?" Sprawled on the floor of the closet, my tears flowed: tears of confusion, happiness, terror, sadness, and incredible wonder.

I pleaded to Dude for an answer, and the image I'd come to know arranged easily in my mind. *Except... what's that glow behind you, Dude? The sun coming up?* There was no answer. As my vision always showed, Dude just sat there at the picnic table, smiling, smoking the cigarette, happily vibrating with feelings of peace and kindness. And gratitude.

Pure, heavenly gratitude.

<<<<<<<>>>>>>

OUTTA THERE
CHAPTER 27

I copied the eighth screenshot of the day, pasting it into the user's manual document in the depths of chapter ten. The new chapter covered a different aspect of the software, beyond the data-entry tasks, and I struggled with writing the copy; the approach had to be different.

When I came up for air, thinking it'd be close to lunchtime, my jaw dropped. It was 2:11. But it wasn't just the eleven thing... it was *worse*. "Oh, no! I missed my appointment!"

It wasn't easy getting appointments with "Dr. Freud," as I called him, my psychiatrist who wrote five different Bi-Polar prescriptions for me. Even worse, I'd planned to ask him for extra refills so I could have more time to find a doctor when I moved. "Shit! I bet there's not another appointment! Then I'll be in Rockville and shit out of luck."

I found the doctor's number and dialed immediately, spending nearly ten minutes on hold, as usual. It was a busy practice, Dr. Freud the busiest, so I planned to ask if another psychiatrist in the group could see me, assuming Freud would be booked.

When Macy, the lazy receptionist, returned to the line, I heard her keyboard clicks as she searched for an appointment. "If you saw another physician, it would be considered a new-patient appointment, and those run three months out. First available is in July."

"That won't do. Look, I'm moving out of state. I either need to see him or get a refill by phone. It's an emergency."

"Not an emergency, Ms. Fox. Doesn't meet our criteria."

"Okay... what if I told you I was thinking of cutting my wrist?"

"Then I'd call an ambulance and the staff doctor at Bayview would see you in the morning."

Sigh. "Do you have a cancellation list?"

"We do."

A cheer rose in my throat. *Problem solved!* "Okay, put me on that list. I can come with only fifteen minutes' notice."

"The problem is... you are number 42 on the list. We average maybe five cancellations per week, usually less." My heart sunk. I couldn't find my voice to reply. "See, Ms. Fox, people just don't 'forget' appointments in this practice. They know how scarce they are." Her condescending tone was like fingernails on a blackboard.

"Thank you for the tip, Macy, but you don't need to add more Shame here. In your business, you should know better."

Macy's answer: "There will be a missed appointment fee of 25 dollars."

Good luck getting that! Screw you!

Incredulous, I huffed, "So you're just going to leave me hanging out to dry? With no meds? Don't you know what that means to my mood? To my basic *health?*"

"I don't make the rules, Ms. Fox."

My jaw ached from clenching it so hard, and my head pounded with tension. "But... what do I do?"

"Perhaps find another physician with a more generous schedule?"

"Fuck you!" I retorted. She hung up.

I dashed to the cabinet and gathered my pill bottles, pouring them on the bed for a count. "Ten days, then I'm out. I'm screwed." I let my mind wander. *What the hell – maybe I don't even need them! I've been so stable lately that I'm boring. They say Bi-Polar Disorder is a lifetime disease, but they also said I'd never be able to stop drinking.*

Somewhere deep in my mind, I saw a red flag, but pushed my "convenient" thoughts of self-sufficiency forward to send the red flag to the Netherlands. I spoke to the empty room. "Yeah, a change in location, new boyfriend, new digs, new outlook... I'll be fine. Besides, what choice do I have?"

Nobody answered my self-talk, of course, but the room still vibrated with tension. "Back to work now, Lela Fox." I took a deep breath and typed another paragraph, moving forward as quickly as I could.

<<<<<<<<<>>>>>>>>

"Ten days to go, baby! How many boxes have you packed?"

"Lots! I haven't counted, but I have lined the walls in three rooms. Tonight, I'll tackle some of the kitchen."

"Keep up the good work! Sorry that I can't be there to help you, and I bet I could pack twice the amount in each box. You know why?"

"Why, Damon." Yawn. *Yeah, I've heard it all before.*

"Because I'm damn-good at spatial relations. In fact, I've been having dreams about how to fit everything in the truck."

"Chill, Mr. Anal. It'll all fit and be organized. It's not my first move, you know."

"You're writing which room the boxes should be unloaded to, aren't you?"

"Of course! In red and circled."

"Good girl."

"But separating the storage stuff from the things going to your place–"

"*Our* place."

"Okay," I giggled, feeling the strength of our connection, "Separating all that has been a real challenge. And something I've never done."

"I know how to make it happen if you've packed right."

"Give me a little credit, huh?" My feathers had ruffled; Damon pissed me off by assuming I didn't know how to pack a for a move. "I'm no dumbass girl."

"Right. You're a *bad*ass girl."

"Actually, you should say 'woman,' not 'girl.'"

"Whatever... don't be so sensitive about it."

"Arg!" He'd flipped my pissed-off switch with the "don't be sensitive" comment, and I jumped on him like a dog would jump on a bone. "Don't you *ever*, EVER tell I'm being too sensitive! Or *any* shit like that. It's like telling me to change my personality! I don't ask you to quit being anal about things!"

"Wouldn't do any good if you did."

"Well, ditto, dumbass. Promise me you won't say that. It's interfered with three of three marriages."

"Ouch."

"Damn-right!" I said, mad enough to spit flecks on saliva on the phone. "As they say... them's fightin' words."

"Yes, ma'am."

"That's not much better. Just back down, Damon. I gotta go, anyway."

"Back to packing?"

"Yeah. Sure."

"I love you. Talk to you tomorrow! Stay busy!"

My pout was full-on; I decided not to return the "I love you" line. "Bye, Damon."

<<<<<<<<<<<<>>>>>>>>>>>>

The day before Damon arrived, I took the full day off from work – for the first time since I'd started the project. I'd worked at least six hours per weekend, a minimum of forty hours during the week. And my paychecks were phenomenal, never ceasing to thrill me when I went to the bank.

All credit cards but the Visa were paid off and canceled. However, my Visa balance was just a bit over $600. If I played my cards right, one more paycheck would bring it to zero.

Everything was packed except the bare essentials, and the boxes for those things were pre-marked with the list of contents and the room where it should go. My Sharpie had barely held out; the marks weren't bold or dark at the end, but the turquoise top of the paper boxes gave enough contrast. I was ready and I hoped Damon would be pleased.

When I picked him up at the airport, he was testy, bitching about the inefficiency of the airlines. I said, "It was just a fifteen-minute delay, Damon. That's not bad! Some people have to wait all day *and* all night for a plane. Count your blessings." But he continued to swear under his breath, ignoring my fantastic mood.

I assumed my medications were entirely out of my system by then, and still I felt great! But I hesitated to tell Damon I was off meds; he was always checking to make sure I took them and took them on time.

My boyfriend's first comment as we left the airport lot: "I made a Tuesday appointment at a car detailer in Rockville, and sideline mechanic, to see if he can do something about the rattles in this piece of shit."

"The Jetta isn't a piece of shit. And I've gotten used to the rattles. Probably just a few loose screws, anyway. Nothing I want to spend money on fixing."

He raised his voice, shocking the hell out of me. "But I am the one who wants it fixed! Don't I get what *I* want, too? Huh? Doesn't *my* opinion count?"

"What the hell, Damon? Relax! *You* pay to fix the rattles, then. And arrange to get it there. Don't be angry with me about something so stupid."

His face fell, almost contorted. "I'm sorry, Lela. I guess I'm just so stressed about the move. I love ya, babe. Didn't mean to yell. It's just... I have it all arranged and don't want you to argue about it."

"So *my* opinion doesn't matter?"

Damon didn't reply. *Chalk one up for Lela.*

We stopped for lunch at one of my favorite spots on the bay and sat outside with the ocean breeze. Our view of a dozen boats docked nearby created the idyllic venue, and the wired-in calypso music sent my toes tapping. When I shared my happy thoughts about it, Damon disagreed, complaining about the fishy smell. "These are the boats that bring fresh fish to the restaurant! What else would it smell like?"

"Well..." He shook his head, squenching up his nose. "It's unpleasant."

"What's *wrong* with you today, Damon? You're pissy as hell and making me mad. Can't you find *one* thing to be grateful for? Did you do your gratitude list today?"

"I'm still doing that. Oakley's idea for everybody, not just alcoholics–"

"And that doesn't start your day with a new perspective? Gratitude galore?!"

"Whatever... it's helpful. Helps me keep things on a positive note, for the most part. And I usually find a lot more than five things to be grateful for, a hundred things about my awesome Lela – always."

"That's sweet, baby. I'm grateful for you, too, and absolutely sure about that! And I'm happy to be going back home. I want to see my parents this weekend. Do you want to drive to the farm with me?"

Damon grimaced. "Sure. I want to meet your parents, and 'convey my intentions,' as the old folks say. I'm sure they're not pleased about our 'living in sin.'"

"Ha! You got *that* right! It's the elephant in the room when I talk to them. They won't tell me their feelings, but they know their beliefs are behind the times. So old-fashioned, but that's just the way they are."

Damon's mind was elsewhere; I could tell. Then he huffed, "The only thing about going there... damn, Lela!"

"What are you talking about?"

"You leave so early! Can't we just go later in the day?"

"It's too short of a day if we go late. The drive is a bummer." I let myself be lost in a bevy of thoughts, keeping a rare silence for a while.

"You know what?"

"What?"

I mimicked a child, "I need my Momma!"

Damon's chuckle was genuine. "She needs *you*, too! And I know your dad wants to see you. He told me how long it would take you to get there, so if we leave at–"

My mouth opened wide with surprise. "You talked to my dad?"

"Yep."

"You called him? Just... out of the blue?"

"I did. Why? Is that a problem?"

"Uh... no. I guess not. I'm just, uh, surprised that you would do that without telling me."

"I need your permission to talk to my future father-in-law?"

It took a moment for that to sink in. *Future father-in-law... so he's planning on us getting married. And he's barging right in on my family as if it was his own. Is that a good thing? Does he think I should do the same with HIS family? I barely know them! And I'm SCARED of his mother – she's tough as nails.*

I asked, "Did you call anybody else?"

"Should I have?"

"No. Not at all." I paused to practice my speech, then cleared my throat. "I'm going to set some boundaries here, Damon. Don't call my family unless you tell me first, and tell me what you plan to say."

"Why?"

"Because it's too... personal."

"Don't you think the two of us have grown beyond 'too personal?'"

"Maybe so. But I've set this boundary and I expect you to stay on the other side of it."

He eyed me as if accusing I'd committed a crime. "Okaaaaay." A quick swallow of his Coke. "Well, I don't get it, but I know you're weird about your family, so I'll–"

"I am NOT 'weird' about my family!"

"But you *are*."

"I am NOT!" My nostrils flared. *How DARE he question a perfectly happy relationship with my family?! How dare he judge me on that? He knows NOTHING about it!*

I realized my heart rate had doubled; I was breathing hard. *Well, you DESERVE to be angry. He's overstepped!*

"Jeez, Lela! Chill out! Don't be so–"

"Don't you DARE tell me to not be so sensitive!" Damon sat back in his chair and gestured a lip-zip. *What an ass! What's happened to my sweet Damon? What am I going to do now?! This feeling is waaaay too familiar.*

I threw my napkin on the table, beside my half-eaten plate of shrimp. "I'm going to the restroom to get my shit together. I suggest you get yours together while I'm gone."

<<<<<<<<<>>>>>>>>

By the time we got to my apartment, all the tension had dissolved – not because we'd talked about it and worked it through, but because I decided I didn't want the tension and simply kicked it aside. The change had gone unnoticed by my boyfriend, though; he apparently hadn't know how upset I'd been in the first place.

Once inside, Damon walked room-by-room, ooh'ing and aah'ing at the walls of boxes. He nodded his head, index finger to his chin. "You've been busy!"

"Definitely. And only basic survival things are still out. We're barely set up for tonight and the morning." I beamed with pride; I *had* worked hard, down to the wire, and things were perfectly organized. I could almost point to the box where you'd find the dessert-sized plates, for instance.

Damon hadn't said much as I babbled about how I'd done all the good organizing, what I left in, what I left out, the red star I'd added to the boxes for my desk, blah, blah, blah.

Then he interrupted me. "But there's a big problem."

Confused, the space between my brows became smaller. "What problem?"

"The boxes are only labeled on the top, not the *side*."

"So?"

"That doesn't work for loading and unloading the truck."

My mind chewed on this fact; I envisioned a packed U-Haul. "Well, that's easy enough. Maybe not ideal... I see what you're saying, but surely it's not a world-ending problem."

"Get your Sharpie and start marking."

"No! And, besides, my Sharpie is out of ink."

"Then give me your keys. I'll go get another."

"Damon, you're being ridiculous."

"But I'm the one loading and unloading the truck. I want to make it as efficient as possible."

I huffed a sigh, breathing long and slow through my nose to control my anger. I counted to five, practicing what Oakley would applaud: restraint of tongue and pen. I spoke slowly and in a staccato tone. "Whatever you say, dear. I want to make it easy for you."

<<<<<<<<<<<>>>>>>>>>>>

"What do you *mean* you don't have a reservation for Fox?! It was confirmed more than a month ago!" My blood pressure shot to the roof the instant the U-Haul man checked his computer, not finding my name. Damon was checking the rattles in the Jetta; he argued that I should wait for him, but the argument ended with me slamming the door in his face.

The U-Haul man re-arranged his ballcap, showing a greasy-black hairline. "I'm sorry, ma'am. And I have no other trucks to offer you today. All booked up."

"Check again." Snippy. And pissed.

He rolled his eyes but pecked a few more keys. "Nope. Nothing in that name."

My stress level had maxed out. Tears came as if flipping a switch. "But you don't understand! Everything's packed! Everything's planned down to the minute! This can't be happening. You screwed up royally, Mr. U-Haul Man!" My voice was at full volume on the final syllable.

The bell above the door tinkled and I jumped, nervous as a cat. Damon approached the counter, acting all bossy and in control. "What seems to be the problem here, sir?"

I answered before the man could. "They lost the reservation! And there are no more trucks! What are we going to do?" The boo-hoo's had begun. I felt like the Wicked Witch in a puddle of water.

Damon gently put a hand on my shoulder. "It's okay, Lela. I've got this handled, do you understand?" He put his index finger under my chin to raise it until I could look him in the eye. "I've got this. You don't need to worry."

I blubbered, "O-kk-ay," and wiped snot on my shirt sleeve.

He turned to the man without letting go of me. "The reservation is in Toomey. Damon Toomey."

Keyboard clicks. "Aha! Here we are! Damon Toomey, a 25-footer with tow trailer."

With my head down, I saw Damon click his heels together. "Correct," he said.

The U-Haul man was all chirpy now. "Yes, Mr. Toomey, it's parked right out front with the keys in it, but I'll need you to sign a few papers first."

"Certainly," Damon answered, then turned to me. "Lela, there's a chair over there. Go and sit. Calm yourself down. It's okay, honey. You've just worked yourself into a frenzy. All is well. Remember, never fear, my dear – Damon is here."

I rolled my eyes. My dad used to say that when I was a kid and I loved it then. But now it sounded like a lie, a slap in the face. "Well, you'll need my credit card, so I'll stay."

"Nope. Have that covered, too. Just go rest."

Tears started anew. I felt so helpless, so inadequate, and ridiculously needy. And there was Damon, scooping up my shit and hauling it away. Efficiently. Suddenly I felt frail, like a sick child who wants to be held. And that feeling tasted like chalk in my mouth.

I am NOT helpless! I am in charge, but he won't let me be! Exhaustion took over, and my thoughts drifted to a more peaceful arena. *But why not let him take the reins? You've done all the packing, handled the Florida end. He knows what he's doing, so let him. Quit being a controlling bitch and relax, for God's sake! Relax and say a prayer of gratitude.*

I zoned out in the chair, focusing more on the music in the background than on the business dealings at the counter. It felt strange to let things happen without me, almost like I was drunk and unaware, or like I needed somebody to take care of me because I couldn't do it myself.

The feeling was eerily familiar, like when I first met Stuart and went along with his every suggestion... only because I had no clue of the reality going on. I knew this wasn't a repeat of that; I certainly wasn't drunk nor unable. I knew what to do, I just...

Damn, Lela! Get over it! He made the arrangements, and that was great! Isn't it nice for somebody ELSE to do the work? Somebody who truly doesn't need your supervision, for God's sake! He's a capable man who likes efficiency, and he loves you... why would that upset you? Chillax, chick.

I wiped the rest of my tears with my t-shirt and took a deep breath. At that moment, Damon turned from the counter. "You ready, Freddy? We're in business!" I smiled at his smile; he seemed so happy, his face cherubic and child-like. He put his arm around my shoulders, guiding me through the door. "I have an idea," he said.

"What's your idea?"

"Let's move you to Rockville! Move in with me and be my forever girl! What'd 'ya say?" Then he kissed my head. Soon after, he started spitting... like blowing through wet lips. He was spitting on my head!

"What the hell are you doing?!"

"I just ate a curl. A Lela curl." He snuggled me closer, rubbing his nose against mine. "We're on! The adventure begins!" Then he stopped, pulled me into his arms for a tight hug. Afterward, gazing deep into my eyes, he asked, "Are you with me, babe?"

"I'm with you. And I'm in love with you, too. I love you from the bottom of my heart."

<<<<<<<<<<>>>>>>>>>

Though we had started early in the morning, it got hot fast. Both of us were sweating and struggling to lift the heavy furniture. Again, Damon told me I should've just donated everything and be done with it. "I mean, you have everything you need already. My condo is fully furnished and fully equipped. Why do you need to keep your spatulas, for instance?"

"Maybe one day we'll need them."

"A dime a dozen. I think you still have some packrat in you."

"Perhaps. But I lost so much 'in the war,' as you call it. What I have left is important to me. And who knows... we may end up in a bigger place and need *all* of this."

"Doubtful."

When the truck was fully loaded, I trudged to the apartment office to return my keys and sign off on the lease. I'd asked Damon if he needed help driving the car onto the tow trailer, but he said no. I walked off, wondering how he could do that alone. *He must know something I don't.*

The apartment manager's rep looked to be about twelve years old. "Sorry to see you go, Ms. Fox. You've been a good tenant. Never a complaint, never a late payment. You're a rare breed."

"I try to be responsible. My Momma taught me well," I said.

"You'll get your deposit back if you've done all these things," and she handed me a yellow sheet of paper. I checked it, knowing I'd cleaned well enough for a full deposit return. I'd painted the walls to remove Stuart's graffiti, of course, and the paint matched perfectly, so they'd never know. "Make sure we have your correct forwarding address." Blah, blah, blah. Done.

I no longer live in Florida. Two years here, and now I'm going home. A chill went down my spine. I was 100 percent ready to attack this second chance with gusto.

The car was on the trailer and Damon was in the truck, checking the switches and adjusting the mirrors, he said. "I'm ready to be a Tennessean again, babe. Let's split this town."

<<<<<<<<<>>>>>>>>

We stopped to spend the night just north of Valdosta and, for the first time, slept together without making love. I considered it a pivotal point in our relationship as I laid awake, listening to his soft snore. I was exhausted but on edge. Couldn't sleep. I suppose it was after three AM before I dozed off, dreaming of a puzzle where none of the pieces fit.

Damon had requested a six AM wake-up call from the front desk, and showered while I pulled myself out of bed. "Coffeeeeee! Coffeeeeee!" I pleaded. It was a cheap hotel with an adjacent Waffle House, and while I wanted to linger over breakfast, Damon demanded we rush.

"We must be at the storage place before five, Lela!" He seemed frantic about this, and said it so accusingly... as if he couldn't understand why I wasn't as freaked out as he was. "We've gotta go! You can sleep in the truck."

We stumbled out of the Waffle House after an argument when I insisted that I pay for the meal. "Damon, it's the least I can do! You've paid for everything!"

"It's all the same money, Lela. Once we get set up, we're opening a joint account, right?"

That hit me like a boulder across the face. "We are? I wasn't... I didn't think... but..."

"What? We're a household now. Double trouble, all for two and two for all."

I laughed. "That is *so* not the quote."

"Whatever." Damon's goofy grin had returned, threatening to sidetrack the topic I considered of utmost importance.

I continued, "But we've never had a talk about finances. If we're..."

"Don't worry, I'll handle it. I have a plan."

I closed my eyes, feeling my stomach take a leap. "No, Damon. It's either *my* plan or *I* handle my own. Nobody in the world will ever manage my money again. Not even you."

He started to answer, then caught himself in mid-breath. "Oh. I get it. Stuart."

"And the other two. *I'm* the money manager. No arguments on that."

He breathed in and out twice, slowly, as if trying to calm himself. "We'll see," he said.

"*You* may 'we'll see,' but *I* know what I'm looking at right now. My money is *my* money. It's non-negotiable." I saw the tightness of his jaw but said no more. This was not the time or place to talk about it, of course, and I knew I could express myself better once I got settled. "We'll talk about it later."

"Yes. We will."

Within twenty miles, I was asleep, my head on Damon's leg. My heart felt free. *This is all going to work. I'm going home. I have Damon, and we love each other. I'll see my parents in just a few days. And my son in a few weeks. I'm happy. I'm going home.*

<<<<<<<>>>>>>

LIFETIME NUMBER 7 BEGINS
THE TRANSITION

Somewhere within the 811 miles between West Palm Beach, Florida and Rockville, Tennessee, my life changed: it took a 180-degree turn. In both circumstances and motivation. Lifetime Number Seven began for Lela Fox.

I felt focused, sober-minded, calm, and firm in my resolve. The insanity of early sobriety had waned.

As this new adventure dawned, I lunged a hundred steps forward in my growth and understanding of true maturity. I aimed for the stars, armed with nothing but pages of inspirational quotes from my sponsor and a strong connection to my Higher Power. That was all I needed, I thought.

Despite the challenges ahead of me, I trudged toward the happy destiny AA promised. I thought my struggles were over... that I'd crossed the bridge, free of pain and chaos.

What's more, I thought Lifetime Number Seven would be my last, and serenity was mine for the taking.

Excitement pulsed through my veins as my eagerness to live and learn shot to the stratosphere. I was ready to feel stability and normalcy 24/7. And most of all, I was eager to grow closer to Dude, and to expand my understanding of the bright light that glowed behind him.

What I didn't know: I was manic as hell.

THERE'S NO PLACE LIKE HOME
CHAPTER 28

Damon started worrying about our arrival time forty miles south of Chattanooga, convinced we'd not make it to the storage place before it closed. I tried to soothe him. Though I was the one nervous and fidgety, I asked, "Would it be the end of the world, babe? Why can't we just park the truck in your condo's lot overnight and go to the storage place in the morning? Why all the drama?"

Damon answered immediately and with a snip in his voice. "First, that's not the plan, and I want it to go as I planned it." I rolled my eyes. *Such a control freak. Harmless, but a control freak.* "Second," he said, "I parked my car next to U-Store-It and got a ride to the airport. That way, we can park at the storage lot and don't have to drive this damn truck at rush hour, see?"

I was squirming, wound tight as a rope, for what I thought was no reason whatsoever. But there was a damn-good reason: A mixture of zero psych meds and a massive dose of frustration.

I held back the sigh to express my frustration to Damon, instead chanting in my head... just to make sure my head was full. I was a zooming whirlwind of Bi-Polar mania.

I halfway knew I was out of control. I feared that the crazy woman in my peripheral vision might be me. As always, I *tried* to control the manic feelings, but couldn't. I felt myself winding tight onto an ultra-springy wire, ready to pounce, then shrink, then pounce, then shrink. Over and over again. I specifically remember wanting to pace, and, instead, "rocked" in my seat while stuck in the cab of the truck. But at some point, I was too manic to know I was manic.

And suddenly, a thought came.

So Damon can take care of it? GREAT! He wants it his way... why not give him his way? I talked to myself about it endlessly for 100 miles, trying to convince myself to let him.

Admittedly, we cut it close on getting there on time. We pulled into the U-Store-It lot at 4:55. I stayed in the truck while Damon checked with the attendant. *Why NOT stay in the damn truck? I'm sure Mr. Fastidious put the unit in his name and has all his ducks in a row.*

Minutes later, Damon burst through the door with a giant smile on his face, folding a sheet of paper in half. As he climbed into the driver's seat, he announced, "Perfect... absolutely perfect. By the way, I only rented it for six months. Who knows if we'll move or not, right?"

"I guess..."

"She said to park on the right, and we'll unload tomorrow, but I have the lock with me and want to recheck the unit."

"That's smart. I'd like to see it, too." Then I laughed. "As if an empty space gives me a clue what would fit inside! I sucked at spatial relations in school. You know, how many triangles fit in this rectangle? It's beyond my understanding."

"I'm a pro, so don't worry your little head about it, sweetie."

That comment ruffled the feathers on my ultra-sensitive anger scale. "Look, buddy: my 'little head' is quite large and self-sufficient, okay? I'm not a dumb princess who needs saving, but a damn queen who has it all handled. Would you please quit treating me like some helpless little girl!"

Damon froze, his mouth open in surprise. "But, Lela-honey, I didn't mean you were dumb or helpless! You're putting words in my mouth! I just thought, well, I thought you like it when I take care of everything."

This is your chance, Lela. Tell him exactly how you feel. Calm and cool, like a real couple communicating in an adult way. "No, Damon. I don't like it. Not at all. I'm a capable woman. And, for that matter, able to jump a building in a single bound. It's not that I don't appreciate your help, I just don't need 100 percent of it. Please don't micro-manage me, Damon. It's demeaning."

"Demeaning?!" His eyes were wide, his face showing incredulous surprise.

I tried to make him understand. "Maybe you don't get it. In fact, maybe it's a woman thing to begin with, but in all my previous relationships, *I've* been the one in charge. Well, except Stuart, but that doesn't count. See, otherwise, I was the one in charge of the money, the planning, the meals, the schedule, the everything! I'm perfectly capable and don't like being controlled by you or anybody else. Surely you can understand that! Put the shoe on the other foot. I don't need a full-time caretaker."

Apparently still confused, Damon's eyebrows were squenched together, and he still stared at his hands on the steering wheel. "I... I thought I was doing the right thing."

"I know you thought so, babe. And I know you mean no harm. But it *is* a bit harmful. Because, well, I'd like to be treated as an *equal.* Surely you can understand that!"

"Of *course* you're my equal! I *never* meant it that way!"

"It's what it feels like."

"Okay, 100 percent turn-around, then. I don't want you to feel, uh, 'less than.' I've heard you use that phrase before."

"Yeah, it's an alcoholic thing. But it applies here, too. Because I'm *not* 'less than.' I'm *more than enough.* The problem, Damon... what if I'm more than you can handle?"

Damon didn't reply as my words evaporated into the stale air of the truck. After a ten-second pause, he pushed the key into the ignition. "More about that later. Thank you for telling me how you feel."

"Thank you for listening. No, thank you for *hearing.* That's much more important."

"Still processing it, but for now, I've got to get this truck parked."

"Aye, aye, Captain."

<<<<<<<<<>>>>>>>>>

We stopped to get a burger on the way back to Damon's condo. Manic, I tingled with excitement in knowing I was back home in Rockville, and though I should have been tired, I wanted to go dancing, go out, go somewhere... anywhere. But Damon said, "Absolutely not" with his foot firmly down.

A flash of Dude traveled across in the inside of the windshield, and I flashed back full of gratitude... so grateful that Damon was my savior, my guardian angel, chosen by Dude as the one to bring me home again.

Thank you, Dude. Thank you for Damon. Help me make him feel happy and free – as happy and free as he makes ME feel.

When I grabbed his hands and thanked him, his face fell. "Thanks for what?" he asked.

"For everything, Damon. Everything."

"Uh, you're welcome?"

"Yep, that'll do."

<<<<<<<>>>>>>

A COLD HOUSEWARMING

CHAPTER 29

I grabbed Damon's arm and tried to drag him up the pathway to his condo. I'd slowed my pace after he pitched a fit about being dragged – twice – but I was frantic to get inside and get my new life started.

I knew I was out of control, though I'd been calmed a bit by Damon's speech of "concern for Lela" on the way home. But he talked to me as if trying to convince a child to behave; I didn't have time for that shit and ignored the warnings. I put on a happy face, planning to keep the mania in control... just my little secret.

I pulled him into the alcove and squealed, "A new paint job on your front door!"

"I painted everything. Wait 'til you see the place. You'll freak."

I freaked, alright. The walls were screaming, glossy white, not easy on the eyes. But Damon seemed incredibly proud. "Nice and bright! And look! All my guitars are in the living room now. I'm going to hang them on the wall over the sofa."

"That'd be nice. You sure need *something* on the walls. Maybe I should pull out some of my framed things that were supposed to go in storage."

"Nah. I hate cluttered walls." *Bullshit. It looks as bare as an igloo.*

"And look at all the clutter everywhere else, Damon! That bookshelf is supposed to be for *display,* not a catch-all for your crap."

"It's all what I call décor, dear, not crap. I like to be surrounded by my stuff."

"Stuff or junk?"

"It's not junk! My guitar picks, extra strings... my nail clippers, these are things I want to be in easy reach."

I thought twice before replying. Maybe Damon kept his entire house like I kept my desk area – full of weird shit and everything in easy reach. I said, "And speaking of my desk, I was thinking–"

He cut me off. "First, we weren't speaking of your desk. And second, I have the perfect spot for it. I scooted stuff around in the spare room. You'll have a nice setup there. Tight quarters, maybe, but it will do."

"No, baby. We've talked about this, haven't we?"

"About where to put your desk? No, we haven't."

My eyebrows twisted, feeling sure we would've talked about something so important. "I guess I've thought about it so much myself that I thought we'd agreed." Then I turned in a swirl, laughing. "I need to be in the middle of things, right here in the living room. We can move the sofa here..." I walked to the opposite wall, pointing along the baseboard. "And I'll put my L-shaped desk here, to here." I walked the placement heel-to-toe.

"No."

"No? Just... a flat no? Why not?"

"I want the sofa where it is." Closing my eyes, I swayed on woozy legs. Never did I imagine he'd argue about where to put my desk!

Undaunted, I rattled on. "Well, I can also clean up the place a bit. Get some of the junk organized. I know a few tricks, see? Ways to keep things straight... ducks in a row, a place for everything, get this place in tip-top order!"

"No."

There was no need to answer. Damon was going to fight me at every turn. "Jeez, Damon! My opinion doesn't count here?"

"Of course it counts!"

"Well good, because–"

"Just not about the arrangement of the furniture. And the things you call junk."

I sighed, trying to control my temper. Finally, I stepped forward. "I'm going to check out the spare room and see if my desk will fit." The room was to the left of the powder room, which I noticed was bare of rugs or any type of décor. *That won't do, either.*

I opened the spare-room door to nothing but a pile of random shit on the floor. No furniture, nothing on the wall. It was a damn storage room!

The louvers on the heat-and-air vent were closed; the air was stale and heavy. Horrible! The 10x10 square would be the worst-possible office room. *This sucks! I can't work in here! I need light! I need air! And more, more happiness! Joy! This will never be right!*

Like a flash from above, I got zapped into a different way of thinking. *Accept it, Lela. You may actually get a real job soon and won't work at home, so drop the insistence. Deep breaths.* I leaned against the wall and followed my advice, breathing until my heart rate had returned to normal and the buzz in my head had quietened.

Back in the living room, I asked Damon where we could store all the stuff that was now on the floor of the spare room. He answered, "What's wrong with leaving it where it is? It's out of your way."

Okay, Lela. NOW you can put your foot down. "My office will *not* be a storage room! I need a *real* office, not a random corner surrounded by ski poles and generators and stacks of magazines. Surely some of that can go, or at least go into the garage!"

"The garage is full."

"How?! It's a crazy-big garage!"

"Come see," he said with a broad and proud grin, taking me by the hand. "Careful on the steps."

Entering the cinder-block-walled square garage, my jaw hit the floor. "Oh. My. God. What *is* all this?"

"All my bank statements, bills, miscellaneous paperwork... organized by date and color-coded by the payee."

"Damon! How many years does this go back?" I was incredulous; the entire wall was full of matching boxes, three shelves high."

"Fifteen years. Plus part of this year's stuff."

Blown away, I snapped my head toward Damon and squealed, "You don't need to keep all that shit! Why would you need a decades-old water bill?"

He kept his mouth in a pout, moving his eyebrows independently. "Well, one never knows."

"Yes, one *does* know. You *won't* need it! This is ridiculous!"

"Damn, Lela! I thought you'd be proud of me! This was *hard work*."

I let my heart rate slow before I answered. "I don't mean to be unkind, babe. I'm sure you worked hard, but it's *unnecessary* work. And now it's blocking space that could be used for more practical things."

He didn't answer, keeping the pout and avoiding eye contact. After a pause, I walked back up the steps and closed the door behind me.

Let him stew down there. What a screwed-up thing THIS is going to be. I plopped on the sofa and grabbed the remote, but couldn't get the TV to power up.

Must somehow need the two other remotes laid out here. What the hell? How can I live in a place where I can't even turn on the TV?!

<<<<<<<<<<>>>>>>>>>

"Goodnight," I said. He replied with the same. I laid there a few minutes in the silence, then turned to cuddle up in a nice spoon. Surprisingly, Damon shrugged me off, citing, "It's too hot."

I rolled back over onto my back, thinking. *This will be the second night in a row without sex. Is he really that tired? Too tired for a quickie? Should I worry? Does he already know it won't work, too?*

The words "Does he already know?" ran through my mind compulsively. I freaked out.

But how can I talk to him about it? He's clueless and stubborn and determined.

I raised on one elbow and lit a cigarette, its ember glow mesmerizing. *Problems... maybe BIG problems to come. In fact, already here. Can I live in this place with him? SHOULD I?*

Halfway through the cigarette, I wondered what I would do otherwise. *Easy answer, you crazy bitch: get your own apartment, and the two of you could just date like ordinary people.*

But he says he has a plan all worked out! Mentioned marriage, even! But in the last two days, you've seen a whole new side of him. The anal side. The persnickety side. But do you love him, Lela? Do you? Are you 100 percent committed here?

The other side of my brain argued, citing that Damon was, for sure, a *nice guy*... no stains on his record of being my Rock of Gibraltar, and I was sure he loved me.

But what about that snarky comment about me not taking my meds? Was he putting me down on purpose, trying to shame me? Yes, I think he was.

I'd told him along the way, somewhere in North Florida, that I wanted to be med-free for a while. His jaw had clenched and he turned away, staying eerily quiet for thirty miles or more.

So he's THAT against it? Why wouldn't he respect my own decision about my own health? I've been stable without my medicine! I know what I'm doing!

Putting the cigarette out, I thought about the possibility of my stability being true to others vs. being true to only me. Did I have symptoms? Anger? It was true that I'd been mad as hell at Damon during the packing and move. *But it's his fault! He's an OCD maniac! Trying to manage me like I'm incapable! It's HIS FAULT!*

I got out of bed, mad as hell, and stomped downstairs. Damon's laptop was set up on the dining room table, and I logged in. *See, he trusts me enough to give me his damn password, but not enough to make a damn U-Haul reservation!*

Two hours into Googling all sorts of random things, my anger was gone, but I looked like a cartoon – a saucer-eyed woman in front of a spinning slot machine. A manic Googler.

The result, among other things: scribbles on a notepad with full info about apartments in the area – phone numbers and prices. Moving out seemed to be the best choice, the safest choice. And maybe the only way to save my relationship with Damon.

Unless, of course, the relationship should have been left as a friendship in the first place. I love him, no doubt, but... being his wife? Living with this anal mess?

As if trying to talk myself into staying, I checked out the hall closet that Damon had deemed to be my clothes closet. He'd made it clear that the Master closet would remain his. I could start from scratch downstairs, he said, and he'd buy the needed organizers.

But when I opened the accordion doors, I gasped from deep in my lungs – it was trashed! The most disorganized mess in the whole place! Papers everywhere, broken hangers tangled in clots along the pole, Junk on top of junk. *What happened to Damon's demand for order behind THESE doors?!*

I looked back into the kitchen for comparison. *Yep, there's his blackboard weekly menu plan, his oversized white-board for a detailed grocery list (written in order of the store's layout, he'd bragged to me once), and a keeper-thing for his keys and pocket change.*

I checked the fridge for more evidence of his organization, and there it was – color-coordinated. The cabinets; as neat as a pin. I half respected his OCD approach to putting things in order, but I wondered if he went too far. *But then, there's the opposite. This closet. What man goes to such extremes in both directions?*

Not a bit sleepy, I sat on the floor and began to organize the mess in the closet jungle. I dared not throw anything away but made neat piles so Damon could decide where to store the things outside of this precious 4 x 8-foot space.

What struck me most was the pile of papers, the majority of them random notes of no value whatsoever – a Post-It-Note that said "Practice, Thurs. 6:00." No reference to date. So that was a throw-away, for sure, but I didn't use a trash bag. Instead, I put these pieces of paper in a separate pile. When he saw the pile, I decided, it would teach him the error of his ridiculous ways.

More paper: "Jesse and Lola Friday. Dinner somewhere. Take can of oil." I laughed. Next was a to-do list that included "Call Mom – don't tell her about motorcycle," and "Make up excuse for Saturday." It was his life, without reference, without context, but endearing. And infuriating.

Two hours later, when I'd finished sorting, I vacuumed the carpet and carefully placed the stacks back inside the closet, prepared to talk about it early in the morning.

"Hell, it *is* morning! I crashed on the sofa and fell asleep around five AM.

I jerked awake at seven, when Damon sat beside me, pushing a warm cup of coffee toward my hand. "Good morning, princess!" he chirped.

I closed my eyes against the sun and covered them with my forearm. I slurred, "I told you I'm not a princess, I'm the queen." Damon laughed.

"Okay... good morning, dear queen. Your king is awake and requesting the honor of your presence." I opened one eye to see his goofy grin. And my heart melted. *What a sweet man... misguided, crazy as hell, but sweet.*

Damon rubbed my back. "Why did you get up last night? I woke to an empty bed and it scared me."

"I couldn't sleep. Too much to think about." I sipped at the steamy cup. "Wow! You make good coffee! I've forgotten your custom mix. How many different types? Three?"

"Perfected now with a blend of *four*. I added a scoop of Café Bustello for more body."

"It seems like a real pain in the ass, the lengths you go to, but it's a damn-good cup of coffee."

"Thank you, dear." His goofy grin exuded charm, and I fell for him a thousand times more.

I'd almost forgotten my overnight task and jumped up to show him my handiwork in the closet. We stood together with the closet doors open. I pointed. "That pile is definitely trash. Random old papers and notes, old magazines, shit like that. But, I'll have you know, I didn't throw one single thing away. I wanted you to see how ridiculous it is to–"

"Hey! That's *my shit!* Not ridiculous shit, but *good shit!*"

"But I need that *closet*, Damon! Your – quote, 'good shit' – has to go!"

Ten beats of silence ticked as Damon stared at the pile of papers. Then he took a deep breath and turned away. "You want eggs?" *What the hell? Now he won't even talk about it?!*

He looked at me in my pause of exasperation, tapping his foot. "So, do you want eggs or not?"

I shrugged, giving up on the discussion about the closet. Within my sigh, I said, "I thought Lola was bringing Egg McMuffins."

"But she's not here, and I'm hungry." There was no apology in his expression.

"I'll wait for Lola. You go ahead. But while you're cooking, go through that closet!"

With his back to me on the way to the kitchen, he murmured, "Yeah, yeah, yeah."

"I mean it, Damon! That closet is for my clothes! And the clothes are coming today!"

Another murmur, softer this time: "Maybe and maybe not."

<<<<<<<<<>>>>>>>>

Lola was beside herself with joy when she saw me, repeating, "Lela's back! Lela's back! Lela's back!" The three of us sat together in the living room as Damon and Lola talked non-stop about the news in town, who was doing who, the new venues and restaurants, new friends in the group, new opportunities.

Lola had *finally* dumped her cowboy asshole boyfriend Mel and had halfway moved in with Damon's BFF Jesse. I assumed the four of us would hang out together a lot, with me as the new fourth in the crowd. Damon was aglow with a list of things we could do on "double dates," but his heart seemed on the opposite side of his excitement. It seemed he dreaded to say every sentence that left his mouth. Curious.

"You okay, babe?" I asked Damon.

"Uhhhh. Last I checked, I was."

"You seem distracted, unhappy."

"Just trying to relax," he said.

The silence that followed was deafening. I saw Lola and Damon pass a look between them, both with a grimace. "What the hell's going on, y'all?"

They both answered with silence. Confused, I thought it best to remove myself from a conversation I didn't understand. I got up to get coffee.

The air in the room had changed when I returned, but I refused to be daunted by their weirdness. Unfettered, I asked about our friend Kay-Kay, who'd been stuck in a bad divorce with custody of her ex's troubled children. Lola assured me things were better with Kay-Kay and invited me to hang out on her deck later that afternoon.

"Sorry, but Damon and I will be unpacking the truck and–"

Damon interrupted. "We can empty the truck *any* day, Lela. The extra rental is only $20 a day. So go on – have fun with your girlfriends! It'll be good for you, and maybe I'll see you there later."

"What? And 'maybe?'"

"I'm riding motorcycles with Jesse today. Our return to town depends on how far we ride. There's no plan really, we're going to ride The Dragon." The Dragon was a road just outside of the national park, with twenty hairpin curves in a row. Motorcycle riders loved it; they loved the danger.

Confused, I wondered why and how Damon had planned a ride with Jesse when, until last night, his plan for us was to unload and return the U-Haul. *What's going on? Has he changed his mind about the whole thing? Does he know that I feel the same sense of doubt?*

I pretended to be undaunted and told Lola, "I do happen to have my swimsuit unpacked and here, so we can get some sun lounging on Kay-

Kay's jungle of a porch. I love it there, always have. Has her green thumb turned greener?"

"Practically neon by now. You have to see her garden plot... and the herbs! Oh, my God! It smells like heaven!" Lola had made me an offer I couldn't refuse.

<<<<<<<<<<>>>>>>>>>

Feeling much less manic without Damon around, I settled on a comfy patio lounge on Kay-Kay's plant-laden patio. "This is the perfect time and place for a little girl talk, y'all. I'm struggling with a decision and need your opinions."

Kay-Kay rubbed her hands together excitedly. "Oh, yeah! Girl talk! Bring it on!"

"I'm not so sure it's a good idea to move straight into Damon's place. There are, uh... issues. And not just practical ones."

Lola sighed. "I wondered what would come down with him. The last time we talked, he said he didn't want – quote, 'your junk' – spread around the house. And he thinks you may be manic–"

I cut her off. "MY junk?" I laughed long and hard. "Oh, I think it goes deeper than that. It seems he doesn't want anything about me there, including the 'me' of me. It's not been discussed, but his behavior has changed over the past few days, since he came to West Palm to get me. And last night – whoa! I'll just use the term 'eye-opening.'"

My friends sat in rapt attention, urging me on. "Like today... according to his meticulous plan, we should be unloading the truck, stacking stuff in the storage room, and taking the rest to his place. But suddenly he tells me to come here because he's riding The Dragon with Jesse. What's *up* with that? I'm not sure what he's trying to tell me."

Silence. Way too much quiet, so I kept talking... rattling on about feeling both rejected and relieved, and details about what I'd found while searching for an apartment of my own. And, again, about Damon and the question of whether or not I loved him enough.

Finally, Lola interrupted me. "Do you want me to talk to him?"

"No! Surely the two of us can get this straight with a normal, calm, adult conversation! I'm just kinda scared. I thought I had it all figured out, ya know? But now, everything is up in the air again. I'm home, but I'm homeless."

"You can move in here!" offered Kay-Kay, her golden-tan face beaming in the sun.

Lola added another option. "Or into my place, 'cause I stay with Jesse most of the time, anyway."

"So you two think I should go elsewhere and not, uh, force my way into Damon's very odd household?"

Kay-Kay lit a cigarette and exhaled sharply. "You two could still date, even seriously. But maybe it *is* too soon to move in together. I wouldn't do it."

Lola agreed. "I'll help you find a place, Miss Lela. And help you move. Whatever you need."

"No! *Damon* will help me move! This is not the end of the road, y'all! I refuse to break up with him just because I'm not immediately moving in. We just didn't talk about things enough beforehand. I didn't know how he felt and didn't tell him what I had planned, either. But I don't want to break up with him! I've hung my hat on this relationship."

My words had been frantic, loud. A tear dripped from my jaw onto my bare belly, on its way to the spot where the elastic on my bikini bottom didn't touch my skin. It was the "sweet spot" Damon liked, just in front of my hip bone.

I watched the teardrop disappear inside that never-never land and knew something else had disappeared, too.

<<<<<<<<>>>>>>>

PARTY POOPER
CHAPTER 30

"Looks like it will fit through the door if you take off the legs," I said, guiding Damon and Jesse as they moved the sofa into my new apartment, Number 111-G at Copper Pointe.

"Why do you have such a huge sofa, anyway?" Damon complained.

"Planning on having a million guests, like us?" It was Jesse, the one bearing the majority of weight.

"I bought it second-hand, Jesse. It is what it is," adding a tease for the new friend/strong man who made this move possible, "And it's a nice sofa, so quit your bitching!" The two men lowered the sofa onto the concrete and reached for the screwdriver I held for them, mumbling under their breaths as they worked to release the legs.

Jesse, Lola's boyfriend and Damon's best friend, had sprinkled his sarcastic sense of humor throughout the move that day. He was smart, quick with a funny comeback, and I'd liked him immediately. As I'd told Lola, we'd be a fearless foursome.

I looked at Damon's face as he focused on his task. The sight of him still filled me with exhilaration. I knew I loved him; the butterflies still flew in my tummy, and our conversation about delaying my move to his condo had gone well. No cross words, no tears. Just facts and laughing about the reality of each of us being set in our ways.

He'd tried to tell me I was too manic for him, but I giggled through that ridiculousness.

We'd ended the talk with "we're just old and stodgy and set in our ways." I didn't feel old or stodgy, but "set in my ways" had an element of truth. "My ways" had become the new phrasing that set my boundaries, and I refused to apologize for setting them. *They're healthy boundaries, and it's about time you stood up for yourself, Lela.*

Lola and I carried the smaller stuff, placing it in the appropriate room as instructed *twice* on the box. She ogled at the organization of it all, asking if Damon had done the job. I doubled over laughing about that; Lola knew what I was up against when it came to Damon's OCD. But in truth, she didn't know the half of it.

"I love the layout of this place, Lela! And right here beside the playground!"

"I chose this particular unit – well, first because it was number 111, but mostly because of the playground. To me, there's no better sound than the tinkle of a child's laughter."

"Awww. See? That just sums up your kindness, my friend. I love you so much! And I'm so glad you're back home where you belong!" We hugged for a long time... until Damon's shouts made us move from the sofa's new home in the living room.

But our arms stayed wrapped together. Lola was such a good friend, my best ever, and she had amazing talents; there was plenty to admire about this mysterious Cherokee Indian woman. She could do almost anything. To my delight, she'd offered to help me decorate. I did pretty well on my own, but Lola had a keen eye.

"Oh, yes! They'd be perfect!" She spoke to me as if I knew what she meant. I didn't answer, just paused for her to explain. "Do you still have those batik sarongs you bought in Cancun?"

"Yes, I do. I couldn't stand to throw them away, but I've never known what to do–"

"They will be your curtains in this place."

I froze, thinking. "Damn, Lola! That's a great idea!"

"That's one of many things I'm going to do for you, dear!"

"Don't you want to do the Fiesta Ware first? You won't believe how much I have now. So many colors!" We chatted about how it would fit on the antique cabinet that faced the foyer.

Soon, the truck was empty, and we all collapsed in the living room to relax. "I'm exhausted," Jesse said. But I doubted it; he had the energy of a Jack Russell Terrier, and never stopped. Then he stood and pulled a bag of weed from his pocket, together with a pack of rolling papers. I watched in amazement as Jesse proceeded to roll a joint on my coffee table.

I could smell the pungent odor of the pot just from opening the bag and, in my mind, taste the hit of the joint I was so tempted to inhale. Mania returned in a heartbeat, it seemed. I blurted, "Jesse! You can't smoke that in my house!"

He looked up, his face relaxed and typically goofy. Then he shrugged. "Okay, I'll smoke outside." That was it. A simple statement.

I can and should stop this. I must put my foot down. I didn't even know he smoked weed! What do I do? The book says no mood or mind-altering drugs, Lela, and that definitely includes weed. Don't smoke, and even don't let him smoke outside! Your patio is within the kid's playground!

With my heart pounding, dreading the consequences of being the bad guy, I said, "No, Jesse. No smoking outside either. You're on the ground floor with no privacy. And... it's not, uh, in my program. I don't smoke anymore, either."

Yep, Lela is now a party pooper. My greatest fear. I'm a dull, boring stick in the mud, destined to put a plug in everyone's fun. What a drag I am.

"But it's not alcohol, Lela! I wouldn't drink in front of you!" he said, licking the paper to seal the joint.

It would be the first time for me to say no to a friend's simple act of smoking a joint, but I knew I had to. And I had to do it fast... my mind was running at jet-speed "No pot, Jesse. Not here. I didn't even know you smoked." I looked at Damon, hoping he'd back me on this. But he simply sat there, watching Jesse reach for his lighter. So I pleaded, "Damon! Tell him no! Tell him he can't smoke that here!"

There was a pause; too long of a pause. I stood, ready to puff out my chest and be a badass. But I guess Jesse saw the look on my face and froze. He slowly took the joint from his mouth, put his palms toward me as if pushing me away. He said, "It looks like *you're* the one who needs a toke or two. It might take the edge off your attitude."

"My attitude is for my own self-preservation, Jesse." Ping-pong balls spun my brain as my built-in anxiety meter hit the red zone.

I looked again at Damon. He smiled at me, at least, but I was pissed at him for staying silent during what I considered a major turning point in my sobriety. I'd been insulated from "normal people" for so long in Florida, where I hung out with AA people almost exclusively.

"Jesse, you'll find that sober people have a different outlook on things. Not just about drinking and weed and coke or whatever, but everything. My books say 'no mood or mind-altering drugs,' and for me, that includes even *thoughts* of them. Or thoughts of cheating and lying, for that matter." I stopped, seeing my three friends' faces of horror. I guess they thought it was the beginning of a sermon, and I didn't want to come across that way.

Backing down, I rambled, hoping to change those looks of horror and confusion, but it didn't work. So I smiled, gathered my thoughts and my craziness, and shut the hell up.

For a minute.

To fill the pit of unknown feelings, I threw out a comment my dad used to say. Through a laugh, I said, "No lying, no cheating, no dancing in the living room, no happiness *anywhere* in this house!" I threw my head back to howl with laughter. Daddy's joke, always said when we were too loud during the news, was a piece of family tradition, and my funny voice while saying it was on-target, I thought.

I stopped laughing, only to see three unamused faces staring back at me. Even Lola's smile was absent. No doubt: there'd been a significant change in the "fearless foursome" we'd only just begun. I could taste the tension.

Why isn't Damon saying something? Why is he letting me play the bad guy all alone? I thought he was 100 percent supportive of my sobriety! This is a critical turn of events!

Silence loomed. Jesse looked at Lola, who shrugged. Damon continued to stare at nothing. I realized I'd been holding my breath and exhaled loudly.

Then Jesse put his hands on his knees and rose; all six feet of him rolled toward the ceiling. "Well, are y'all ready? Let's go smoke this thing and get some dinner."

There it is. I'm excluded. Because I don't smoke pot. And Damon is just letting this happen. Speak up, serious boyfriend! Let me and my sobriety be a part of your social group!

But he said nothing. In fact, he followed Jesse in standing, and stretched his arms high, groaning as one does with a good stretch. "Damn,

I'm beat! But I'm ready to split." He put his arms down and flashed me a way-too-casual look. Lela? You're all settled? You need more help?"

Surprised and hurt, I mumbled that I'd be fine. I shot a look at Lola, her face full of pity for me. *Don't pity me, Lola! Stand up for me, my friend! Get these guys to sit back down! Let's talk – about anything! About the weather, about the price of eggs in China! And why can't I go to dinner with you guys? Huh? Suddenly I'm chopped liver?*

At least Lola never took her eyes off me, coming forward to hug me goodbye. "See you tomorrow, Miss Lela! We'll fix this place up nice and cozy. Be ready, 'cause I'll call you in the morning." Her words were sincere, but there was an edge... as if she was speaking to placate a child.

I rather doubted she'd call, but answered with a thank you. The truth was... I was in a fog, wondering what the hell had just happened.

You know what happened, Lela. You're now an outcast, a weirdo, a stick in the mud. And crazy as hell. Your AA program has caused you to lose friends with normal people, not just party animals. It's not like Jesse is a good-for-nothing, but you couldn't let it slide... you couldn't give him an inch, could you? You Goody-Two-Shoes. Your mom would be proud.

They left without fanfare. I'd never felt so alone, suddenly plopped into an apartment bare of my personality and love of any sort. I cried for a while, talking aloud to myself while trying to move forward from the yucky frame of mind.

"I think I'll go to a meeting, dammit!" A sudden decision, but exactly what I needed. Checking the time – yep, perfect for a rushed trip to the West 40 club for the 5:30. I dashed to the bathroom to splash water on my face, found a clean shirt, and hopped in the Jetta.

Rockville recovery, here I come.

<<<<<<<>>>>>>

On the way, I remembered my first meeting at the West 40 club years ago, when I still lived in the G-R-E-E-N house and before I met Stuart.

Way back then, I knew I was an alcoholic in desperate need of help but hadn't admitted it to anyone, and definitely not myself. And how quickly I dismissed the "teachings" of the people in that room! I thought they were liars, purporting "Life is grand" bullshit from their thrones of an impossible sobriety.

I laughed about it on the way, speaking to the rattles in the car. "You believe them now, Lela? Hell-yeah, you do! And here in Rockville, they'll think you're a newcomer, so you have a lot to prove. Start it right. Put on your best sober face right now, and speak the wisdom you have. It may not be experience, but there's definitely strength and hope. Share what you know."

THE WEST 40 CLUB
CHAPTER 31

The room was smoky, full of fresh-looking faces, about fifty of them. I took a seat, arriving just as the chairman said, "Let's have a meeting."

I smiled at the girl beside me, realizing with a start that it was Barb, an old drinking buddy. Silently, we reacted with laughter and surprise. Then I whispered, "You too, huh?" and she shook her head with enthusiasm. Another whisper from me: "Fourteen months. How 'bout you?"

Barb counted on her fingers, which cracked me up. "Two years, four months."

"Good for you! I got sober in Florida. Just moved back two days ago."

"Welcome home. You'll love this club. Lots of good sobriety here."

I scanned the room but saw no other people from my former life. *I wonder what happened to them, anyway... are they still drinking or already dead? What the hell, they may be normal people and happy grandparents for all I know. Your life has taken three U-turns since you've seen those folks, but aren't you glad you ended up HERE instead of "out there?"*

Hell-yes, I was glad.

I listened carefully to the first half-dozen who shared in the meeting: first, a gray-faced old-timer, and a little too gruff for me. His serenity was not my brand, that's for sure. Then a few shared who said a word or two that proved smart, sober thinking.

Then, a guy about my age, broad-shouldered and incredibly nice-looking, claimed the floor. His face was scarred from childhood acne; I'd seen people like that before, but his confidence shined along with bright blue eyes. After sharing his name (Gil; a Fox family name, so I noticed), he talked eloquently on the topic of honesty, weaving what Oakley called "a

239

verbal tapestry." He made sense and eased my worry about the quality of the meetings at the West 40 club.

A few women shared, summing their experience with honesty as it compared to their drinking days. I could totally identify. Again, I listened carefully, keeping my eye out for a sponsor. I didn't plan to wing it in Rockville – it would be too risky. I needed guidance and somebody to keep me moving forward in the program.

I made a mental note to also call my old therapist, Kate, so she could see the "new me." Ta-da! I hadn't seen a therapist since rehab and felt in need of a major checkup from the neck-up. Mostly, though, I was curious to hear what Kate would say about how much I'd changed.

About halfway through the meeting, I shared, weaving in that I was new to town, back among those who suddenly knew nothing about me and my new life. It was a half-hidden plea for friendship in the program and within the West 40 club. To compare my drinking life to my sober life was "like a movie," I said, a movie of total transformation with a guaranteed happy ending.

At the after-meeting in the parking lot, I chatted with my old friend Barb. When I let her get a word in, she corrected me on her name. "They call me 'Butterfly Barb' now."

"Why? Because you're nervous? Butterflies in your stomach?"

"No, butterflies fly *out my ass*. I'm too damn happy, they say. Life's too good, and they bitch about it... say it scares the newcomers."

I laughed with my head thrown back. "That's hilarious! But I remember my first meeting, which was *here*, by the way, and I thought everybody was lying. I never thought *anybody* could be that happy without drinking. I ran away, literally, and it took another two-years-plus before I met my bottom."

Barb said, "We ought to hang out. In fact... hey! Thursday!"

"Thursday?"

"A whole bunch of us go up to Cades Cove in the Smokies for a Full Moon meeting every month – you know, at that first cabin in the loop?"

"I know the place."

"Outdoor meeting, of course, and this month, the weather will be perfect for it."

"I'd *love* that."

"Cool. You can ride with me."

"Meet you here?" She nodded. "What time?"

"Around 6:30 unless we go to eat first. I guess you noticed the 'Crack House' across the street. That's where we go."

"I love Cracker Barrell, especially after being away from southern cooking for so long. But I get to see my parents this weekend, and I've requested chicken and dumplings. My mom's is yum-yum-yummy!"

We talked about food for a while, just chatting, then the big guy with acne scars interrupted. "Hey, Butterfly Barb! How's it going?" He was speaking to Barb, but looking at me.

Barb said, "Hey Gil, meet my old friend Lela. We used to drink together. She was a wild one, for sure!" she laughed, "And something tells me she's *still* a hoot. I can't wait for us to start hanging out. She'll love all the gals here, don't you think?"

Gil's eyes drilled into mine; after a few seconds, I had to look away. *Jeez, back down, you sonofabitch.* Yet something about him stopped me from correcting his gaze.

Gil beamed a broad and genuine smile, and asked, "Are you going to the Full Moon meeting? It's going to be a big crowd this month."

I answered with a sultry tone, an accidental accent... I guess because I was nervous. "Yes, I'm riding with Barb, as a matter of fact."

Barb interjected, "And about four others. It'll be a tight fit, but there's no sense in traveling that far without a full load."

"Yeah, I'm riding with Corncob... maybe Pharmacist Mark and TVA Bob."

I laughed. "Don't you love the stupid names we give each other? Like 'anonymous' taken to the extreme!"

Gil chuckled. "They call me Railroad Gil, by the way... or sometimes just Railroad. I work at CSX as a train conductor."

"Wow! My brother-in-law works for CSX, too. Out of Deerfield."

"The Deerfield terminal? Well, hell! I'd know him. I was in Deerfield for years. What's his name?"

"John Swag."

"Oh, hell-yeah! I know John! They call him Little General."

"That's hilarious! And I bet I know why... short little guy, in charge of everything? OCD with a too-ethical work ethic?"

"Exactly!"

The good-looking railroad man was glowing with excitement, brimming with it. *Either he really likes John, or he's trying to impress ME. The new girl, fresh meat for single AA guys.* I caught a glimpse at his left ring finger. Yep, single.

I don't know if Barb caught a whiff of "wow" between Gil and I but she quickly said, "I gotta go, Lela. Tomorrow at the 5:30?"

"Uh, sure. Good to see you!" Barb dashed to her car, leaving Railroad Gil and me standing alone. I didn't want to start the gossip sure to come in a new club, so I left, too. "Nice to meet you, Gil. See you around, I guess. Do you always come to the 5:30?"

"Mostly. So I hope to see you tomorrow, okay?" He waved goodbye like a homecoming queen in a parade as I disappeared into the depths of the parking lot.

What a wimpy wave for such a big guy! But he's nice. Interesting. And such eyes! Oh, my God! But you're taken, remember? You'll have to learn a way to make that known. Damon is still the man, unless today's scene killed that, too.

Still, I hate being the new meat and being hit on. Gil was the only one who came to talk to me, but how many geezers eyed me up and down? Practically ALL of them.

Oakley and I had talked about how to stay a single woman in a crowd of AA predators, but it was a short-term lesson. Damon came pretty soon after the breakup with Bear.

I left West 40 with a new perspective, new confidence in myself and my sobriety. My mind had slowed down. *That's always what happens, Lela. Stay close to that club, close to Rockville's recovery community. Sobriety also helps your moods be stable.*

The drive home took longer because of a crash on Valley Pike, and my mind wandered. I hated that things were up in the air again, just after feeling like I'd landed on solid ground. *You've got to face facts: not just maybe... PROBABLY it's not going to work out with you and Damon.*

I shivered with the thought.

No! Please, Dude... let this one last. Just like everybody over forty, I want a long-term relationship! Finally! Don't I deserve it?! Surely, after all the shit I've been through? And I'm ready to settle down! Please let this one last!

<<<<<<<>>>>>>

LOLA'S MAGIC ACT
CHAPTER 32

The rest of the week, I worked to get settled in my new place. My office was the first task; I had work to do and a deadline that wouldn't change. The DSL internet connection was set, so, I set up the computer, organized my desk meticulously, and capped the room by hanging my red, 3D vowels on the feature-wall.

I stepped back to admire my work and spoke to the room: "This will work beautifully, and still earning sixty bucks an hour! How lucky you are, Lela Fox!" I performed a silent hats-off to Dude.

Next on the list was to unwrap the Fiesta Ware. Lola was coming later to help me arrange it on the antique cabinet and two new wall shelves that matched beautifully. As I unpacked each of the 100+ pieces, I checked it off on my inventory sheet. Later, I planned to recheck the values to see if the prices had increased in the short time I'd owned the pieces.

Correction: the investments. You didn't waste that money, right? It wasn't a thrill-buy or online shopping addiction, right?

I hung a few pictures, having to toss a few that'd been damaged in my Florida storage unit. It pained me to throw things away; it was like giving Stuart Weinstein a point on my demise scorecard. I wondered if he knew I'd moved away, be it back home or another apartment down the street.

Thankfully, I'd learned to not let the possibility of him spying on me dictate my behavior, but since he'd called from the sober house in Texas, there hadn't been any in-my-face suspicious stuff. Still, I'd set up a private, unlisted, and restricted home phone number and changed my cell number to have a Rockville area code.

Surely you've slipped it all by him... or maybe he's finally given up. Or maybe he found serenity, hooked up with a good woman, easily re-gained custody of his son, and his life has turned out peachy.

Still, thinking about Stuart still gave me the heebie-jeebies when my mind was at full-speed. *Whatever happened to you, Stuart Weinstein, just leave me out of it! Don't follow me to Tennessee! Please!*

Lola arrived around three PM and spun around the apartment, rushing from room to room. "It looks fantastic!" She eyed me sideways and reached for a high-five.

"And now – drum roll, please – Lola steps in for the finishing touches! You, my friend, are the one that makes a place look charming. In doing your magic, move anything anywhere. The décor pieces are already unpacked and stacked on the floor, waiting for your mystic touch."

I caught a look on Lola's face... something sad was on her mind. "Lola, babe, what's going on? You need to talk?"

She snapped her head toward me sharply. "No."

"That's it? Just 'no' and no explanation? *Some*thing's on your mind, come on!"

"There is, but I don't need to talk about it!" Again, a little snippy tone was in her voice, so unusual for the typically cheery lady I knew.

"Ohhh. It must be *bad!* Jesse?"

"No."

"Your son?"

"No."

"Kay-Kay?"

"No."

"Then... something about work?"

"Look, Lela, just go away and let me do this. Otherwise, we'll do too much chit-chatting. And you said you had a deadline?"

"I do. And... let me tell you about it." Lola sighed, then plopped on the sofa and lit a cigarette, as if giving up. She stared into space as I manically barfed details about the training presentation I'd designed with a series of cartoon dancers for "section dividers," the font I'd chosen, the pencil icons... blah, blah, blah. I saw her eyes glaze over, but she didn't tell me to put a plug in it.

But the exact moment I paused for a breath, she stood. "Great ideas! Now let me get to work." I felt like an ass. Shut down and shut out.

As she started arranging the Fiesta Ware. I tiptoed out of the room to get out the batik sarongs for Lola's curtain idea and slithered back to my office.

I don't know what's up your ass, Lola, but I hope you know I'm here for you. It's almost like you're treating me like a non-friend.

I sat at my computer and opened the user manual document, losing myself in the process of writing for almost two hours. Then Lola stuck her head in the door. "Time to hang the curtains in here. Just a purple valance so it won't be dark." Very matter of fact.

I smiled, pushed myself toward the center of the room, and asked if she needed help. "No, I've figured it out now." Again, there was something too snappy, too distant in her tone. It wasn't normal at all. I'd purposely *not* talked about what happened with Jesse's joint on move-in day, hadn't asked about their night after leaving my place, and I'd kept Damon's name out of the conversation from the get-go.

But now... is Lola stepping away from our friendship? Did I mess up that bad? Did the guys say something to warn her away? Shouldn't such a close friendship be able to endure a lot more than that?!

Was I paranoid? Maybe. Thinking it was all about me? Probably.

But something – everything – had changed, and I had a sinking feeling about the cause. Lela Fox, a no-fun alcoholic, brought the crowd down.

It never occurred to me that I was driving everybody crazy being a manic Bi-Polar maniac... making them afraid to confront me about taking meds again. So instead, they ran from me.

<<<<<<<>>>>>>

TO THE FARM
CHAPTER 33

The phone rang five times. Just before his voice mail clicked on, Damon mumbled a greeting.

On the flip side, I was chirpy and in a fantastic mood. I sang, "Good morning, my love! You're just now getting up?"

"Yeah, I'm, uh... sick."

"Sick? But I thought you were going to the farm with me today, to see my parents? I mean, you took the day off just to go."

"I just don't think... Lela, I feel like shit. Stayed out late last night, had one of my weird beers and those all-hops brews always give me a hangover, ya know?"

"No, I didn't know that," I snapped back.

"Well, they do. I'm just not feeling up to it." I smelled a skunk; he was lying to me and covering the lie with another lie.

I pursed my lips and spoke in the most sweet-bitchy way I could muster. "Well, have a nice, non-existent hangover, dear. Maybe I'll call you in a few days. Or maybe not." And I hung up fast.

Like a slap in the face, Damon had lied and avoided meeting my parents in one sentence. I stayed on the sofa with my phone in-hand for another five minutes, hoping he would call back. But, no. The phone was silent.

My tears began. *Another screw-up, Lela. Here you go again. What is wrong with you that you can't keep a man? What do you do WRONG? Every time!*

The phone rang in the middle of bashing myself. Damon said, "I can be ready in a half-hour. Is that cool?"

Flabbergasted, I didn't answer. "Hello?" he prompted. I still didn't answer, but he continued, "I'll be there with breakfast biscuits at nine. Be ready." The line went dead.

<<<<<<<<>>>>>>>

We ate the biscuits in the car, heading northeast to the farm. "So tell me what happened this morning, Damon. Why did you turn me down then change your mind?"

"Baby, I heard the hurt in your voice and decided I was being 100 percent selfish. Three Tylenol and a cold shower fixed my headache... I just wasn't up for it when you called. Will you forgive me? Can we act like it didn't happen?"

Silence. Then I spoke carefully; I wanted to make sure he heard my words. "It was like a blow-off, Damon. And I know you were lying, dipshit. I felt abandoned. And unimportant."

"But you *know* you're important to me... surely I don't have to tell you more than a hundred times a day! And I'm sorry you felt abandoned. I hope you never feel that way again because, hey... I'm your partner, your pal, your knight in shining armor, right?"

I smiled as my eyes rolled to the back of my head. "Riiiight. So, where's your white horse?"

"I thought you didn't need saving, Ms. Queen of Everything."

"Oh yeah, right. I guess I can't have it both ways."

Damon's intense frown seemed to fill the front seat. "Seems like 'both ways' is *exactly* how you want it. You're hard to figure out." He paused, letting a mile pass before completing the thought. "But I'm *trying* to figure you out. Just don't give up hope on me yet."

"I'll try. You'll not exactly an open book yourself, Damon Toomey. But there's a long list of things we just haven't discussed yet. I mean, I've known you for so long, I assumed I knew everything about you. But obviously, I don't. I need to know what makes you tick, Damon. Emotionally, sexually, financially, technically, and entertainment-wise. I just don't have the info, and that shocks me. So, despite our twelve years together, we're a long way

248

from knowing each other, much less living together in the same happy house."

"I'm hoping to learn a lot about you by meeting your parents today. You've described your mom as both a saint and a disgustingly squeaky-clean prude. Which is it?"

I spoke through a chuckle, "I guess it's truly both."

Damon continued, "And your dad – all I know is you love him so much that the thought of him makes you cry. Overwhelmed with gratitude, I guess. *He's* the one that sounds like a saint, and one of a kind."

"He is definitely different... different from anybody I've ever known. So silly and corny. But probably what I love the most is how he treats my mom. He absolutely *adores* her, even after 53 years together. And that adoration is was what I grew up watching. So be forewarned: my ideas about romance and love – plus about the distribution of what I'll call power – those two are my example. It may make you run away from me, to be honest, but I can't help but want exactly what they have."

"Noted." After ten seconds of silence, Damon said, "And I come from the polar opposite environment. My parents barely spoke to each other."

"Tell me about it."

Damon talked for a half-hour, telling me more about himself than he'd hinted at otherwise. I sat on my hands to keep from interrupting. The more he talked, the bigger the red flag became. Damon had no life example of what I considered true and equal love, mutual respect, or calm compromise. Pretty big shit, a red flag with a long kite's tail.

Always an idealist, I thought meeting my parents would make him want what I wanted. Who *wouldn't* want that?! If he liked what he saw, I knew I could easily teach him how to get it. The result: Damon and I could be the second-generation Mom and Dad.

Oh, how perfect that will be!

<<<<<<<<>>>>>>>

We entered the back door of the farmhouse. I shouted a greeting, wondering why Mom wasn't in the kitchen and Daddy in the Lazy-Boy, where they always were. Then I heard Mom's voice coming from the back bedroom. "Yay! Lela's here!" Footsteps coming forward, with Daddy's clomp just behind. Dad was ho-ho-ho'ing down the hall like Santa Claus, being his regular silly self.

Big squeezes from both of them preceded the "presentation" of Damon. Daddy shook his hand in a tight grip, telling him he'd heard only good things, then teased him with a line threatening to strangle him if he tried to eat all the chicken and dumplings.

"Daddy, you're such a dweeb! And maybe Damon thinks you're serious!" My father made a funny face at Damon but didn't speak.

Then, speaking to Damon, I said, "Just don't let him try to snip at your ankles like a dog. He used to do that to my high school boyfriends."

Daddy bellowed, "But I was trying to run them off! None of them were good enough for my favorite baby daughter!"

Damon loved that line and repeated it several times during our visit. He said he could instantly see the love Daddy and I shared. In fact, he said it "vibrated in the room."

Mom was her oh-so-appropriate self, saying precisely the right things and nothing more, asking open-ended questions so Damon would feel free to talk. And talk he did!

It seemed Damon felt 100 percent comfortable with my folks, and I reveled in the ease of our meeting. Lunch was yummy, as Mom's meals always were, then Daddy and Damon discussed the union before abruptly switching to the topic of my sobriety.

"The sober Lela is *my* Lela, and I'm not willing to let her step back into being that crummy-drunk Lela. I support her in every way, and will always be there to protect her." Blah, blah, blah. He said everything my Daddy wanted to hear, and I ate it up, too.

I felt loved by all in the room and absolutely glowed with happiness. My mind was running on jet fuel as I darted here and there to show Damon the dumb shit of my childhood that was still displayed at the farmhouse.

After lunch, we moved to what my family called the party side of the room and continued a variety of conversations. Mom kept bragging on how good I looked, "healthy," she said. I reminded her she'd seen me at my worst. "But what an astonishing difference, Lela! God has blessed you!"

The room fell silent. I didn't want to respond to that. Mom knew about my Dude and disapproved. They both called my Higher Power sacrilege, thinking that giving God a name other than God, with a personality other than an ethereal glow, was a slap in the face to The Almighty and a thumbs' down to my upbringing.

I saw Damon fidget, then he picked up the Rockville newspaper he'd brought, passing it to me. Anxiety had sent my manic mood to a new level, and soon, I found myself absorbed in the classifieds, again checking "Dogs for Sale." For the first time since I'd been sober, I could actually own a dog and I was chomping at the bit to get one. *As soon as possible.*

I gasped, finding exactly what I wanted. "Yay! Long-haired dachshund! Six weeks old and just $150! That's exactly what I want, and the ad just started today! It's like I was *supposed to* discover it."

I immediately ran to the front bedroom to call the number listed in the ad. Sure enough, I would have a red long-haired dachshund, to "replace" my *wire*-haired dachshund from marriage number two. The lady said the red one, a male, had all his shots and a thorough vet check, and the low price was because one of the parents was only half-dachshund. Like I cared about that!

"I just want the perfect pet, ma'am."

"He would be perfect, and seems to be the most independent of the litter."

"Will you be home in about two hours?"

"I'll be here all day."

"Great! I'll call when I get back in town."

Running back to the living room, I announced my intentions. Nobody told me I was crazy. Nobody reminded me that spending the cash may not be a good idea. Nobody said I had made a knee-jerk decision or reminded me that I was manic or that I'd have to pay a pet deposit to Copper Pointe. They all just watched me with their mouths open.

I was firing on all cylinders, ready to go, and craving "motherhood" of a little red dog to call my own. Something that offered unconditional love.

I said, "Damon, let's go," then kissed Mom on the forehead and Daddy on top of his bald head. "I want that dog ASAP." The ceremonious routine for goodbye was cut short; I was hell-bent on leaving right that second. Mania.

On the way home, Damon told me he had plans for the evening and couldn't go with me to see the dog. Shocked, I said nothing. But my mind worked overtime.

Plans for WHAT? Dare I ask where he's going? Or with who? Would he ask ME to explain if I was the one who blurted that out? What kind of honest relationship is this?

The distance between us tasted like bile for the full hour's drive. I was confused as hell; it had been a good day until I got excited about the dog.

I guess I'm losing him, but he seemed to really like my parents! Wouldn't that connection strengthen the relationship instead of sever it? What do I do now? He's so independent, but just a week ago, he was sucking my own independence out of me?! What have I done? How do I fix it?

I prodded a bit, trying not to nag. "You liked my parents?"

"Very much so."

"Did it teach you more about me?"

"Absolutely. And you're right – your parents' example is a lofty one. I'm not sure I could ever, uh, do that."

I *had* to ask but feared the answer. "Do what?"

"Be like your dad. He's..." Damon cleared his throat. "He's, uh, subservient to your mom."

"*Subservient?* Hell-no! It's just that Mom takes charge of most stuff. And that's where I learned it. Daddy has an iron fist about 'his stuff,' but you didn't *see* any of his stuff today. I admit, he's mellowed with age, but still, the word 'subservient' is far from true." I paused for effect. "And hardly fair to say."

Damon didn't reply. The next twenty minutes of the ride was silent. I fidgeted.

"Oh!" he said, "You got some mail. It's in the door compartment." I flipped through the envelopes. *Shit! My Visa statement. Lela, "almost" paying it off doesn't count. Quit using it, and pay the last $600. It's stupid to have a balance and pay the interest. What the hell are you doing, nitwit?*

My thoughts were swirling, but I said nothing. Damon dropped me off at my place and didn't come in. My mind went into defense mode, trying to harden my heart, I suppose.

So be it! Easy come, easy go. A dog won't leave me.

<<<<<<<<>>>>>>>

In the checkout line at Walmart with a full shopping cart: dog food, a leash and collar, a small-ish dog crate, a rubber-chicken toy, a t-shirt that said "Top Dog," poop bags, food and water bowls, a dozen more things.

Then I dashed to the breeder's house and fell in love with a miniature dachshund I named Pork Chop.

He fit in a basket that had held magazines in a former life and peeked over the edge as I sat beside him on the sofa. He wasn't a whiner and didn't seem hungry or upset like many newly-weaned puppies. And the cuddly monster didn't chew on my furniture or poop on the carpet, nor act scared or lonely. Instead, he stayed on my lap, cuddling between my elbow and torso, or on my shoulder licking my neck.

Now I had somebody to talk to in the empty apartment

R.I.P. Pork Chop. You happily offered comfort in the days when nothing or nobody else in my life did.

The day you died was the third saddest of my life. And I'm sorry I moved from the house where you are buried in the backyard. I often think of your grave and hope the new owners haven't disturbed your shade tree.

You're forever in my heart, but I know I'll see you again... up there where you won't have cancer or pain. Until then, dance and play with a thousand tennis balls. And say hey to Murphy, my fat Sheltie.

<<<<<<<<>>>>>>>

FULL MOON
CHAPTER 34

I folded a spare comforter to make a bed for Pork Chop in my office, and rigged a ramp and landing so he could peek over the patio railing to watch the kids on the playground. Everybody in the apartment complex knew and loved Pork Chop. The consensus: the most people-friendly dog they'd ever known.

His constant needs kept my errands short; I didn't want to leave him alone for long. Pork Chop's puppy bladder was tiny and quite active, but I was determined to go to the Full Moon meeting in the mountains. The second meeting at West 40 had been better than the first, and I wanted to get to know those people better. I'd met dozens of the folks, and with just a few exceptions – namely, Blake the Playboy – I liked them all.

On Thursday, I skipped dinner at "The Crack" and met the group at the club just before 6:30. Obviously, the parking lot was the meeting place for many carpools because it was crowded.

Railroad Gil made it a point to speak to me and introduce his friend Corncob. I'd never seen such an *old but young* man in my life! His eyes were foggy with cataracts, and he had no teeth – seriously, none. Neither top or bottom. His skin, leathery from the sun, stretched over a semblance of bones; he was as thin as a toothpick. But, like all the West 40 people, he was nice as hell and overly cordial. "We love *old* newcomers," he'd said, grinning.

Barb turned to touch my arm. "Ready, Lela?"

"Absolutely. I guess it's too late to call shotgun."

"You're first to call it!"

"Hell-yeah! I know it's just not even an hours' drive, but those mountain roads are hard on the belly if you're in the backseat."

"Yep, it's hell to get there and heaven when you arrive. You'll love this meeting, girl. Always spiritual and powerful, lots of old-timers to keep the newbies in line. And could the weather be more perfect?" Barb spun around with her arms wide, shouting, "It's gorgeous! It's amazing! It's perfection!"

"Definitely a beautiful night in East Tennessee. Dude is good."

"Who?"

I grimaced, having said that without thinking. "Just pretend I said 'God is good.'"

Barb looked at me with a questioning wrinkle in her brow but didn't ask anything further, just agreed that God was, indeed, good.

At that moment, three other women entered the group, the three for the backseat. Amanda the Nurse, Crying Kathy, and one who barely spoke, Laurel. She seemed so uncomfortable and unhappy that it gave me the heebie-jeebies. Haunted Laurel, I thought that name suited her... and wondered what her story was. Laurel huffed a cigarette like it was life itself, pacing in a small circle. Weird. Haunted Laurel haunted me.

Butterfly Barb drove a massive SUV, now filled with the banter and jokes of five women and a silent ghost, mostly a ton of gossip about West 40 people, teaching me who to stay away from besides the obvious ones. The sun slowly set during the drive, and with each mile higher in altitude and deeper into the mountains, the moon glowed brighter.

An hour later, we parked in the lot at Cades Cove and joined the other people in the caravan, walking (and skipping) to the first turn-off in the road's ten-mile loop. There it was: the famed John Oliver cabin, built in 1820 by the area's first settlers and the last family to be kicked out by the Park Service.

The front yard was massive and pockmarked with wildflowers under dozens of centuries-old Scarlet Oak trees. The moon was so bright it seemed you could reach out and touch it, and the only sounds were crickets and the rustling of the leaves.

True and utter peace. Mother Nature at her finest.

Laurel spoke for the first time since we'd piled into the SUV. "Bears don't come out at night, do they?"

Nobody answered, but I felt obligated to say *something* to ease her fears and include her in the group. I said, "No, Laurel. Bears hibernate at night," having no idea if that was true or not. I didn't want Haunted Laurel to be any more nervous than she already was.

Our group of sixty-plus gathered on the porch of the cabin, spilling to the log steps, and spread onto a dozen blankets in the front yard. Silence encompassed us; I'd never seen a bunch of alcoholics so reverent and quiet.

After five minutes of near-silence, somebody from the dark side of the porch said, "Let's have an AA meeting." There were no readings, just people sharing what the twelve steps meant to them, why they were grateful for the traditions and the program, and how the promises had come true in their life. The words rang true in my mind, offering a personal touch to what had become rote memorizations. Our voices were low and respectful, as if gratitude vibrated our vocal cords.

There were long silences between people who spoke. Sitting on a plaid blanket with Barb and our carpool group, I heard subtle sniffling. It was the girl named Crying Kathy, who soon shared about her wealth of gratitude for being sober and able to be a good mother to her daughter. "I'm like, an example for her, and suddenly understand what I'm supposed to teach her. It's quite literally a miracle." Her words were laced with tears, happy tears, and I immediately began to cry, too.

My sister had always teased me about crying when others did, accusing me of being a "sympathy crier," but Crying Kathy's words moved me. She said what was also in *my* heart. The miracles of sobriety.

Then Railroad Gil shared and blew me away. He shared the pain of his seven-month-old son dying in his arms. Only God could lead him out of that dark place, he said, but it had shrouded him for more than a year. Crying Kathy was openly sobbing by then, and I'm sure many tears dropped in the darkness during Gil's seven minutes, not to mention his own tears – his voice gave his emotions a voice.

Also admitting his gambling addiction and devastating financial bottom, Gil seemed to be a sensitive soul with a strong dependence on his Higher Power. It moved me and made me want to know more about this railroad guy's spirit and soul. He seemed so vulnerable and joyfully spiritual.

Ask Barb if he's one of the nice guys. He's good-looking enough to be one of the Playboys, though. Maybe this much humility is a front because it's almost too good to be true... too much angst in his story to be followed by so much peace.

I'd been to many gratitude meetings, but the Full Moon meeting in Cades Cove topped them all. There wasn't a dry eye in the circle for the closing prayer, guys included. One by one, the blankets were folded and legs stretched after an almost two-hour meeting.

Nobody wanted to leave, it seemed. Jokes began, but slowly. Laughs were guarded at first, each of us humbled by the venue and heartfelt gratitude we'd shared.

When Barb and I reached to main loop road, I whispered a question. "What's the deal with Railroad Gil? As spiritual as he sounds? As humble?"

"Pretty much. A little effeminate for me, though. I guess you'd say I'm still into the bad boys. But men seem to shy away from me, anyway, I think because they're scared." A few yards further into the walk, she asked if I was hooked up with anybody.

"Officially, I'm in a relationship, but I expect it to explode any day now, if it hasn't already."

"Are you okay? I didn't hear any Guilt, Shame, or Remorse in that comment."

"Yeah, well... I think I handled the very beginning of the relationship wrong. I've known him for almost thirteen years, but I'm thinking he's just not who I'm supposed to be with. What I'd like to do, finally, is be single for a change. Three failed marriages already, okay? Plus another botched relationship in my first year of sobriety."

Barb said, "I've learned a lot from being single. Learned I can do things by myself, and knowing that has empowered me to do more and to reach out more." Then silence loomed; I walked, strongly considering a lone start in Rockville, knowing I didn't NEED a partner in the same way I used to.

Stand on your own two feet, Lela. It's about time! Don't jump back into needy mode like you tend to do. Old habits.... latching onto somebody and expecting them to do the same at the same pace. The only way you'll break that habit is to be WITHOUT a man. Commit yourself to that. Right now.

Railroad Gil and Corncob caught up to us, Gil's boots digging into the gravel with a sturdy step. "Hey, Lela! Great meeting, huh?"

Barb said hello to both the guys, and I blabbed in a loud voice, "Honestly, the best meeting I've ever been to. And I've had my fair share."

"Oh. I thought you were pretty new."

"New back to Rockville, but I have a one-year chip. Drilled a hole and keep it on my keychain."

"I carry my ten-year chip on my keychain, too. Hard to drill those metal ones, ya know?"

"Ten years!"

"Actually, twelve."

"Good job, Railroad. That's a big deal. Hope I get there."

I asked Barb, "Is he lying, my friend? Is Railroad really an old-timer?"

"A *young* old-timer, maybe. He's not lying."

"Is he a nice guy?" I asked, teasing Gil by asking in front of him.

She laughed, sliding her eyes toward Gil. "Let's just say that heart of gold is going to waste, 'cause he won't sponsor anybody, even though newcomers kiss his feet. I wouldn't trust him, Lela."

Railroad Gil exploded in laughter; a hearty laugh that came from deep within. "Hey! I'm trustworthy! Ask anybody!"

"Anybody but your sponsees, right?"

"Look, Barb. My sponsor is in Louisville – Willie, and he saved my life. He's the one who said I shouldn't sponsor anybody."

"What's the reason?"

Gil looked at his feet, kicking errant rocks on the road. He hesitated to answer. "Well, hell. If you must know... because I absorb all their problems, try to make them sober or else. And get all crazy myself."

Barb huffed; in the light, I'm sure I would've seen her eyes roll. "A likely story. You're just lazy! And scared. I don't believe a word you say, Railroad!"

"Barb, your suspicious nature is, uh... cute."

Barb's tease turned serious. "Cute? You're the first damn man who's *ever* called me cute. Because 'cute' isn't in me, Gil." She pointed her thumb at me. "Now Lela here, *she's* one who's cute. She's funny as hell, knows her shit, and I think she likes you."

"Barb! I never said that!"

"Oh, Lela! You didn't *need* to say it out loud!"

I play-swatted at Gil's arm. "Trust me – *she's* the liar. Besides, I have a boyfriend."

Barb talked louder, aiming her comment at Corncob. "Hey, man, don't you think Lela's cute?"

He said, "Of course! So cute all the guys are scared of her!" And he laughed hysterically.

"*I'm* not scared of her!" Gil spoke loudly, obviously wanting a crowd to hear. The look on his face was a combination of pride and embarrassment, coyness and boldness – and wonderfully charming. I felt my face tingling, happy to have the attention, even though I knew I'd say the same about him. Because I was scared of him. Scared of how I felt about him, anyway.

Soon, full laughter took the group to the edge of the loop road and spilled into the parking lot.

Gil said, "Breakfast at the Pancake Barn! We always go there after the Full Moon, and it's so pretty tonight that I think we can sit outside on the terrace."

My jaw dropped. "All these people? It must be a big place."

Barb answered. "Actually, it's small. We take it over, like cockroaches in a dark kitchen."

Gil spoke up immediately. "Ewwww. Oh, my God! Give me *anything* but cockroaches. I hate them!" Then this gargantuan strong-man shivered like a girl. I was amazed. And intrigued.

I said, "Hey, man, I just came from Florida, land of the giant Palmetto bug! I agree – they're prehistoric enemies. Not in *my* house!"

Gil said, "I saw one in my kitchen once and ran. Didn't go back in there for a week. Stayed at Corncob's place wearing the same clothes."

"That's a pretty serious fear of roaches."

He shivered. "Don't even say the word! Why are we talking about this, anyway? Let's go to Pancake Barn. And I'll just warn you, I'll fight for a seat next to you. I want to hear your story. And wow... I liked what you shared tonight."

"My story isn't so special."

"I beg to differ."

"How would you *know*, Gil?"

"I hear the pain in your voice."

At that moment, Barb shouted backward to Gil and me. "Lela! Hurry, we must be first in line or we won't get a seat!"

"See ya, Railroad," I said, jogging toward Barb's SUV.

<<<<<<<<<>>>>>>>>>

Even outside, the noise on the terrace echoed against the trees. So many loud and laughing voices, you had to shout to be heard. We had three servers, who quickly got pissed at us with separate checks, special requests, and multiple demands for coffee and more coffee.

I got to know many others from West 40 and had a good time, but I squirmed in my seat after we'd eaten and talked for a while. I needed to get back to my puppy.

As promised, Railroad Gil had finagled a seat next to me. Thankfully, he wasn't overly flirty but made his interest in me apparent. Not pushy, just all-smiles and all-ears. I told him about my puppy and how I wish I'd known it would be such a late night. "He has a little-baby bladder and hits the newspaper maybe five of ten times, so who knows what I'll go home to."

"Corncob and I can take you home early. Now, as a matter of fact. You ready?"

"No, I don't want to make a scene by leaving too early. Besides, I'm having a good time." I beamed at Gil for a half-second before realizing that could be interpreted as a flirtatious line. .

"You're having a good time, huh?" *Shit. Dammit, Lela. Quit acting interested!* "Well, I am, too!" Railroad Gil's baby-blues sparkled, but he said nothing further and didn't flash weird looks or do anything to make me uncomfortable.

I blurted out, "I have a boyfriend, you know." No intro or reason to bring it up, just laying there on the table flashing like neon. It was meant to keep him at a distance, but it came out like an admission of interest in him.

"Boyfriends come, and boyfriends go. Do you two live together?"

"No."

"That's good."

"Good? Good for who? For what? Good in what way?" The more I said, the more I buried myself. Gil chuckled, a little one then a big one, but he didn't answer.

The first to leave was Blake the Playboy, who said he had a late date. Gil immediately whispered in my ear. "You're not the first to leave now, so the coast is clear. Let's go."

"But does that asshole guy count? He's leaving because he's a..." I let the comment whip away in the breeze.

A laugh, sharp. "You pegged him right. My advice to you: stay far away from Blake the Flake."

"Do you have a name for everyone?"

"Pretty much."

"Okay, what's a name for me. Besides 'new girl.' Been there, done that."

"Sweet Lela?"

"No way."

"Lovely Lela?"

"Watch yourself."

"Lela from Florida?"

"That fits, not so catchy, but it fits."

"I know! Railroad Lela!"

"Ha, ha, mister. Don't you wish!" *Oops. Dumb thing to say!*

"Yes, I *do* wish. But for now, you just need a ride home."

"Right, Gil. And that's all I'll ever need."

He eyed me sideways, silent for a full five seconds, longer than I could hold his gaze. "Let me get Corncob," he said and pushed himself back from the table.

I turned to Barb and waited for a break in the six-way conversation she had going. Finally, I put my hand on her arm to get her attention. "Hey, Railroad and Corncob are taking me home because... well, my puppy has been alone for a long time."

"Railroad? Corncob? You just might be in trouble, girl."

I panicked. "Seriously? I thought... I mean, uh, they seem nice... and, well, Railroad offered, and I just–"

"Oh, he *is* nice. That's the worry."

"Oh."

"Be careful out there."

I stood when Railroad and Corncob stood behind me, Gil bidding loud farewells and Corncob shouting, "Have a blessed night" to everybody. Then Gil made a big deal of pulling my chair out like a 1950s gentleman, and my face turned beet-red. Feeling like a giant flashing sign, I stood beside them to say "nice to meet you" to dozens of people.

Gil and Corncob never said, "Lela's going with us," but I felt so labeled. Just the opposite of what I needed. So, of course, I felt like I had to explain to the group, and I did just that, using Pork Chop as my excuse. An honest and legitimate explanation, but a few comments of "A likely story..." and "Riiight, good one!" floated from the crowd.

Keep your head up, Lela. You're legit. You're not doing anything wrong. Or shady. Or flirty. You're just getting a ride home.

The drive was longer going back to Rockville; we'd zigged and zagged to get to Pancake Barn and ended up further away from the interstate. Corncob's truck was full of trash and tools. He tried to straighten things up, laughing about it being a work truck and not a people truck, but I kept my foot on *top* of the circular saw, making sure my toes were protected. Railroad Gil sat in the back with his head between the seats to talk to us. And he talked practically the whole time.

About halfway through the ride, I decided he was selfish, doing all the talking, but the tides soon turned. He asked all the open-ended questions that could determine the "quality of my program," and, somehow, I felt comfortable telling him I had invented a Higher Power named Dude. I almost told him about my vision – I was *that* comfortable – but I'd told very few people the story, always fearing judgement. I couldn't do that in Rockville yet, I decided.

Gil said, "I wish I could design my own HP, but unfortunately, I was raised Catholic, so guilt is part of my make-up. I feel obligated to praise the plain ol' halo-wearing Jesus Christ. Like you, I often wish he was more like me, more casual and friendly. But it sounds like you have a reverence for your Dude, and that's all that counts."

Corncob spoke up. "The fact that both of you losers have a Higher Power is pretty amazing. Mine comes and goes. And these days, he's gone. Hasn't been around in a while, in fact. I'm just floundering around, looking for some sense of peace."

Gil replied immediately, I'm telling ya, Cob, you've got to work the damn steps! You haven't had a drink in five years but still want one! And why is that? Because you aren't working the program! My offer to help still stands."

"And my refusal of your help still stands."

I spoke up, confused that a twelve-stepper was stepless. "You haven't done a fourth step?"

"Nope. And don't plan to."

"But doesn't Guilt eat you up? Do you understand your motivations? What makes you a different person than when you were a drunk?"

Gil interjected, "Listen to her, Cob! She makes sense!"

"Y'all get off my ass. I have a sponsor. I go to meetings. I'm on the damn Board of Directors at the club! And here I am, trudging toward happy destiny, and it's none of y'all's damn business."

"True," I said, "But this is a program of *twelve steps*. Going through those steps, one by one, is what keeps people sober. Unless everything I've learned has been a lie."

Gil asked, "Where are you, step-wise, Lela?"

"Well, things kept happening so I've done a verrry thorough fourth, and made amends to a few key people, but she told me to stop. I need a sponsor in Rockville. You know of one?"

Both men spoke at the same time, saying the same name: "Vickie."

Gil followed up with "Black-haired Vickie."

"Does she go to the 5:30?"

Gil answered fast. "She'd be perfect for you! But she only goes to the Stitch and Bitch."

"Oh! You have one here, too?" I was amazed! I could probably do embroidery a lot calmer now.

"A women's meeting? Everybody has a women's meeting!"

"Do they really stitch?"

Both men laughed. "No! We just call it that." I shrugged, then explained the Florida meeting I'd attended. They both thought it was hilarious and probably based on the long-term nickname for women's meetings."

"What do I know?" I admitted.

"Well, the Testosterone Club meets Wednesdays at seven, but we don't whip 'em out."

"Not even Blake?"

It was as if this line made me one of their crowd. Gil's strong shoulders racked with laughter, and he removed his wire-framed glasses to wipe the tears from his eyes. And I realized that when Corncob laughed, his "no teeth" jaws filled out so much that you'd never guess he was toothless.

<<<<<<<<<<>>>>>>>>>>

The West 40 parking lot was empty and dark, even with the bright moon reflecting on the fenders of cars. Everybody was still at the Pancake Barn, I supposed. Gil and I got out of Corncob's truck at the same time, then Gil walked with me to my Jetta. "It's late. Do you need an escort home?"

"That's the most ridiculous thing I've ever heard."

"Well, I want to be sure you're—"

"You're sweet, but I'm fine."

On my last syllable, a car turned into the parking lot.

Railroad Gil shouted and waved, "Carter!" Then he turned to me and said, "Stay and meet Carter and his wife Carolyn. There's some good recovery in that Cadillac."

Knowing I should leave and take care of Pork Chop, something made me stay, and before long, the five of us were sitting on the curb in front of the club, talking about sobriety and serenity.

Gil's delivery was smooth, his words wise and practical. Carter, a man my age and an avid TSU basketball fan, shared the serenity of his life and love for his strikingly beautiful wife, Carolyn.

Our connection was instant.

Already, Lela... good AA friends in Rockville. You're going to be okay. My only worry was that Gil paid a bit too much attention to me, and I didn't think his focus was because I was new. He never outwardly flirted but wanted to know everything about me in one hour. He explained, "Your life has taken so many different turns, like different lifetimes."

"Each markedly different from the other" was my answer. I told him coming back to Rockville was the latest "markedly different" phase, and I felt ready to grow into myself even further.

"That sounds exciting! Can I watch?"

I couldn't tell if it was a play on words or a phrase of encouragement, so I didn't answer. Instead, I bid the folks goodbye. Gil stood to hug me, but he also had the sideways hug technique down-pat, down it was a long-distance hip-to-hip and funny as hell. We locked eyes and laughed. "See ya around, Railroad," I said.

"I hope so," he answered. I felt his eyes on my back as I walked away.

ESCAPE FROM MYSELF
CHAPTER 35

I got up early to work a few hours, then escaped for a day of fun – another day on Kay-Kay's "patio in the trees" with Lola. Pork Chop was my passenger and had no idea that going bye-bye could be so exciting. His tail wagged all the way across town.

"Hey, Miss Lela!" Lola was happy to see me and relieved that I'd made it up the mountain of Kay-Kay's curvy gravel driveway. It had rained overnight and a few places had washed out.

"What are you going to do about that driveway, Kay-Kay?" I asked, "Does it do that every time it rains?"

"My cousin is still working on it."

"Well he better work harder."

Kay-Kay laughed. "You get what you pay for." I grimaced, remembering she had a huge family, all living on the same used-to-be-the-family-farm property, and according to Southern ways, to hire an outsider was worse than blasphemy.

For three hours, we talked and laughed, sang dumb songs at the top of our lungs, and roamed the herb garden. Kay-Kay smoked a joint a few hours into the afternoon, but it was her place, so what could I say? If I'd been overly tempted to take a hit, I would have left, but I refused to be tempted. I didn't want my sobriety to hinder my friendships more than it already had.

My mood had stabilized a bit, not so manic, but I felt a little outside of the crowd. I realized I was, quite literally, coming from a different place than they were, and as the afternoon progressed, it became more and more apparent.

Kay-Kay talked about the awful problems with her marriage and recent divorce, the issues with her wayward children, and spoke of impending doom. I hoped Lola would level the playing field with some happiness, but she also complained of problems in her relationship with Jesse.

Come on, Lela. This is more normal than you're thinking it is. Bitching about men is what women do when they gather – bitch, bitch, bitch. Did you really think Rockville would embellish you with happiness around every corner? Face the fact that most people aren't happy. And just because YOU are, you can't isolate yourself from others, or you'd have no friends at all.

With a lull in our conversation, I told the girls about the Full Moon Meeting. "I met some interesting people."

"Well, good for you, Miss Lela!" Lola always called me that, making me think of my nanny in Florida who called me the same. I hadn't told Lola, or any non-AA Rockville friend, for that matter, details about my life just before I hit bottom, nor did I want to. The whole scene with Stuart and Baby-Daddy made me feel stupid, and I didn't want to re-live the stupidity.

But as Oakley had insisted, I'd written all the stupidity down... and prayed to be able to forgive myself. Eventually, it would happen, I knew, but in the meantime, I still struggled. I simply chose to struggle in silence.

Shaking off the Shame of the past, I focused on the present, decided to *be* present, as Oakley advised. So I kept talking about the meeting, even mentioning the AA stuff I knew they wouldn't understand. But something else came out of my mouth, almost without thinking. I said, "And I met a guy. A fascinating, good-looking guy."

Lola gasped. Kay-Kay huffed a "Whoa!"

Catching her breath, Lola challenged, "Do tell!"

"Well, he *is* good-looking, but he's a bit overweight. And has acne scars, big ones."

Kay-Kay piped in. "Yeah, probably from cystic acne, it's called. I knew a guy like that. What horrible shame to live with!"

"Shame? Not him! Very confident, and obviously very sober." Lola didn't reply, and Kay-Kay used the pause to excuse herself. "He lost a child, Lola, and talked about it. He cried, and made *lots* of people cry."

As if in a daze of memories, I breathed, "His seven-month-old baby died in his arms when he was seven years' sober."

"And he's still sober after that? That's some kickass strength!"

"That's also what he shared – about the strength it took to make it out of that darkness. He's very spiritual. But open-minded. I even told him about Dude."

Lola knew how "secret" my Dude story was to me and raised her eyebrows, shocked.

"Yeah, imagine that. The guy made me comfortable enough to tell. But I didn't tell him about the origin, the vision, but you *know* I don't tell that."

"Right," Lola mumbled.

Then I chuckled, remembering the conversations on the way home in Corncob's truck. "And he's funny as hell, too!" Five minutes later, I was still talking about Railroad Gil.

Lola ooh'ed and aww'ed, maybe trying to make me feel okay about rambling on about him. I continued, "And you'll love this part – his best friend's name is Corncob!"

Lola threw her head back to laugh. I told her all the funny nicknames I'd learned of the West 40 people, realizing how much I liked the people. Being with them was like being home. "I was with like-minded people, Lola. Has AA made me a freak? Only able to associate with other alcoholics?"

"You're here, aren't you?"

"But everything is so... different. I think about things in a deep way now, always investigating myself and my motivations. And always measuring the motivations of others."

"Why is that?" Lola seemed honestly interested.

"Because I know more about human nature now... or something. Hell, I don't know! But I think I'm forever going to be weird. And obviously boring."

Another hoot of a laugh from Lola. "Miss Lela, you could never, ever, ever be boring. You've got a sharp mind and quick wit. You crack me up!"

"But not today. Today, I'm all up in my head."

"So you're thinking too much... wouldn't that be a *good* thing?"

"No! Not when I over-think and drive myself crazy. And that's what's happening. My sponsor often said, 'No thinking!'" I laughed. "As if it's possible."

"But maybe you're thinking about the acne guy."

"Yeah..." My mind turned to memories of the night before, and I turned dreamy. "He works for the railroad, on some crazy schedule I don't quite understand."

"But, what about Damon? I mean, I know you two are–"

"I don't know *what* is going on with Damon!" My anger rose in a flash. "He's hot, then he's cold. We haven't made love since we left Florida."

"Whuuut?" Lola drew the word out, adding her Southern twang. I would have laughed if the topic hadn't been so serious.

She turned even more serious. "Listen, Lela. This is important." I turned to look into her beautiful brown eyes. "Has Damon tried to talk to you about... uh, Bi-Polar? About your meds?"

The question didn't register as something to be concerned about. I answered honestly and plainly. "Yes, but he doesn't understand... so, whatever."

I saw Lola grimace and squirm. Just as she opened her mouth to say something obviously hard for her to say, I started blabbing again. "So Damon met my parents, right?" She nodded. "Then on the way home, told me he had 'other plans' for the evening, but didn't say what those plans were. I feel very shut-out."

"But you know he's with Jesse today, right?"

"Not until *you* told me. Those early-morning 'I love you' calls don't happen anymore. It seems I'm on my own."

"But the way he talks about you – to me, and to Jesse – it's like he's still ready to make everything work!"

"Would you do me a favor and get to the bottom of this for me? I feel like I can't ask."

"Well, I know *one* of the problems, Lela. But I don't think you want to hear it. You're manic as hell. I hope you know that."

Nothing sparked a need for me to answer that comment. I didn't think my "yes, I'm a little hyper" attitude had anything to do with Damon, and I told her exactly that.

Continuing, I said, "And here's the deal, Lola. Something, uh, snapped as we packed that damn U-Haul. He was acting so damn anal, it was driving me crazy, seriously crazy! We had words. Then when I tried to put my two-cents in when setting up the condo to accommodate *me*, the shit hit the fan. I think it goes well beyond us both being set in our ways... I think his way doesn't include me at all. Maybe it doesn't include *anybody*. And the motherfucker keeps telling me to calm down! I *hate* that!"

By the time I was finished, Lola's jaw was slack, her mouth open in disbelief. But the moment had passed. I was unreachable.

Kay-Kay opened the sliding glass door and shouted to Lola, "Jesse's on the phone for you."

"He calls the home phone?" I asked.

"Yeah, he's weird."

Soon, Lola bounced back outside, happy. "Jesse and Damon are coming at five! They're bringing pizza!"

Something within me broke in that instant. I didn't want to see Damon. I didn't want pizza. I didn't want to be there. What I wanted was to go back to the West 40 club and see if Railroad Gil was going to be at the 5:30 meeting.

I glanced at Pork Chop, now awake and panting in the heat, despite the shade tree that protected him.

"Lola! I need you!" My voice was frantic.

She rushed over, maybe hearing the mania in my voice. Then she sat on the edge of my lounge chair, her soft hand on my arm. "What?"

"I want to go see the alcoholics at West 40. And the acne guy. I can't see Damon and deal with the anxiety it causes."

Silence. All three of us lowered our heads.

What a change in thinking since you left this morning! You've been through the full spectrum of emotions today, hearing the girl's complaints, trying to explain Damon's odd behavior to an unbelieving Lola. Wondering if you're losing your shit...

I sat up, feeling weak. I noticed that my hands were shaking, and things became clear in my mind. *I can't handle any more of this. I need a meeting. I need to be around my own kind. And, maybe, HE will be there. I have no idea why, but I want to see him. Damon, be damned!*

I gathered my things, slid a tank top over my head, and stepped into my shorts and sandals. "It's been fun, y'all, but I gotta go."

"Are you okay?" Lola and Kay-Kay spoke simultaneously.

"I'm fine. I'm just... overthinking."

"What should I tell Damon?" Lola asked.

I froze in my tracks. *What to tell Damon? Tell him the truth? Through Lola? No! But be honest. You MUST be honest.* The knot in my belly relaxed. "Tell him I said hey, and I'll talk to him later."

Putting Pork Chop in my tote bag and gathering his bowl, I headed for the Jetta. Kay-Kay called to my back, warning me to be careful on the driveway.

<<<<<<<<<>>>>>>>>

I cried most of the way home, wailing to the dog. At first, the poor thing had his ears back as if I was scolding him, but he relaxed when my sobs included baby-talk comments of "Good boy!" and "You're my best friend, Pork Choppy!"

I wasn't even sure *why* I was so upset. My emotions just flowed, feeling needy, then strong, then pitiful, then powerful. *What is wrong with you? Where is your gratitude? Where is your HEAD? You're going crazy for no reason!*

A hot shower stopped my tears, and a sense of stability in mood and thought had returned. Trying the find the reason for my breakdown, I carefully considered the fact that I wasn't taking meds anymore. Others kept talking about it, but I'd never seriously considered the problem within my own mind.

After thinking, I decided lack of treatment had nothing to do with my craziness. It seemed very specific to Damon, and definitely not the typical generalized mania or depression. I wasn't angry, which is how my Bi-Polar spikes usually started. Whether going up or coming down, anger was the beginning. But anger wasn't the problem. I was a ball of anxiety, and the only thing that made me feel in control was to be at a meeting. *What if I get addicted to AA?*

I sat down and gazed into my makeup mirror for a long time, studying my face, and noticing the golden glow of today's sun. I talked to myself out loud, arguing on a dozen topics. But the consensus was I was growing, yet afraid to grow

It made sense.

I felt I had no choice but to move on from Damon... living in the great unknown caused too much stress. But I'd talked myself out of focusing on Railroad Gil; that wasn't moving on – that was moving backward.

"Stay single for a damn change, Lela!" Pork Chop thought I was talking to him and wagged his tail, so I continued the soliloquy. "Stand on your own, find out who you are, and dig on that. You're capable and smart, with no reason to *need* a damn man, right? You don't need a plumber or a handyman, so what would he bring to the table, anyway?"

When Pork Chop didn't answer, I added, "You haven't even learned to compromise with yourself, so how could you *possibly* think you're ready to compromise with a partner?"

My getting-ready routine began. Without knowing why, I took extra care to look my best. I carefully coated each lash with "Blackest Black" and dusted my cheeks with new, "Sugar Melon" blush. A kiss of "Mauvelous" and I was ready. Just in time for the 5:30 meeting.

<<<<<<<<>>>>>>>

TORN IN TWO
CHAPTER 36

Gil noticed me as soon as I got out of the car, making me think he'd been on the lookout for a white Jetta. He waved high in the air and shouted, "Hey, Serene Lela!" *Oh, so that's my nickname, huh? What a hoot!*

The pre-meeting was in full swing. Naturally, I trotted toward the biggest group in the parking lot, and, naturally, the biggest group was led by Railroad Gil.

Even from a distance, I heard his "speech" to the crowd as he loudly pontificated about being painstakingly honest in all our affairs. But he didn't sound like a Big Book thumper or know-it-all; he'd said that as the punch line of a joke. His constituents roared with laughter.

It was evident Gil was one of the movers and shakers at West 40, and definitely in his element socially. His easy-going "leadership" style turned my crank, and, despite my will to stop it, a buzz started between my ears – half anxiety, half excitement.

But I noticed I felt different, not so manic and out of control when Gil Justice was around. I was in charge of myself, feeling capable of being myself without harsh judgement from others.

Feeling better because of Gil? Don't, Lela! You promised Pork Chop you'd stay single.

That night, confidence seemed to vibrate from Gil's chest, filling his red Polo. I also noticed the polo covered a larger belly than I remembered. *But it looks like Stuart's belly... starting way up high, the result of a hiatal hernia.* I used to tease Stuart about having a "shelf" for a bib, and Gil's looked the same. It wasn't pretty, but it wasn't a deal-killer, either.

Killing what deal? Stop it, dammit!

As I walked into the circle of West 40 members, Gil shouted to everybody, introducing me. "Hey, y'all, this is Serene Lela. She's almost two years sober, just new here. From Florida."

"Actually, I'm from Rockville, just... well, I got sober in Florida," I corrected him, also speaking loud to the group. I didn't correct him on the length of my sobriety, but who wants a demotion, right?

"Welcome, Lela," was the happy reply from 25-or-so voices. A friendly group, all the same Caucasian good ol' boys (in Tennessee, "good ol' boys" includes redneck women, too). Everybody seemed friendly in their boring uniformity.

In Florida, there were jihads next to toothless bikers, mohawks next to crew cuts, Cubans next to sophisticated French women – diversity to the extreme. But Tennessee was the polar opposite. Per tradition, a "real" Tennesseans was a staunch Republican, redneck gun owner, 100 percent heterosexual, and dyed-in-the-wool Christian with slam-shut distrust of those outside of those restrictive boundaries. I had a difficult time accepting that uniformity again, and knew the only way I could define myself as open-minded was to act that way at every opportunity. But, of course, I'd then be seen as a radical, even in AA. *So be it. I yam what I yam, folks.*

Maybe that's why I liked Gil so much. From our discussion on the way back from the Full Moon meeting, I knew he was a fired-up Democrat like me, and a railroad union man. Plus, he'd lived in large-ish Midwest cities despite his Kentucky roots. Gil seemed to be accepting of everybody and everything, honestly interested in every bit of diversity he could find.

I was staring at him, I realized, as I thought about how open-minded he was. Suddenly, his eyes looked directly into mine. *Oh, wow!* Something flashed between us... the wind stopped blowing, all sounds paused, and my peripheral vision became a blur. It was just me and Gil in the world for a moment, connected instantly and purposefully. Suddenly, my armpits were damp and a silent vibration filled my head.

Then he smiled. His eyes, *so damn blue*, sparkled with an ethereal flash of light behind them. When sounds returned, I heard somebody say, "Don't you think so, Gil?" but he didn't look away from me. His eyes pierced me like daggers, and I couldn't have looked away if I tried. And I didn't want to try. I was awe-struck and frozen in that moment of peace.

Then Butterfly Barb touched my arm, jolting me back to reality. *Dammit! Go away, Barb!* The aggravated thought surprised me; I wanted a friendship with Barb; I just didn't want the eye contact with Gil to go away.

"How's your puppy?" Barb asked. "Why don't you bring him next time? He can be Pork Chop, the Long-haired Alcoholic. The club really does allow dogs." Her words didn't register in my mind; it was as if she'd spoken from miles away. My happy new friend tried again. "Lela? Did you even hear me?"

Finally, her face came into focus. "Uh, no, I guess I didn't hear."

"Bring your dachshund! The club allows dogs. Corncob brings his all the time."

Ignoring her comment, I blurted the most critical question on my mind. "Tell me about Gil."

"I've told you!"

"Tell me again. He's a nice guy? Because I find myself... just, really, attracted to him."

"Lela, back down! Don't go so fast!" She play-slapped me on the bicep. "Can't ya just keep it in your pants, girl?"

"Uh, I'm not thinking *that* far. It's just... I caught him looking at me and it was a, well, mesmerizing moment. For both of us, I think."

"Watch yourself, Ms. Newcomer."

"I'm not a newcomer!"

"You are at *this* club!" Slowly, I nodded. *Yes, Lela. You know Butterfly Barb is right. Don't move fast about anything, and mainly because he's just going to be a good friend, right? That's what you promised! Or maybe a date or two, but nothing more than that. Barb's right – keep it in your pants.*

Barb again interrupted my thoughts. "But, let me tell you... word on the street is he's quite taken with you, too. He's been talking around about you, warning the other men off. I quote: 'Hands off, you slobs! She's mine.'"

"No shit?"

"Lela, but you know: hooking up with somebody immediately? That's not recovery."

"You're right. And recovery is my gig. Actually, I had a long talk with myself about my determination to stay single. It's not in my nature, but you're right that recovery must come first. Growing in sobriety is my goal."

"Then quit staring at him."

"Was I?"

"Of course, you dumbass. At the very least, play hard to get. Don't be such a... uh, a *girl*. Walk the walk and save your reputation."

"Ouch." *Oh yeah, my reputation.* My lips twisted in a face filled with Guilt.

"Right. I mean, I'm not your sponsor or anything... just saying what I think my sponsor would say to me."

"Speaking of that, I'm looking for a sponsor. Who would you recommend?"

"That easy. Black-haired Vickie, if she's available. She'll only sponsor one at a time."

"Gil and Corncob recommended Vickie, too. She's serene enough for a not-yet-serene Lela?"

"Vickie is awesome, and I admire her 'one sponsee' rule. Me, I have four sponsees, *all* driving me crazy."

"I can't wait to become a sponsor myself! How exciting is that! To build somebody up, teach, and help them see the light."

"Sorry, but it's nothing like that."

"Still, I'd like to get a sponsee. And my Florida sponsor taught me to *never say no* if someone asks."

"You're in deep shit around here, then. So many newcomers! But, of course, you have a lot to prove first. Especially a history of *being single and cool with it*." She emphasized each of the final words with a poke of her finger on my chest. Then she cleared her throat.

<<<<<<<<<>>>>>>>>

The meeting was just so-so. A first-step meeting for the most part, but I learned the short version of a lot of old-timer's recovery stories. Both Barb and Gil shared, and they both roused my heart.

But at the closing prayer, something odd happened, maybe something that could only happen at a club focused on the social aspect of recovery. While we were still holding hands, a 30-ish blonde woman shouted, "Poker Party at my place! Nine o'clock. Be there or be... oblong."

People laughed at the lame joke, but I was astonished that a poker party would be announced at a twelve-step meeting. And I thought of Gil, the gambling addict.

Poker wasn't my thing in the first place; I'd dipped my toe into the casinos as a drunk, but my Mom taught me to fear gambling. Her father lost thousands during the depression – when thousands were few and far between. Even worse, it was her mother's inheritance that the sonofabitch gambled away. She still hated him for it, and rightly so, according to me. When I got sober, I pledged to make gambling a no-no, too. So, no poker party for me.

Gil practically accosted me in the parking lot as we all smoked cigarettes and joined in various groups. I was still trying to find the group that fit me best, so I followed Butterfly Barb around like a puppy. She was good to introduce me to everybody and said nice things, but twice she said I was not available for dating. It pissed me off, no matter how much she may have been trying to protect me.

Gil touched my arm; I turned and he said, "I was hoping you'd share tonight. You have a great story to tell, and I'm sure it would help a lot of the new girls."

"There sure are a lot of new girls around here. What's up with that?"

He shrugged. "You get what you get. You'll find the church meetings have a lot more sobriety. There are quite a few, so... hey! Maybe we could go to one together?" It was a tricky question; asking a "date" to a meeting isn't a date. But it's not just a meeting either.

"Maybe." It was the only safe answer.

"But, everybody, and I mean *everybody,* is going to Christy's tonight for the poker party. Even me! And I don't play cards at all."

"Neither do I."

"She only sets up two tables, and the rest of us hang out in her huge living room or on the back patio. She's got a thing for flowers and green stuff, and it's really nice out there."

"So her parties are a regular thing?"

"Every other Friday. I always go unless work interferes." Then his eyes widened with a hopeful smile. "I hope to see you there?"

A question, not a statement. And something in Gil's face made it all seem so innocent, so easy to say yes. "Does Christy live around here? I won't go to Timbuktu."

"It's nearby. Timberbrook Apartments, off Lonas Road?" I nodded, knowing the area. "Number B-11."

I chuckled, "Eleven..."

"Eleven?"

"It's a thing with me. My magic number, apparently."

"Cool! That means you're meant to be there... Ms. B-11." The joke fell flat, but I laughed, pushing on his arm. *Wow! Where did that electricity come from? Just touching his skin? Shit! What IS it about this man?*

<<<<<<<>>>>>>

HAPPY HAIR

CHAPTER 37

The B-11 apartment was packed with people, some gathered around the poker tables, some in the back, and some crowding the large living room's sectional sofa. Nerves took over at first; I was stiff and shy in meeting the dozens of people who warmly introduced themselves.

Corncob shouted a greeting from the other side of the living room, ending with, "Y'all need to know Serene Lela. She comes from Florida, but she talks like us."

"I'm from here, Corncob!"

His skinny shoulders shrugged. I made a dash for the empty seat on the sectional and learned a lot about Corncob in that ten minutes – first, most people just called him "Cob." He did odd jobs and spent every dime he had, no matter the season, and he'd been accused of killing a teacher in the fourth grade when he kicked a ball and it hit her in the head. The teacher died of a stroke, maybe-or-maybe-not because of being hit with the ball, but he'd been teased by the students and shunned by the staff for the rest of his years in school.

Pharmacist Mark had told me the story. I said, "Ouch!" That'd screw somebody us for life! PTSD and all that, right?"

Mark said, "He seems to handle it better than most. His brand of 'crazy' is hilarious, and he'd give you the shirt off his back. No shit. Cob's a good guy."

"Too bad about his teeth," I said, which took Pharmacist Mark aback.

"Funny, but I don't even notice anymore. Cob is just... Cob."

I couldn't let it drop. "But sometimes his face looks full of teeth... it's only when he frowns, or, uh, something, that it looks all caved in. Curious, huh?"

"Never thought about it, but you're right."

Mark started talking shit with a guy on the other side of the sofa, turning his back on me. It wasn't rude or anything, but the girl on the other side of me also had her back to me. Still nervous, I guess, I got the "Lela's a weirdo" feeling big-time, and stood up.

Mark glanced my way as he felt the weight of the sofa shift. "Gonna get a drink," I said. He nodded. The coolers were by the back door. Grabbing a Diet Coke, I wandered onto the patio, lured by a gentle scent of... *wow! Something's blooming!* I looked around. The smell could have come from anywhere.

Gil said Christy had a green thumb, but this... oasis... is spectacular. I love how Tennessee has such a variety of plants and flowers, even tropical plants can grow in the summer, but this is beyond beautiful. I stuck my nose into a massive bloom at eye height and breathed deeply.

"Smells awesome, huh?" The voice was deep, coming behind me at an angle. I turned to find Gil, red Solo cup in hand, wearing a shy smile. "Flowers are *everywhere* out here. You oughta see the orchids around the corner!"

"Those are hard to grow, man! I don't know much, but even my mother complains about hers year after year."

"I don't know much, either, but I know orchids. I've had success, but my damn work schedule makes it hard to be a good plant daddy."

"Plant daddy?"

Gil chuckled. "Yes, I have green children."

"No other kids?"

"Yes! Thanks for asking. I have a son and daughter, twelve and ten."

"Cool. I have a nineteen-year-old son."

"Wow. You started early!"

"Yeah, but on purpose. I thought a family would keep me away from alcohol."

Gil laughed. "I'm sure *that* worked out!"

"About as well as any other technique I tried," I admitted with a smile.

"They say you went to a rehab center in Florida. I wish I could have done it that way. I was robbed."

"Ha! Are you kidding?! Rehab damn-near broke me. It's like hard-core boot camp, where they invent ways to keep you in line and on a schedule. It was a dual-diagnosis center, though, and I finally got my meds straightened out." *Why did you say that, Lela? Are you advertising Bi-Polar, for God's sake?! And you're not even on meds now, so why in the hell would you offer this information to a stranger?*

Gil took a drink of what looked like ice water, smiling over the cup. "Bi-Polar?" I could only nod. "Me, too," he said, offering his cup for a toast. "Here's to better living through chemistry!"

I clicked his glass and drank from the icy-cold can. "I thought self-medicating with vodka was the answer for a long time. And it *worked* for a long time, with a few exceptions."

"Ditto on that. But my moods been stable since the day I quit drinking... since I rolled myself into the West 40 club, crying like a baby."

"You got sober there?"

"Many years ago. But I still roll in there crying sometimes. Living sober is tough."

"I'll drink to that!" I said, offering my glass for a toast.

Gil laughed. "You're funny." I thanked him, then the conversation hit a dead end. Discomfort rose from my gut to my throat as I shifted my weight from foot to foot.

"Gil looked over his shoulder. "The garden table is empty. Want to sit?"

Knowing it was somewhat of a commitment to be one-on-one when I'd promised myself to focus on the whole party, I agreed for some unknown reason. *Maybe because you're mesmerized by the man? That you find him sexy and exciting? That you want what he has, in more ways than one?*

The bar-height table accommodated only two people, and the umbrella atop it insulated us in privacy among the crowd. Gil began a chirpy running commentary about the flowers on our side of the patio, proving he'd lied about "knowing very little" about blooming plants. I called him on it.

"Well, Christy has given me the tour."

"And you remembered all the names, even the Latin names of these flowers?"

"Well..." his voice trailed off.

"Face it, Gil, you're a flower guy. A big, strong, broad-shouldered flower guy! I love the dichotomy of it all."

"Die-what-a-me?"

"Dichotomy. It means opposites. Polar opposites."

"Your college education is showing."

"It's just a word. And I like words. I'm a writer, in fact."

"Cool! Fiction? Mysteries? Please, don't tell me you write those stupid romance novels!"

"No! And nothing you'd find in a bookstore. Now I'm doing what's officially called technical writing. A software manual for the end user. Trust me – boring stuff."

"But that takes smarts. Smart girls turn me on."

I scolded him. "Gil! You're not supposed to say things like that!"

He answered quickly. "You're right. I'm sorry. That was out of line." His face was fire-engine red. "It's just... you're so..." He took a deep breath in and out. "I can't..." His eyes roved my face, my curly hair, and what I hoped was my pink shirt instead of my boobs. "It's just that... see... I..."

"What, Gil? Spit it out!" I acted perturbed, but I knew he was trying to offer a compliment that didn't cross the line, struggling to find the right thing to say, and it was cute.

I glowed with a grin as he continued to stumble and mumble, not able to finish a sentence. It was funny as hell, watching his nerves take over.

But he wouldn't stop trying. "See, you're just so... your eyes, uh... your hair... yeah, that! Your hair just..." Gil paused, licking his lip nervously. "Your hair looks *sooo* happy on your head!"

"What!?" I cracked up laughing. "All that effort and you end up with 'my hair looks happy on my head!'"

"Oh, God! I'm so sorry! Such a damn idiot!" As his dimpled face reddened even more, my smile broadened.

What a cute, sweet man! Being so careful to be discrete that he's more obvious than a brazen cad! He's a gentleman – and adorable! Yep, Gil Justice is a genuine man with a cute-as-hell crush on me!

Though I knew, I asked. "Gil, are you trying to flirt with me?"

"I just..."

"Don't start the stuttering again, please," I teased.

"Well, I just... okay. Well, how do you tell a beautiful woman that's she's beautiful and you like her? What would *you* advise?"

All I could do was laugh, lovingly so. "Just the way you did. It worked. It made me smile. But it definitely embarrassed me. Mark my word: one day I'll quote you, and you'll be embarrassed, too."

His eyes widened. "Just you saying 'one day' is enough for me. Like 'one day' I'll still be around you?"

I cocked my left eyebrow. "Watch yourself."

Gil back-pedaled verbally, apologizing and ending with, "The last thing I want to do is make you uncomfortable."

"Well, the thing is, Gil, I plan to stay single and happy for my first year back in Rockville. Because I haven't been so successful in, uh, let's just say *several* marriages in the past."

"Hey, I'm a two-time loser myself. What could be worse than that?"

"Uh, well..."

"What? *Three* times?"

"Yep."

"But you were drinking. Those don't count."

With a snort of a chuckle, I said, "If you say so, but also two boyfriends since I've been sober. One an overeater and one an OCD freak. So maybe, just maybe... I'm thinking it might be me."

"Maybe it's what my dad used to say about me. He said that my picker was broke."

"My picker is broke?"

"Yeah, bad choices... *picks*. But the fact that you think it's your fault is just like a newcomer!"

"I am *not* a newcomer!"

"I did it, too."

"Did what?"

"In early sobriety, I took the blame for everything. Maybe it was 'just in case' because I didn't want to blame anybody else. But my sponsor said blaming yourself is usually wrong, and you know why?"

"Do tell."

"It's another symptom of 'It's all about me.'"

"Oh." *Yeah, I can see that. Actually, I KNOW I didn't do wrong with Bear. It was his decision to leave and because of his food addiction. Other than that, he was a kickass choice. With Damon... hell, who knows what had happened there, but I don't think I did anything.*

"You sound full of AA, Gil."

"To the brim. My AA sponsor is also my GA sponsor. Good 'ol Willy. He's in Louisville – I've only been back to Rockville for six months myself. And I can't bring myself to find a local sponsor because I love Willy so much. He's tough, but fair... a hundred years old but more spirited than I am."

Gil lit a cigarette and took a deep hit. "Lots of love there. He taught me to love myself, and I was hard to love."

"I'm still working on that, too. I think when that happens, it'll be Katy Bar the Door. I did a lot of, uh, stuff... hard to forgive myself for most of that. It's stuff that still brings Shame."

"Oh, yeah... our old friend, Mr. Shame."

"*Ms.* Shame, in my case."

Gil laughed and elbowed me. "Good one!"

"It's not *that* funny, but thanks for laughing."

"I have a feeling there will be many times we'll laugh together."

"You're sure assuming a lot."

"Am I?"

"Yes. And stop it! I'm not looking for a relationship, okay, so no matter how happy my hair looks, it's going to remain my hair. Understand?"

Gil's face fell hard and he looked away, mumbling something under his breath. I dared not ask him to enunciate, not sure I wanted to hear it.

So I sat back in the chair, struggling to find a way to change the subject. The truth: I was so flattered by his interest in me, and so interested in him, that I decided to ask an open-ended question, for my own selfish curiosity. After a polite pause, I asked, "So tell me about you. Give a one-paragraph summary of Gil Justice."

"One paragraph? That's a lot."

"No it's not!"

"Well, I'm not that much different from any other alcoholic. Started drinking in my early teens. Had an asshole for a father who kicked me out when I was seventeen and a sweet mother who sneaked behind him to make sure I was okay. Spent a year at a junior college, partying beyond crazy limits, dealing weed by the kilo. Then the Logan County Sherriff organized a raid on my best customer, who was also dealing, and I was *convinced* he'd name his source. Scared shitless, I took off for California.

In a broken-down car, with just a handful of dollars and lots of stupidity. My mother couldn't save me then."

"What happened? This story ends where?"

"I made it to the coast, got robbed twice, and had no money at all. Worked odd jobs while walking the streets and holding a 'Will Work for Food' sign. I just kept moving east. I wanted to go home. But my clunker of a car officially died in Laramie, Wyoming of all places."

"Not a thriving metropolis, huh?"

"And cold as hell. I don't know how or why, but a guy hired me to work the midnight shift at the only convenience store on the long highway. It wasn't *me* that got the job because I was a big mess. I've always thought it was God who put all that in my lap. *Had* to be God, because it gets better."

Eager to hear the rest of the story, I rushed him through the pause of lighting another cigarette. "The railroad had a Job Fair kind of thing in Laramie, and I applied, twenty years old and strong as a machine."

He chuckled, patting his middle. "I didn't have this back then. And lo-and-behold, they hired me. I was on a work crew, building track across the damn snow in the wilds out there. Ended up crew chief."

"What a blessing! And unless I'm wrong, the railroad pays good money, right?"

"Best around there, for sure. But it was hard. I slept in a converted boxcar, heated at least, but twelve guys to a car. No shower, no way to cook or anything. But God intervened again, I guess you'd say, and I was, uh, able to come back to Logan County to see my mom, transferring my two years of railroad seniority to CSX, which has a big hub in Loganville where we lived. It all fell together like magic. Again, *God*."

"God is pretty much *all* magic."

"True in my life, for sure."

"So that's when you got sober?"

"Hell no! I drank for another fifteen years, drinking on the job, drinking all day and all night. Our usual end." He looked at me dreamily, which kinda creeped me out, but he had a kind smile, and that odd sparkle of his eyes flashed in the porch light's glow. "That's much more than one paragraph, Lela. So it's your turn."

"No. Let's save that."

"For when? Tomorrow night? Dinner?"

"Gil! I *told* you!"

"Sorry... had to ask, thinking maybe I could trip you up."

"You'd take a date even if it was a trick?"

His eyes shot to the left, with no head movement, then returned to drill into me. "Uh, yeah. Yes, I would, but only with you. You're the new kid on the block, see, and the bachelors are waiting in line. I have to put my best foot forward and not give up before I lose you to a more charming suitor."

Suitor! How funny. And who could be more charming than THIS guy, huh? But tread softly, Lela Fox. Don't lead him on or try to tease him like you used to do to men. Enjoy the attention, but keep your distance. You're going to be joyously single. And if you think otherwise, call Oakley tonight.

When I "snapped back" after being lost in my thoughts, Gil was looking at me with a broad grin. "What?" I asked.

"Nothing. Just watching you think, hoping you're not thinking about your other choices."

"Gil!" It was accusatory, the beginning of a scolding sentence.

"No, forget it!" He waved his hands in front of his face as if erasing the comment from the air. "Just... maybe I was just wondering what goes on in that beautiful head of yours."

"That's just as bad, Gil. Seriously, stop. Just be my friend."

He sat up straight and spoke in a much louder voice. "I would *love* to be your friend."

"Good!"

"And anything more would be a bonus." Flattered and amused, I knew I had to keep up the act of defying his interest in me. I shook my head as in disbelief. He was so obviously smitten, but thankfully willing to keep himself in line with my wishes.

I laughed; he did the same. Gil's glances at me were still a little too dreamy to be comfortable, but I knew I was in control and had earned his respect. *Good job, Lela. You know how to do this after all.*

Four people spilled onto the patio, laughing and talking. One guy was who they called Round-Table Ray, who always sat at the round table just inside the door at the West 40 meeting room.

Another guy was a grouch, a younger version of the crotchety old man, still old but not as cranky. Bob Night, with pure white hair and lots of it, a stiff, well-trimmed moustache, and a rock-solid body. I thought he was

288

probably in his mid-50s, retired already, so obviously he had some bucks. A sharp dresser. And he was heading my way.

Gil whispered. "And the parade begins. Don't fall for Bob Night's bullshit, Lela. He's full of it."

"Hi, pretty lady. You're Lela, right?" It was the smooth line of Bob Night himself. I could have strung him along as I did Gil, but I decided to put him in his place.

"Don't call me pretty lady, please. Would you like it if I called you a pretty man?"

Bob's face turned as white as his hair, and Gil's laugh could've been heard two buildings over. He slapped his knee. "I guess she told *you*, Bob!" The man's white face faded into the shadows without another word.

Gil's laugh continued, loud and strong. "Oh, Lela! You crack me up. You've got *words,* girl! You cut him to the bone!"

"Serves his sexist ass right," I said.

"Old men don't understand that, ya know."

"Then they're too old for me."

"Good for you!" Gil shouted to the others now pouring from inside to the patio. "Lela just put Bob in his place! We've got a smart, sharp-tongued girl here. Damn Bob didn't have a chance!"

Then Gil reached up again with his red Solo cup, asking for a toast. Three other people stepped in to share in the click of cups and cans. Gil led the chant. "Here's to Serene Lela – don't piss her off!"

"I wasn't pissed! I just didn't want him to turn on the fake charm, know what I mean? I hate that crap."

Christy, our host, spoke up quickly. "And that's exactly what he came out here to do... to put a move on you. He was watching you two through the window."

"A voyeur, too! Jeezus!"

More people poured through the doors; obviously, the players had finished the card game. I hung out for another hour, having fun and laughing, and got to know more of the crowd than I'd been able to do at the Pancake Barn.

I decided it was time to go, using the puppy as my excuse again.

Gil asked, "When can I meet the puppy? Bring him to the club – seriously. Maybe he'll mate with Corncob's dog, the puff of fur named Marley."

"Should I point out that it might be hard to mate two male dogs?" I laughed with my head back as Gil moaned. "But seriously, I really might bring Pork Chop. Everybody would go crazy, and he'd love it, too! He's such a people dog."

"Tell him goodnight from Railroad Gil Justice." Chuckling, I assured him I would. Gil added, "And tell him to remember my name because he'll be hearing it again."

I rolled my eyes. *He's not going to give up, Lela. You may need another tactic.*

In the car, I ran the evening through my mind, replaying Gil's story and flirty comments. To the empty passenger seat, I said, "My hair looks happy on my head? What the hell is that supposed to *mean?*" Then I laughed long and loud.

What a cute man! And harmless, it seems. So why are you pushing him away so hard, Lela? Chillax, maybe, huh? And remember, a date isn't a relationship. I mean, he's fun. And funny. And polite. And filled with gratitude that he's willing to share. What could be wrong with that?

<<<<<<<<>>>>>>>

TWO FORWARD, ONE BACK
CHAPTER 38

The next morning, I called Oakley for the first time since I'd been in Rockville. The first news I shared was the evident end of my relationship with Damon. She said, "I thought that might happen."

"You *did*? Why? How? It hit me from left field."

"Too good to be true, maybe. And *of course* you're going to fight being controlled. That's what breaks up more couples than anything."

"Well, hell. I thought I really had something going. I'm so ready for a calm and peaceful life, Oakley."

"Tell me why you haven't called until now. You trying to go it alone?"

"No! I just... haven't. Things have been happening so fast, and now all the guys at this new club are honking and snorting all over me."

"Danger! Danger! Danger!" Her volume was loud, and the tone *did* resemble a siren.

"Oh, don't worry about that shit. I've got it handled. There's only one guy who could possibly interest me, anyway, and I told him tonight that I planned to be joyously single for at least a year."

"Did that stop him?"

I froze. *How does she know what happened?* "No. It didn't."

"Keep fighting. And don't just play 'hard to get,' Lela... play '*impossible* to get,' and mean it."

I chuckled. "Still running my show, Oakley?"

291

"Trying to. I think you still need, uh, let's call it guidance. Have you found a psychiatrist yet?"

"Jeez! Give me a minute to do that. But I'm okay without my meds, for the most part."

"Bullshit."

I ignored her comment. "And I've been asking around for a good sponsor up here, as you told me to do Three people have recommended the same person. She goes to the Saturday women's meeting. Tomorrow, so I'm going, too. Her name is Vickie. Black-Haired Vickie."

"Sounds good."

"And Railroad Gil gave me an official AA name. You'll never guess! Oh, Oakley, you'll laugh your ass off!"

"Tell me."

"Serene Lela."

She did laugh, and for a long time. "Well, don't laugh *all* your ass off at my expense!"

"I hope it becomes a very fitting name, Lela," she said, stifling giggles.

"Maybe I'm not so far away from being serene. I'm still walking the walk, you know."

"You're coming along. But you still think too much. Waaaay too much to be serene. That has to go, Lela. I hope a new sponsor can help you live in the present."

"Maybe..." I said, but I still had a hard time understanding the concept, to be honest. I thought thinking ahead was smart. "Oh! And I got a dog! I'll never have to sleep alone again, thanks to Pork Chop.

"Pork Chop – cute name!"

"Isn't it?!"

"So let the *dog* be the one who gives you unconditional love, okay? Instead of expecting it from some AA playboy."

"He's not a playboy!"

"I'm just afraid you'll expect the same amount of what you give. You're a giver, a go-getter, an all-or-nothing girl, Lela. And other people just don't operate that way. I don't think you understand that fact, and sooner or later, you'll fall for the first-date attention, if you know what I mean."

"Are you saying I'm not *cautious* about people?"

Oakley laughed, and I imagined her generous belly jumping up and down. "Oh, girl! You crack me up! Sorry to tell you, but you're the *least* cautious woman I've ever known. You think people are pure good, *always*. One day that will bite you in the ass."

"I don't get it.

A deep sigh came through the line and I stiffened for a piece of advice I wouldn't like; that's how Oakley acted when she was frustrated. "Just don't expect other people to have the same big heart you do."

"But why not?"

"Lela, wake up! You're a walking target! Toughen up and remember the bullshit other people have put you through. Didn't you *learn* from all that?"

"But those people were drunks!"

"You're saying AA people have no character defects?! Only Pork Chop has no character defects. Think about that, ding-dong!"

"Okay, I get it."

"Yeah?"

"Yeah."

"And everything you've learned about yourself – the woman you call 'the new me?"

"She's around sometimes," I said, smart-aleck.

"*Use* that knowledge. Expand on it. And keep redefining yourself as strong, honest, devout... but also a woman who sets and keeps boundaries."

"I know I'm strong."

"Yes, you are. You've survived what most wouldn't have... emotionally, spiritually, and physically. You've come up swinging from a rash of bullshit betrayals. You're definitively strong. And now you have to be even stronger.

"I remember the quote... the one in red? My favorite one."

"Which one?"

I said it with all the power I had. "She didn't know how strong she was until being strong was her only choice."

"Absolutely! That's a great one. And now, your choices don't include being weak. Fight, Lela."

"I'm staying sober, staying honest and kind, and staying strong."

"Good girl! So fight to also stay *single!* And call to tell me about the black-haired Vickie girl."

"I will."

"And will you share something with her? From me?" Her voice went up in tone at the end. My sigh was exaggerated. Cautiously, I asked what she wanted me to say. "Tell her that you're a classic two-years' sober sponsee, a naïve, over-trusting, over-thinking, codependent AA visionary."

"Hey! That's not nice!"

"Truth hurts sometimes. And I said 'classic.' You're not so special."

"Why would I tell her that? Said all in one sentence, it sounds like I'm a Looney Tunes."

"No, it says you're a challenge for a sponsor. But also tell her you're eager to learn."

"But, Oakley–"

"None of it is bad, kiddo. Just tell her. It proves you're a challenge. And if she accepts after knowing that, you've got a winner."

<<<<<<<<<>>>>>>>>

She was easy to spot. To-the-waist black hair, straight but shiny and healthy. Younger than me, but not by much. Giggling about the circuitous route to the front, she reached the chairman's desk and spoke confidently with one the opening readings – appropriately, the promises. Yep, she was Black-Haired Vickie.

I eyed her off and on through the meeting, noticing a striking heart-shaped face and tiny but perfectly shaped lips. She carried the perfect amount of plump, and carried it beautifully. No lipstick. No makeup at all, in fact. But she was drop-dead gorgeous, even with the sloppy outfit she wore. Then she shared; the topic was struggling to be honest, and she blew me away. Her words took me to the AA moon, described how *I* felt, then led me to what could be the ultimate solution, the ultimate serenity.

To put it mildly, I wanted what she had.

After the meeting, I made a beeline for Black-Haired Vickie but she already had an entourage surrounding her. Younger girls and older women, all seeming to hang on her every word. A tinkle of a laugh came from her smile, like wind chimes in a summer breeze. Effortlessly, she twisted her hair into a sloppy bun and stuck a pencil in it, bidding the group goodbye.

Brazen as hell, I stood in the doorway to block her way.

She focused her dinner-plate-sized green eyes on mine. Nervous, I blurted everything in one run-on sentence. "Hi Vickie, my name is Lela Fox and I'm two years' sober and I'm new to town, well, back home, actually, and I need a sponsor, and three different people have said you're the one.

My old sponsor, in Florida, I talked to her last night, and she said to tell you I was very teachable and if you could handle the challenge of a classic naïve overthinker, then I'd found a winner, so would you be my sponsor. Please?"

Her face had shown nothing but amazement during my "speech," and afterward, she cracked up laughing. Then she spoke as frantically as I had as a joke. "Hi Lela Fox, classic, naïve over-thinker from Florida but really from here." More laughter, that tinkle again.

I laughed, too, finally letting out my breath; I didn't know I'd been holding it. "But remember, I'm teachable. And red-hot for the program, Vickie. I've come a long way. I know the literature. I've done a fourth step and 25 percent of my amends. That's when I found out I was moving and my sponsor said to stop and probably start over with a Rockville sponsor because phone calls can only go so far. I want face-to-face. And, just to be honest, I'm blown away by you. The phrase, 'I want what you have' is like a throwaway phrase –that's how bad I want what you have. So will you be my sponsor?"

"Do you *think* as fast as you talk?"

I huffed a chuckle. "I'm a little nervous, actually. But mostly excited. I need a sponsor as soon as possible. People said you only took one at a time. Am I too late? Or can I be on the side for a while, if you need that. I'd give almost anything if you'd be my sponsor. You sound like Oakley – that's my sponsor now – she's awesome, but she's just... so far away."

I realized I hadn't stopped talking fast and was now repeating myself. I lowered my head. "Sorry. I'm not as crazy as I sound."

Vickie's laughter was genuine as she reached to lay a hand on my shoulder. "How about this: I just give you my number and when you settle down a little, we'll talk, okay? I do have a sponsee, but... well, it's rather complicated. And 'teachable' is about my only requirement – that is, if you can meet my demands."

"Demands?"

"You'll see. Call me." She tore a scrap of paper from a notebook she carried and scribbled on it. "I meet weekly with my sponsees, go through the Big Book and Twelve and Twelve, starting on the title page of both. Is that a problem?"

"Uh, no."

"And there's homework. Worksheets, lots of them, gratitude essays, chapter reports, journaling, and required attendance at our meetings and this one. Every week. You'll be busy, 'Ms. Eager to Learn.'"

"I can handle it! It's a lot like what I've done bef–"

She didn't let me finish. "People say I'm a tough sponsor, and I agree. Because I sponsor the same way mine does. It's hard work. Are you up for that, Lela Fox from-Florida-but-not?"

By then, I was moving in slow motion, realizing I may have over-stepped into a realm I wasn't ready for. My "no problem" answer must have come out in eighteen syllables.

Then Vickie bounced out of the door, leaving an echo of that tinkling laugh, stopping to speak to a group of women outside for the after-meeting.

<<<<<<<<<<>>>>>>>>>>

It rained that afternoon and I found myself angry about it, though I had no plans. *Maybe you're just plain ol' angry, for no reason. You deserve a little of that after what you've been through, Lela.*

Though it felt a little more "unstable" than everyday anger and anxiety, I justified it. Just the rainy weather, I thought. Or maybe it was that I had no plans.

I called Lola, and surprisingly, she answered. The rain had dampened her plans for working in a client's massive garden, she said. But she spoke in a staccato tone, acting tense and irritated, the same as she'd acted the previous two conversations we'd had.

I suspected she was mad about me cutting it off with Damon. *But I'm not really the one who cut it off, am I?*

After a while, I raised my voice. "Lola! Come on! What's *wrong* with you?"

She hem-hawed around, trying not to answer, and I had to ask her two more times.

"Lela, it's just... I'm just tired of babysitting Damon since you broke his heart."

"*Me* breaking *his* heart? Are you *kidding* me? Lola, you know that's not what happened. I told you the whole story."

"Well, he's not happy, and he's blaming you and you not taking your meds. Feels betrayed, he says." Then her voice raised an octave. "And he's expecting me to fix it! To call you and fix it."

"What?" I was baffled. "Call me to change my mind? What bullshit!"

Lola sighed. "That's what he wanted, but I refused."

"Let me point out that he hasn't called me himself!" I was the one to sigh that time. "And Lola, I *want* to talk to him, just to make sure we can stay friends. It's just clear that we don't work as a *couple*. He knew it too, at the same time I did. He said everything except the direct words."

"But what about your meds?"

"Meds have nothing to do with it!" I snapped.

Lola's silence was eerie. "Ooookay..." she said, "I guessed you'd say that."

"Of course!"

"But you haven't even had the decency to tell him you've written him off. You just disappeared!" she said.

Did I do that? Yes, but he hasn't called me, either. Did Lola or Kay-Kay say something that day when I left?

Lola interrupted my thoughts. "And your descriptions of this Railroad Gil character... it seems like you're moving on pretty fast."

"No! It's not *like* that! I'm planning to stay single – finally, for once in my life. It will be a period of growth for me. I think I've already found a sponsor, in fact."

"That's good, I guess." An angry sigh this time. "I don't even know what that means!"

Surprised by her anger, I immediately felt a wall build up between us. *Oh, no! Not with Lola! She's my best friend! I can't lose Lola, please, Dude. How do I fix this?*

"She's like a therapist, in a way, but more of a life coach."

"So I'm not good enough now? You can't trust *my* advice?"

"Oh, man... you have it all wrong. It's an AA thing. You can't coach me on how to stay sober, babe. We study AA literature, study the program, get down and dirty about feelings and motivations. Like, even deeper than you'd get with a therapist. You can't possibly understand."

Silence.

The last line echoed in my mind. Telling somebody close to you that they "can't possibly understand" is like adding a layer of stone to the wall already between you. "I'll try to help you understand, my friend. It's just... different, but it goes hand-in-hand with listening to your advice, too! Of *course* I trust what you tell me."

"But you won't listen to me about your meds *or* about Damon." *Oh shit... here it comes again.*

"It's not going to work with Damon, Lola, no matter how much you want it to."

"And no matter how much *Damon* wants it to?"

I laughed. "Trust me – Damon doesn't want it to work, either. Well, maybe if it works exactly as he's planned if I was his puppet. But I'm not going to be micro-managed, see. And surely you'd know that!"

A silent pause, then I pushed forward. "I love you, Lola. Whether I'm with Damon or not can't change *our* friendship, right?" My voice squeaked in hopefulness. *Please, Dude, let her agree with me.*

But she dodged the question. "When is your doctor's appointment?"

"Always that! Quit bugging me about it! I'll get an appointment soon."

Silence on the line. Only heavy breathing from my end – the result of my angry outburst. Lola said, "Well, I've got to get off this horn. I'm cleaning the house today."

My heart sunk; I saw it like a Dali painting, slumping over my knee bones and dripping to the floor. "Lola, no! You're my best friend!"

"Of course," she said in the flattest tone possible, "but the kitchen floor needs a mop."

"Are you, uh, breaking up with me?"

"Oh, don't be silly." It wasn't a friendly comment but a terse, almost hateful one.

My heart continued to slump within my body, and I did the same by slumping on the sofa. The burn of tears came to my eyes and my throat closed up, making me unable to speak.

I didn't want to hang up before we'd put things back the way they were, and my face contorted like a begging child's. I fought to tell her to wait, to not hang up. But she didn't give me a chance. "Talk to you later, Lela." And the line went dead.

I fell to a prone position, in slow motion. *What just happened? Did I just lose a friend? My BEST friend? All because I've chosen a different path – one she doesn't agree with? All because she doesn't understand AA? Supports Damon instead of me? Thinks I'm crazy without a doctor?*

A tear rolled from the corner of my eye, and I closed them. A bevy of tears fell as I imagined a mutating wet spot on the leather of my sofa. I didn't care if it would leave a stain, couldn't afford to care, I thought. *My "old friends" are no longer a part of my life. Just because I'm sober and have boundaries.*

That's all I thought was wrong.

Then I spoke aloud to Dude, "I just want to be a normal person who doesn't drink! I just want to be normal!" I rolled over on my stomach and let the tears flow, my emotions at an all-time low.

And the rain continued to fall.

<<<<<<<<<>>>>>>>>

In my office that afternoon, I clinked and clunked on the keyboard, not accomplishing much, but going through the motions. My tears had dried, but my heart still felt as if it'd been stomped and drowned in acid.

Work-wise, I was still stuck in Chapter 10, which would be the longest and most technical of them all. Despite that challenge, I'd been slack in my work hours that week and knew I had to get *something* done to report to Jeffrey on Monday's phone conference.

Mike Barton was also going to be on the call, too. I supposed he wanted to check on his long-distance contract writer, making sure I wasn't cheating on my timesheet.

I hadn't cheated. It showed ten hours over the past workweek. I closed my eyes and shivered. *What the hell are you doing, Lela? TRYING to screw it all up? This opportunity was a gift from Dude, and you don't want to mess with a miracle!*

I sighed, and moved forward, still half-distracted, but some progress was made. Though I'd only worked four hours, I noted 6.25 on my official timesheet. When I focused on that number, my peripheral vision clouded. It seems my writing throbbed in a beam of sunlight that hadn't penetrated the room. *Watch yourself, Lela Fox. Be honest, be sincere, be sober, be happy.*

Before I dared to change the 6.25 to the correct number, I jumped from my office chair and dove into the shower. *I'll go to the 7:00 speaker meeting at West 40. Evidently, your only friends are going to be AA friends anyway, with Lola out of the picture. The Lela/Lola magic has been broken. What will I do without her?*

I felt betrayed and misunderstood. Abandoned.

You need a meeting, girl.

I never talked to Lola or Damon again after that day, and slowly lost touch with Kay-Kay and almost all the folks in my early-back-to-Rockville days.

I heard through the grapevine that Damon/Lola/Jesse continued their three-pronged friendship for another year... until Jesse got fired from the Post Office for insubordination.

He filed a lawsuit for discrimination, hiring a lawyer who was an old, old friend of ours, one of the drinking crowd but not an alkie. Slowly, Jesse's pie-in-the-sky lawsuit traveled to the federal level as he lost in each lower court.

The longer Jesse was unemployed, the more he changed. Over a years' time, he morphed into an angry and bitter man, and soon after, Lola moved out. A few months later, Damon sold his condo to move in with Jesse, helping him with the bills.

Then Jesse had a stroke – almost died. Lola and Damon both rushed to his side, but the part of Jesse's brain that loved people was gone. He became a shell of himself, angry about everything and distrustful of every person on earth.

Except for one crazy woman he met online.

This nitwit woman – 100+ pounds overweight, "butt-ugly," and mean to dogs, according to rumor – convinced Jesse to sign everything he owned into her name, appointed herself Jesse's power of attorney, medical decision-maker, and pushed him in a wheelchair to the Rock County courthouse to get married.

All this happened within a two-day period.

Of course, Ms. Butt-Ugly immediately kicked Damon out on the street, filing an order of protection against him and lying about his threats to harm her. All Damon wanted was the best for Jesse, and that, of course, threatened her authority in taking over Jesse's life.

That was the last I heard for many years. Somehow, I felt fine in not contacting my friends to find out more.

But twenty years later, as I write this book, I friended Damon on Facebook and we ended up living within five miles of each other. So we started hanging out every so often, going to lunch, talking about the twists our lives had taken in our years apart, and talking about our adventures and mis-adventures of the past.

I like him, wish him the best. And I still consider him my guardian angel for bringing me home. But I'm also sorry about what I put him through, and made amends as best I could.

In breaking up with me, he did what he had to do. I don't blame him at all. A Bi-Polar alcoholic is never easy to manage, and I added a few more wrinkles to that. I still love ya, Damon, and hope you find a woman who'll be what you want her to be.

<<<<<<<>>>>>>

SEVEN DAYS LATER
CHAPTER 39

The second I parked the Jetta, Railroad Gil was at my car door. He wore a bright-royal shirt, which I knew would set off those incredible eyes before I even saw him. He looked fabulous, happy. And, despite the dampness of the day's rain, he wore shorts. Baggy ones.

His calves were massive, but I noticed the tiny little ankles and narrow feet at the end of his sturdy legs. *How do those little things support such a big man? His shoulders are even bigger than my dad's... but he has ankles as delicate as my mom's.* It was a disconcerting sight, yet somehow... charming. Just like his personality. A little quirky and fun.

He took my hand to help me get out of the car, which made me roll my eyes. He looked at me quizzically, but blurted words as if he'd been holding them inside for a week. "I heard you talked to Black-Haired Vickie! She asked me about you."

"She did?" *She did? She did! Wow.*

"She said you were funny." Suddenly, a breeze passed us, a surprisingly warm breeze. The front must be blowing through, I thought.

When I looked back at Gil, he was smiling at me, glowing in that half-dreamy look he'd had the night before. I asked, "What? Why are you looking at me like that?"

"There's that beautiful, happy hair on your head again. Your curls make me smile. You must work hard to make them so perfect."

"I spend zero time on my hair. Just squeeze it with a towel. No brushing or combing because it has a mind of its own."

"I love a girl who can get ready fast."

I chuckled. "Well, the face is another matter."

"And a beautiful face it is..."

"Stop, Gil. No compliments. You're making me uncomfortable."

His mouth opened in surprise as his face reddened. "Okay, okay. Forgive me, it's just... I..."

"And don't start the stuttering again, either." I was teasing but said it with enough force to get my point across.

"Okay then... since we're 'friends' now, can I sit with you at the meeting? You sit on the smoking side, right?"

"It's not an AA meeting if I can't smoke and drink coffee!"

"Spoken like a good alcoholic!"

He put his hand on my shoulder to gently lead me toward the club entrance. A gentlemanly move which reminded me of my father, how he "ushered" mom in and out of everywhere. I vacillated between thinking I should shake his arm away or enjoy the hell out of being treated so kindly.

There's something about this man... like John Wayne but ultra-friendly. The strange comparison shook me, but it was very descriptive, and the thought ran through my mind several times during the walk to the gathered crowd.

The speaker was excellent; Gil said he was a good friend of his: "a good buddy with good recovery" had been his quote. The speaker, "Danno the Manno," had overcome seemingly impossible circumstances while sober, yet didn't drink. Crisis after crisis, yet he stayed sober.

The speaker mimicked squeaky voices for the self-talk going on both sides of his head, like a puppet show. I got so tickled; I almost fell out of my chair. Gil got the giggles from laughing at me.

On the other hand, I recognized what those voices were saying. I was my own worst critic, and that was his point. It turned out to be a strong message. Acceptance is key and all that good stuff.

Our speaker Danno the Manno joined Gil and me outside, and Gil gushed with thanks and compliments for Danno. It was as gushing as his weirdo "happy hair" compliment. *So maybe that's just how he is. Maybe he doesn't particularly like me at all.*

But when he walked me to my car fifteen minutes later, he asked, "Hey, since we're friends, let's have dinner on Monday night. At OCI Tavern. See, just a burger."

"But, Gil... I *told* you–"

"Just as friends. What's a burger between friends?" he said quickly. To turn him down, it seemed, would be rude. I didn't want to piss him off, but I didn't want to give him any ideas, either.

"Friends only?"

"I promise."

During the pause, my brain was on overdrive. My gut felt light and airy... and no with direction found, I said, "Okay. Sure. What time. I'll meet you there."

"Parking sucks on campus. Let's meet here. But, fair warning: my work schedule is unpredictable as hell. I'll tell you why at dinner. So if I have to cancel, please know it's *not* because I don't *want* to go."

Confused, I asked, "But why is your work schedule so unpredictable? I thought the trains had to run right on time, every time."

Gil laughed. "Good one. No, basically, I'm on a roster that rotates with the other guys 24/7. I get only two hours' notice and I have to drive to Pipertown, an hour away. That's why I carry a beeper." He paused, then grinned. "I bet you thought I was a fancy business executive, carrying a beeper."

"You're not?" I laughed, looking him directly in the eye. "I admit, I wondered about that beeper when I saw it on your belt. Not many of those around anymore."

"Keeps work and social life separate. But – this sucks – I'm always on-call, and sometimes have to stay overnight in Loganville. Hell, sometimes it's a 48-hour shift! It sucks. And that's why it's hard to have a family life."

I thought about that on the way home. *Never knowing when you'll work? A 48-hour shift? How does he manage life around that? Does it include holidays, too?*

I said of prayer of thanks to Dude for giving me the freedom I to work when and where I wanted. *What a blessing!* Then the voice UNDER the voice in my head spoke: *Then why aren't you working, Lela?*

<<<<<<<<>>>>>>>

CHEESEBURGER CLASSIC
CHAPTER 40

OCI was an acronym for Old College Inn, the historic tavern and grill on the TSU campus. Some would call it a dive-bar – it was exactly that in the late seventies when I was a student – but they'd remodeled several times, each an improvement in looks and what you'd call acceptability. Yet OCI was still as casual and rowdy as a tavern hangout should be, even that night in 2001.

Gil and I both ordered the Cheeseburger Classic and watched the students playing video games as they downed pitchers of beer. Though they were loud and probably drunk, it didn't bother me because... well, they're students, doing what students should do.

When I told Gil I'd graduated from TSU, he was more than surprised.

"I thought you would've gone to some fancy New York school."

I crumpled my brow. "Why would you think that?"

"Because you're so well-spoken and obviously. And so worldly, it seems."

With a sideways look, I rolled my eyes. "What you don't know is that at heart, I'm just a simple Tennessee girl with old-fashioned values. Honestly. I discovered it when I got sober. It turns out, I want to be like my Goody-Two-Shoes mother."

"No shit?"

"No shit at all. It took a lot of good sponsorin' to give me permission to find my own way, but my parents are ultra-important to me. Pleasing them is a must, in my mind."

"Good for you to have a good family. Not many alkies are so lucky."

"I know. I was shocked to find that out at first, with my Beaver Cleaver example growing up. Are your parents still in Loganville?"

"Dad died three months to the day after my son died. And mom passed two years later. She died alone and lonely and it broke my heart. But with my work schedule, it was hard to see her."

"That's sad. I'm sorry you had to go through that, Gil. I can't imagine losing my parents."

"It sure put my life in a new perspective. My mom was my hero. My dad, not so much. I couldn't even go to the hospital to say goodbye."

I froze. *Another man with a lousy dad relationship. Like Bear. Like Miller McKeown. Like a million wounded men.* "Oh, that sucks."

"Yeah..."

Okay, Lela, change the subject. "So tell me how you know my brother-in-law John, the Little General."

His face went from zero to sixty in one second flat. "He's a damn-nice guy! And the union rep at his terminal office, did you know that?"

"I knew something like that. Not exactly sure what it means, but..."

"Well, I served on the union's Safety Committee with him a few years ago. We'd howdy-up at conferences in Nashville and stuff. He's good people, John is."

"By the way, his mother died yesterday."

"Yesterday? Oh, no! That's bad."

"He and Karen are on their way for the funeral as we speak."

"Well, at least the railroad has good bereavement pay. He'll be off for five days, full-pay."

"That's good." Then it hit me: Karen had tried to tell me about John's weird schedule on the railroad, but she had always taken it in stride. There'd been Thanksgivings without John because he had to work. I couldn't remember a Christmas without him, but many times Karen would show up at the farm alone. I just seemed to not bother her, and I never asked about it.

The server brought our burgers and the conversation turned to moans of delight in the taste of the burgers. Gil said, "Nothing better than the OCI

Classic Cheeseburger. I wish I could bottle and sell them." I got a vision of a burger in a glass bottle and laughed. It became a ten-minute discussion of how ridiculous it would be for us to go into business together in building a burger like a ship in a bottle, how to market them, the advertising, and follow-up.... all kinds of dumb ideas. We laughed long and loud.

"You're so much fun, Lela Fox. Sharp as a knife, but so down to earth. I really-really like you." I'd been looking directly at him when he said that and my stomach took a flip. My cheeks reddened because I realized that I really-really liked him, too.

So now is the time you start scolding him about liking you, Lela... reminding him that you're together as friends only. You're not going to jump into a relationship, dammit, no matter how nice this Railroad Gil happens to be. Right? Right. Remember what Oakley said. Chant it if you have to, just... chill. Even Barb told you to keep it in your pants. And definitely don't get your heart involved. Please!

Yet I said nothing.

"Ya know, I should take you to the yard office where I work sometimes. It's just down the road a piece."

"Your Kentucky is showing... 'down the road a piece.'"

Gil laughed. "Yes, it's still in there. I try, but the guys I work with are 100 percent country-fried. If I don't speak Kentucky at work, they make fun of me, call me Fancy-Pants and shit like that."

"A tough group, huh?"

"The worst. Manly-men from hell."

"You really don't seem like a... what's the word? A laborer? I mean, you're well-spoken yourself, and I know you've spent time away from the buckle of the Bible Belt we live in."

"I had a little college. Mostly I'm an autodidact."

"What? Auto-what?"

"I know a word you don't?!"

"Never heard of it."

"Just means self-taught..."

"Cool word, I'll use it somewhere. Do you have a note pad?"

He laughed. "You serious?"

"As a heart attack." We laughed about being graduates of the School of Hard Knocks. I said, "Aren't we all those kinds of grads, really? Especially alcoholics. We've all had some knocks or we wouldn't be sober."

I fell into a memory bank of the knocks I'd taken... the hell I'd risen from, seeing visions of Stuart Weinstein the night he said he was foot-raped, the night I fell into the campfire on a camping trip, the night I cried in a janitor's closet at a Halloween party – wearing a bee costume. I'd been convinced that my husband was flirting with a princess on the dance floor. *What a pitiful drunk you were, Lela. And how blessed to be sober!*

I looked up at Gil, beaming with a smile. "I'm just so grateful sometimes I think I'll explode."

"And it shows all over your gorgeous face."

Dammit! "Gil! Stop! No flirty compliments, remember?!"

He backed down immediately. "Sorry, sorry. I won't do it again. But hey..."

"Hey what?"

"Let's get out of here. I'm serious about going to the yard office. You can see the trains, see what I do. And I can check the computer to see your brother-in-law on the roster."

I thought about it. It was a weird request, an odd place to go. "To tell the truth, Gil. I'm afraid of trains. When I was little, I was afraid of loud noises and called them 'bigs,' cried and cried over the bigs."

He chuckled. "They *are* big. 200 tons each car if it's fully loaded with grain."

"Damn. That's definitely big." Another thought struck me about trains. "And, once, just a week or so before I got sober, I sat by the railroad tracks, trying to time my jump before the train passed. Death by train sounded like the way to go. Much better than living like I was living."

He paused, rubbed his five o'clock shadow, thinking. "You know, as the conductor, I would have been the one to walk to the front of the train and find you. I know several who've had to do that. Thank God, not me. And those guys are all screwed up seeing that. Complete PTSD."

The buzz started between my ears, this one based on Shame. In a fog, I marveled, "I never thought about what it would do to the train people."

You were a selfish drunk. But the bottom had fallen out of my stomach, the taste of rotten cheese arose, and I feared I'd lose the burger. *What kind of shitty thinking was that? What were you thinking? How COULD you?*

"Whew!" I shook my head. "Bad memories."

"Another reason to be grateful. You don't have to feel that way ever again."

"Right." But the churning in my head had begun. I was shaken up. *Gil walking on those rocks to see my squashed and bloody body, seeing my ugly life splashed on the metal rails.*

<<<<<<<<<<>>>>>>>>>>

We climbed into his Burgundy Maxima serendipitously parked right outside the door, and I decided it was cool to say what I thought the first time. "Do you, like, *live* in this car?"

Gil laughed. "Looks like it, I know. But like I told ya, I have to dash to Pipersville at any given moment, so I keep clothes and stuff with me."

"But you don't have, um... a suitcase?"

"Works just as well to keep them spread all over, I guess."

I could have noted that messiness as a character flaw or I could've laughed. I chose to laugh.

We parked in the gravel lot after Gil got out to open the pad-locked fence gate. The "yard," as he called it, was *huge*, filled with various lengths of train segments, sitting silently in the dark. An eerie sight, hard as steel; it looked like a haunted movie set, and I shivered.

Seeing me reacting to the threat, Gil commented. "It's between shifts, or you'd also be hearing the 'bigs' you fear. Yardmen here build the trains for the local runs. That's my goal for the end of my career – to have enough seniority to claim those jobs. And stay at home instead of being on the road like I am. A predictable six-hour shift sounds like gravy compared to those damn overnights."

Not knowing what to say, I said nothing, anxious and eager to get inside the metal building and out of the dark, away from the scary place called the yard.

I stepped inside on worn linoleum. *Oh. My. God.* What a dump, a mess. Like an I-don't-give-a-damn bachelor pad with cast-off furniture and molded plates of food on every surface. The only difference was two rows of lockers.

"Welcome to my home away from home!" Gil said, spreading his arms wide to show the room. "Chill for a minute. I'll make us some coffee. It sucks as far as coffee goes, but it's free."

I paused too long. "I'd pay for decent coffee in a decent place!" I said, but he'd already disappeared into the dark side of the trailer, out of sight. I dared not sit, waiting for a rat to scurry across the floor and climb up the leg of the broken-down desk.

Even the computer was decrepit, a decade-old machine at best. The sofa was brown and gold plaid, from the seventies, with a missing foot. It sat at a curious angle, seemingly ready to tip. The mismatched trio of chairs looked like they came from a sleazy doctor's waiting room. Only one was not upholstered, a molded plastic scoop like from a high-school cafeteria, in pumpkin orange. But that's the chair I picked, the only one safe from bed bugs and other such cooties.

I waited. And waited. Wondering what was taking him so long... what was in the dark side of the metal trailer that would stop him from "entertaining his guest."

Minutes later, he appeared with two Styrofoam cups. "Your beverage, madame," he said with joking formality, then passed a cup to my waiting hand. "I assume you're black."

That struck me as hilariously funny. I laughed hard enough to spill a drop or two of the coffee. "Actually, I've been a Caucasian all my life."

Gil hadn't realized he'd make such a dumb comment, and the grin that followed was a heartwarming smile from the core of him, it seemed. "You know what I mean, ding-bat."

"Hey! Only *I* can call people ding-bats. That's my dad's line, actually."

"My dad, too. Maybe it was the phrase of the times. *All in the Family*, wasn't it? Archie Bunker?"

"Yep. I think you're right." Then I took a new stance. "Okay, then, I'll call you a doomus. My son's invented word for dumbass. He was about eight when he came up with that."

"Funny."

"It *was*. Doesn't sound so funny now."

A tense silence filled the room... as if we'd run out of things to talk about. I couldn't stand the silence and summed up the situation. "I'll tell ya, Gil, this is a funny place to take a girl on a first date."

He spun around in the desk chair, creating a metal-against-metal shrieking sound. "Ah! She calls it a *date!* A *first* date! Yay! That's what I was hoping you'd think! Because that's exactly how I see it. The first of many more."

I sunk into the orange plastic scoop of a chair, realizing I'd screwed up royally. "I didn't really mean it like that, Gil! Please don't think–"

He interrupted with a mega-excited voice. "Oh yes, I *can* think that! Because you said it with*out* thinking! So that's what you're *really* thinking. And I'm happy! Very happy!"

I looked at my feet, wondering how to answer his exuberance. He was right, though; I realized about halfway through dinner that I wanted it to be a date.

Gil was a great guy. An interesting guy. And genuinely crazy about me. The butterflies in my belly had begun about an hour ago, still fluttering through the fear of the rail cars, the shivering fear of the railroad track memory. *And now he says he's happy... and I think, oh, Dude, I think I'm happy, too.*

Interrupting my scary/happy thoughts, Gil asked in a rushed voice. "Lela? Do you believe in love at first sight?"

The metronome of fear swung hard. "No, Gil, I don't. And don't say that. You're scaring me."

But you're not scared, are you, Lela? You were thinking the same damn thing, weren't you?

<<<<<<<>>>>>>

RESISTING ANSWERS
CHAPTER 41

The next morning, I called early, knowing she'd just be getting home from an overnight shift at the hospital. "Oakley, I think I'm in trouble." I wrung my hand together, worried about letting myself be swayed too early in a relationship.

Alarmed, she shouted, "What kind of trouble? Tell me!" She must have thought it was something outside of my head, like I was in danger or something.

"No... nothing *external*. I'm fine in that way. But I'm all-in, I think, for the guy I told you about. Railroad Gil."

"No! You promised to go solo!"

"Yeah, but... Oakley. It's just, well, do you believe in love at first sight?"

"Not for *sane, practical, sober people*."

My stomach sunk. I didn't really expect her to understand, but decided to give it my best shot, hoping for a word of Oakley's approval. "But he has twelve years clean! He's *surely* sane, practical, and sober."

"I don't care about *his* attitude! My point is, dear, *you* aren't acting sane, practical, and sober!"

In reply to her deep, exasperated sigh, I asked, "Are you getting fed up with me?"

"Definitely fed up when you take backward steps on something you know to be wrong."

"Wrong? It's not *wrong,* maybe just too fast."

"Moving too fast is wrong! Trust me. I know you."

"But..." I blew an impatient sigh. "It just feels so *right.* He's a nice guy, a real social butterfly type, a leader in the club. He's been nominated for the board! Everybody *else* respects him, why can't I?"

"Respecting him doesn't mean screwing him."

"Whoa, there... I'm not ready for *that!*"

"Uh, do you think you can date somebody forever without sex happening eventually? Even scared and sober, how long did you wait with Bear? With Damon?"

I sighed. Of course, Oakley was right. "But what do I do? I find myself thinking about him *all the time!* He's so sweet! And so cute! Just charming as hell, Oakley. He's strong and good-looking. In fact, he looks a lot like Bear – *that* big and powerful. Evidently, it's what I like."

"Stop talking! Did you talk to the new sponsor lady?"

"You're changing the subject?"

"Why wouldn't I? You're not listening to a word I say," she said with a huff. And her comment gave me pause. Oakley was right. I'd made my decision, despite my sponsor's advice. That was unlike me, really.

But Oakley never warned me against dating Bear! I chuckled at my own thought, knowing it was ridiculous. *Well, because she knew him personally, nit-wit. And you'd told her so much about Damon before you two became an item, she had to admit he was good for you.*

This... Gil is just something too new for her. If she knew him, she'd encourage you to go for it. Oh, I wish she was here!

"Oakley, I miss you."

"Doubtful."

"Oh, Jeez. You're mad at me. You're mad as hell."

"Just disappointed. Sometimes you seem so sane and sober-minded, then you go off the deep end. Are you taking your meds?"

I dared not tell her the truth, so I lied. "Of course I am! What do you think? That I'm crazy?" Then I laughed. "No pun intended."

"No pun taken. This is serious."

"I know! But I'm fine, Oakley, just fine. I wouldn't make a decision this big without thinking about it hard. And praying about it, which I have."

"Why don't you pray for another week? Just seven days. Will you at least do that? I'll stoop to say I'm *begging* you to do that. And maybe in that time, you'll talk to the new sponsor you told me about...?"

"Oh. That. I've already talked to her. I sounded like an idiot when I asked her if she'd sponsor me, though. I couldn't stop talking... rambled and rambled."

Oakley laughed. "Like you always do when you're nervous?" More laughter. But, as part of the seven-day favor, talk to her about this railroad guy. She may confirm he's a nice guy for all I know, but remember – *that is not the point!* Do you understand?"

"I think so. *Timing* is the point, right?"

"Bingo."

I paused in the silence that followed. "Okay, Oakley. You've never led me astray. If you feel that strongly about it, I'll wait. I can do seven days. Not only that, I have tons of work to do on the software manual. I've got to stay home and work instead of going to two meetings a day."

"Work, then. You're settled in and ready, surely."

"I barely faked my way through this morning's conference call." *And I lied on my timesheet.*

Oh shit! Don't tell her!

I cleared my throat, putting on my best front. "Overall, I'm doing okay. Staying honest. Making progress."

"Let's hold it to five meetings in the next seven days, okay? And – do it, dammit! – forty hours of work, like normal people do. Okay?"

I could feel Oakley pressuring me to re-focus my energy, but I couldn't let the focus go. "But Oakley, I just feel so ready for a new chapter in my life!"

She laughed! I was incensed. "A chapter in a bad novel. If you want a story, let Dude turn the pages, my dear. The chapter you're on is exactly seven days long.

"He's not always around, anyway. Works crazy hours at the railroad."

"His schedule doesn't determine yours in *any* case."

"And I'm making tons of friends at the AA club. Even better, I'm going to a big-time church meeting on Sunday night." I dared not tell her that Gil had asked me to go to that meeting with him – just the two of us.

With my head hung low, I signed off the call, kicking myself in the ass for lying to Oakley so many times.

Why, Lela? Why? It's Guilt that makes you lie, right? So you KNOW you're doing wrong. The only answer is to lie about it. It's about lying, not about taking your psych meds, not about your timesheet, and not about the next scheduled date with Gil.

And you didn't mention Gil's gambling addiction because you knew she'd freak and send out Oakley's Army.

I spoke to the walls of my office. "Okay, Lela, get honest. Right now. Get out your journal." I wrote for a half-hour, not stopping to dot my i's or correct the punctuation – a squeamishly tricky thing for a writer to do. I poured another cup of coffee before reading it back to myself.

With emotional ouches in every sentence, I realized I was heading down a dangerous path of dishonesty and self-serving behavior.

"Starting today. I change. Today. But for now, I work, and keep an accurate timesheet, carving the 2.25 hours I cheated with last week. Then I can hold my head high. I'll be okay."

Affirming a more-righteous path, so to speak, I felt the weight of a zillion pounds lifted off my shoulders. Free, open, ready to tackle new challenges, and more determined than ever to stay on the wise side of sobriety.

My prayers were typically tearful and silent, and I rarely "said" a word, even in my mind. Just the connection was a vibrating wavelength of communication between Dude and me, beautifully understood on both sides. But that day, I spoke aloud, overcome with Willingness and Gratitude.

In a much more formal tone than usual, I asked for help and opened my heart to answers. I sent a flurry of thank you's and felt them absorbed by the incredible peace above.

To tell you the truth, Dude hadn't changed since the first time I'd seen him. He simply sat there... at the same picnic table, smoking the same cigarette, with the same ultra-peaceful smile. Behind him, though, the curious yellow glow was pulsating, more orange at the edges. Like somebody or some*thing* was there and also connecting with me. And maybe like Dude was directing it.

In my mind, I asked Dude what the orange glow was supposed to mean... and the entire vision faded away slowly. Like a dream, but so very, very real.

<<<<<<<<>>>>>>>>

BLACK-HAIRED & BAD-ASS
CHAPTER 42

I did as I was told. I canceled the date with Gil for the Sunday night church meeting and kept my head in the computer to finish the difficult Chapter 10 of the user's manual.

On Tuesday, I called Black-Haired Vicki for the first time. After the greeting, she said, "I was wondering if you'd ever call. It's been three days since we spoke."

Surprised, I answered, "I didn't know that was part of the deal, uh, to call immediately."

"Depends on how badly you want me to be your sponsor."

Oops. Lela, you screwed up. "Vickie, I can tell you a thousand percent that I want you to be my sponsor. And, in fact, I've found out in these three days that I need you even more than I thought. I won't miss a day again. You can trust me on that."

"Good. So tell me where you are in your program." It was said in a happy voice, but it wasn't a friendly question. All-business.

I tried to be all-business, too. "I've done a comprehensive fourth step – a full notebook's worth. My old sponsor, Oakley, had me go deeper than most do, I think. No bullet points. Instead, multiple paragraphs to detail what I did and how I feel about it, what should've happened, what to do next time, etcetera, etcetera. And I've made amends to the key people: my parents, my son and my sisters, a few more."

"And how did that go."

Instantly terrorized, remembering pain I'd never shared with anyone, I started crying. "My son, Bo, is only nineteen. And my sponsor said that after my, uh... speech, I should ask if there's anything *they* want to say."

"I agree."

I wiped my nose with a Kleenex. "Well, turns out, Bo had three specific events that still pissed him off, he said. And he told the stories, with details, and I don't even remember!" I stifled a loud boo-hoo. "Vickie, it absolutely broke my heart."

"Then it was a good amends, I'd say."

"I thought it was supposed to make me feel *better*, not worse!"

"The 'better' comes in the long run. And the truth hurts sometimes, Lela."

"That sure as hell did."

"No cussing, please."

I froze. *What did she just say?* "Uh... really?"

"Absolutely. Sober, productive citizens have more to offer than nasty words. And they say you're a writer? Surely you have better ways to express yourself."

"Okay..." I was shocked. *Is she a Goody-Two-Shoes? Some kind of church freak?*

"It's also a discipline thing, Lela. A sponsor-to-sponsee exercise. Didn't you go to treatment somewhere?"

"Yes, in Florida."

"Then you understand discipline for discipline's sake. I'm not trying to be bossy – it's just that cussing is one of the things alcoholics can change to raise themselves from the depths of the lower echelon. Plus, it's easy and it's free."

I still couldn't reply, wondering if I'd just met the biggest challenge of my sober life.

Vickie continued, "It's not that I'm so much *against* it as just... I'm not *for* it. I mean, don't freak out. But, repeat: No cussing."

"Uh, that will be hard for me. I have what my dad calls a potty mouth."

"Then you get the concept. If you can not cuss around your parents, and your son, I assume, then just carry that forward to your daily life."

I sat in amazement at the turn of the conversation, half-worried about having such a strict sponsor, and half-excited about the opportunity to change in ways I'd not yet envisioned.

"I'll try my best, Vickie. Because I want you as a sponsor. But how's my timing? They say you only sponsor one woman at a time."

"One is fading and there's no one in line, so yes, I can be your sponsor. The question is... can you be my sponsee."

"Yes. I'm sure of it." *Damn-sure, actually, but you can't say that.*

"So call me. My work hours vary, but I'm always off on Wednesday nights and weekends. So just call whenever. Every day. Leave a message. And always-always call back if you need to talk. Where is your head?"

The line struck me as funny. "Right here, balancing on top of my neck."

She giggled, the tinkling laugh that endeared me the day I met her. "You're silly. I like that."

"Yes, I'm silly. But most people groan instead of laugh."

"I guess I'm silly, too. But, actually, that was a legitimate question. Where is your head? What are you thinking?"

I thought about telling her of my aching for Railroad Gil, and asking her what she thought. Maybe, just maybe, she'll give me the go-ahead. *But for now, fake your sanity, highlight your readiness for a relationship, tell her you're strong in recovery.*

"I'm strong, and not just because I have to be. I'm determined to excel sober. In fact, I have a sign on my refrigerator that says exactly that: Excel Sober. But my story is a series of jagged peaks and valleys, even since I've been sober."

"We'll get into that soon. How's Wednesday?"

"*This* Wednesday?"

"*All* Wednesdays. For our study session. How about Perkin's, the one near Bluff Drive?"

"Works for me."

"Okay. 7:00, every Wednesday, with absolutely no exceptions. Well, unless your grandmother dies."

I laughed. "You *are* tough."

"You'll be glad about it later, I hope." Then the tinkling laugh. *How could such a hard ass be so cute?*

"I need you to make a gratitude list every day, too. Bring them to our meeting."

"My former sponsors made me do that, too. Five things with no repeats."

"Then make it *ten* things for now. And we can talk about it. Remember, no repeats or simple stuff like the roof over your head. Be silly if you want."

"That sounds great! Oh, Vickie, I'm fired up as hhhhh–" *Oops. No cussing.* "I'm fired up as heck!" Then I sighed, "'But 'heck' doesn't express how excited I am!"

"You'll find ways to rephrase things, Ms. Writer."

"I'll be working on it."

I hung up the phone and sat in amazement for a minute or two. *Do you want to get better really quick? Then you've found the right sponsor. Even if she turns out to be an AA Nazi, you'll learn. And isn't that what you want?*

I spoke aloud. "Yes, that's what I want. Big time."

<<<<<<<<<<>>>>>>>>>>

We started on the title page of the Big Book. Vickie said, "Get a pen." I did. "Circle the word third from the last in the subhead. Notice it says '*recovered*' from alcoholism. *Past tense.* Not 'recover*ing*' like we usually say.

Then she pulled out a sheet of paper, a photocopy of a dictionary page, with the definition of 'recovered' circled in red: "Write this down, too: 'Recovered' means... to regain something lost or taken, to reclaim from a 'bad' state, to regain health and strength after illness or trouble, and the fourth – to regain former *or better* state."

As I scribbled, referring to the paper now and then, she said, "According to definition number four, it's not just getting back to what you had, but to gain more than you lost."

She paused so I could write. I asked for a few reminders, then huffed a sigh. "With all this discussion on just the title page... are we going to study each *word* in this book?" My attitude was a mix of awe and disdain.

"You have a problem with it?" She pursed her lips, but somehow the friendly look remained. Vickie's beauty couldn't be distorted by her hard-ass tactics.

"Uh, no. I guess not."

"Then let's continue."

And continue we did. Vickie had me draw the cycle of RIDS: Restless, Irritable, Discontent, Serenity, repeat, and repeat, and repeat.

With the first "real page" in the book, Vickie noticed mine was already colorful; marked with highlighters in various colors and a variety of pencils. She showered me with compliments of my study in the past. But I could already tell that her brand of study was above and beyond anything prior sponsors had taught me.

I used a black pen this time, underlining everything Vickie pointed out, and it was pretty much everything. I asked, "Can you recite this book in your sleep."

That tinkling laugh again. "Parts of it, probably. But it's our guide to staying sober, our 'Bible,' so to speak, and it deserves my respect. Yours, too."

"I just don't want to be a Big Book thumper. I can't stand those people."

"You have a choice in the matter, silly. You can choose to thump or not thump. But having a foundation of what this book is about, from beginning to end, results in strong recovery. It is your future, and if nothing else, the basis of your goals. How many times have you heard the promises?"

I shrugged. "Every meeting, so hundreds."

"But do you really know how to obtain them?"

"Keep coming back? It works if you work it? Don't drink and don't die?"

"Of course all *those*. But to be... call it 'painstakingly honest,'" she said, "Honesty requires practice. Work. Baby steps until you convince *yourself* that being honest is what scares the demons away."

"I love that phrase!"

"Without honesty, we have nothing... can't go forward. So every time we meet, I want you to tell me a little secret about yourself... something you're ashamed of, maybe. Something you think may drive you to places and into thoughts you know are unhealthy. You don't have to suffer alone. Don't let Shame rotate forever in your head and stifle your growth."

"I have a lot of Shame. *A lot!* In fact, it all started from Shame, too, at age thirteen with my first drink."

"Shame can only go away by forgiving yourself, and forgiving yourself is a process. Will you let me help you with that?"

"Oh, Vickie! You don't know how much I'd *love* for that to happen!"

"Then that's our plan, our treatment goal."

I froze. Are you ready for this? Can your Shame really be eradicated? By somebody who says things like "treatment goal?"

And what's under all that Shame? Oh, God! I'm afraid to see, dammit! Oh – and don't say dammit.

Vickie Reagan taught me more than every word in the Big Book; she taught me about life, love, bravery, faith, discipline, and how to live sober and free while having fun.

I found out who I was, and with Vickie's help, I didn't run away from the real me. I embraced her and learned to believe in her. I took several steps backward over the years, but I wouldn't be sober today without Vickie's support.

If nothing more, I credit her with the next phase of my sobriety, the one that blossomed within me for a decade.

Her heartwarming-but-heartbreaking story, however, interrupted our intimate relationship for nearly 15 years. She became too busy, unable to be free on Wednesday or any other day.

Here's what happened:

When Vickie and I first met, she'd just broken up with Bart, her self-described *soulmate, love of her life, her future wrapped in tinsel.* She broke up with him after three years of dating and waiting, at last deciding that she couldn't give up her lifelong dream of being a wife and mother to 2.25 children. Not to mention a spring flower garden and white picket fence.

After their breakup, she met another man, and after a time, fell in love with him and his promise of marriage and a houseful of kids. They were engaged on August 31, 2011.

I attended an impromptu engagement party for them on the second day of September.

Then, nine days later, on 9/11, the day New York's twin towers were destroyed by terrorists, Bart called her to say the tragedy had changed his perspective and he wanted to marry her and be a father to their 2.25 children.

In angst, she broke up with her fiancé and married Bart, *her soulmate, the love of her life, her future wrapped in tinsel.* Lo-and-behold, they soon had twins, one with a developmental disability.

Vickie's focus was on her children, and rightly so. She quit her job and gave up her sponsee, even cutting meeting attendance down to one a week. My phone calls were hit or miss once the kids started crawling.

Though I missed her terribly, and still do, I took what she taught me and became a badass sponsor to a dozen-plus other girls, taking Vickie's example to a new generation.

<<<<<<<>>>>>>

SHARING MY SECRETS
CHAPTER 43

I worked all day Sunday, having spent my seven days without an official date with Gil. Not that I didn't flirt with him at meetings; I did, when he was there. And I thought about him constantly. In fact, I thought the love at first sight thing may be a real thing with the two of us.

As I also promised to Oakley, I went to only one meeting a day, always hoping he was there. When I didn't see him, my heart hurt, and I knew I had it bad.

I'd been to dinner with big groups from West 40, ate many Grand Slams from Denny's, and hit a few buffets at China Pearl, and Gil was at two of those dinners. He always sat beside me or straight across. And though I never asked them to, everybody seemed eager to save a place for him near me. (I heard somebody say, "That should be Railroad's seat.) But instead of being embarrassed, I was excited. *Rumors be damned! They seem to be fine with it!*

Our "meeting date" was at 7:00, appropriately called "Sundays at Seven" and held at St. John's Cathedral, directly across from the Episcopal church where I'd been so disappointed with my baptism only sixteen years before.

The meeting was a tenth step meeting! Finally! Words of wisdom from people farther along in the program. I absorbed every word. It was a beautiful night when Gil and I wandered to the garden area behind the cathedral. The statue of St. Francis of Assisi was an original, Gil explained, chiseled by a Gatlinburg artist specifically for the cathedral.

The animals that surrounded the statue, also carved by local artists, created a showy display. To me, it was odd to have a statue of a *saint*, because I knew nothing of such things, and told Gil so.

"Catholics are strange people. Mostly they shuffle in and shuffle out on Sundays, but there's an inherent sense of guilt and obligation involved. It's pretty messed up."

"I find Christians, all Christians, pretty screwed up, too. That's why my Higher Power is... uh, of a different variety."

He looked at me and cocked his head, a question mark in his eyes. Then he sat on a small concrete bench and patted the empty side. "Sit down and tell me about it. What's your Higher Power all about? Is it/he/she a doorknob?"

I joked, "More like a Pop-Tart."

"Ha, ha," he said, his voice flat but his face glowing with a smile. "Seriously. And judging by the tears that just came to your eyes, it seems your Higher Power is a big deal to you. Tell me what you believe."

His eyes were bright; it seemed he really wanted to know. And for some odd reason, I felt comfortable telling him. I still had, hmm... should I call it Shame, or embarrassment?... about my "vision" so long ago on the back patio at rehab, and I still feared people would mistrust somebody who believed in a non-traditional Higher Power.

"You won't like it. My mom says it's sacrilegious. And being Catholic, I'm sure you–"

"I'm only Catholic by birth, not by belief. I just haven't been able to invent anything better than what I was taught growing up. Family tradition reigns. But knowing you, you've created some wildly creative, fantastic, science-fiction, kind of Higher Power, custom-designed power to fit your every need."

My eyes widened. "How did you know?"

He looked dumbfounded. "I'm right? I was just joking about your creativity, but of course, anybody's Higher Power is self-designed, really."

Did he just say that? Self-designed is okay? "Well, it's not like I made him up *completely*. Not fiction! But, uh, my Higher Power came to me in, like, a vision." I put my head down, gazing at the mosaic-glass bird on the birdbath, ready for Gil to laugh at me.

But Gil didn't laugh at all. He interrupted my Shame and anxiety with a question. Or maybe it was a command. "Tell me what keeps you sober, Lela Fox. I want to get to know you." His voice was gentle, supportive.

I swallowed hard, realizing *I* also wanted to know him better, and knew I'd only get the chance if I also did a tell-all. So I began from the beginning. "Well... when I was about six, in a Sunday school class – we went to this tiny Methodist Church in Burgess – there was a picture in our little workbook-thingie. The picture was a break in the clouds with a sparkling beam of light coming through. Know what I mean?"

"There's probably a million pay-per-use photos just like it. In many Sunday school books."

"Agreed. But it struck me as so, so special at the time. And underneath the photo was a caption. It said, 'God is here.' For whatever reason, that photograph stuck in my mind for decades, and even when it was a joke, even when I was drinking, I quoted the caption every time I saw the sun breaking through the clouds. It happens a lot, you know?"

"I guess, but what does that have to do with–"

"I'm getting there." I stretched my neck, nervous. "So, I was in rehab, just after a pretty traumatic breakdown having to do with my husband."

"Now ex-husband, right?"

I laughed. "Maybe, maybe not. That's a whole 'nother story. I'll tell you sometime."

"I can wait, hopeful for many 'sometimes.'" I rolled my eyes. "But please... go on. You had a breakdown and..." The end of his question went high in pitch, urging me to complete the story, but I had begun to feel silly again. He tried again and finally kept his mouth shut as I explained.

"Well, my Higher Power is a guy. Just a regular guy. A hippie, actually, who looks exactly like my cousin Lewis Balyum."

"Your cousin is your Higher Power?"

"Do you want to hear this or not?" Gil made the gesture of zipping his lips together. "This... man... sits at a concrete picnic table in the sky, holes in his jeans, an old flannel shirt half-buttoned. Pretty sloppy, really. And he smokes." Gil had looked away, and I sensed he was laughing behind his hand. *Oh, I KNEW I shouldn't have told him!*

Then he looked back at me with big, bright eyes. "A God who smokes! *Cool!*"

Relief. He believes me! Should I keep going? Tell him everything?! "But I don't call him 'God.' Because, after he, um, appeared, I said something so calm and casual, like I'd say to a regular person."

"What was it?"

"I said: 'Dude, I need some help down here,' and just talked to him like he was my cousin Lewis, having a regular conversation. But I could feel some kind of... vibrations, almost. Some unexplained power, and I knew this Dude had all the answers. I didn't even have to ask the questions. And, Gil, it still feels like that. There's a connection between us that's like – everything good and powerful and happy. The ultimate peace and comfort. And one time, the first time I was ever around alcohol as a sober person, another vision came at the exact right time, no shit, and he squinted his eyes, showing 'displeasure' about the champagne. I swear!"

Gil touched my cheek, wiping a tear I didn't even know had fallen. "What a beautiful story, Lela. You know, a Higher Power is 'as we understand him,' right? And it's no joke. If Dude is your God, then Dude is your God. You have nothing to be embarrassed about."

My body went limp with relief. I wasn't even sure why I was crying, and sure as hell didn't know why it would be okay to cry in front of Gil. "Some badass woman I am, huh? Crying like a baby..."

"Don't think that way. Why do you think you can't cry about it? If it's meaningful, it's worthy of tears."

"I'm just embarrassed. I mean, to be all filled with snot and mascara on my cheeks in front of you. I wasn't planning on this happening; bet on that."

"Sorry, I don't bet anymore." I was caught off-guard by a bad gambling-addict joke, laughing just enough to stop my tears. I wiped the last of them with my left sleeve. He moved forward and I freaked; I thought he was going to kiss me. But he kissed a tear just before it dripped off my jaw. "You missed one." A wink. "But I got it."

Gil sighed a big one and smiled, looking further down the garden trail, saying nothing. Just sitting and feeling peace. After a few minutes of feeling weird as shit about feeling peaceful with him, I accepted it.

I was with my man.

Okay, here goes, Lela Fox. So maybe it's not just Gil that thinks my vision is fine. Like... instantly acceptable. I've held it in for so long... I feel so free. Oh, my God! And so RELIEVED! I had held so much Shame for my beliefs.

I said, "So if that's the case, I need to tell you a few other things."

"If what's the case? And what other things?"

I laughed nervously, afraid the "if that's the case" comment had shined a spotlight on my scenario of our newly defined relationship. But I needed to test if Gil would still want to be with a screwed-up woman like me... a woman with so many secrets and so much Shame.

So I spilled the beans.

"First, I'm not even sure if I'm divorced or not."

"Not sure? How the hell..."

"Because I had to hide from him. All I know is that when he left Florida, we were still legally married. Texas is in the possibilities of where he is, and that's about all I know."

"But... haven't you filed for divorce?"

"He filed. I never answered the complaint, trying to get money." I chuckled, "But that fell through in a big way. So... even though the divorce could've been granted 'in absentia' – Latin for me being absent – he left the state. And has to file again in whatever state he landed in and list my address as 'unknown.'"

"How would you find out, then?"

"My mom's lawyer-friend said to just keep Googling it, state by state. And/or to invest in a people-finder subscription of some sort to find him, eventually, then I'd know which state to focus on when searching."

"Wow. I bet that makes you feel–"

"Disgusted. Dirty. Used. In limbo. And, still, scared. If he finds me again, he'll restart the harassing and the stalking, I'm afraid. An unlisted number only goes so far."

"Sounds like you have a story to tell."

"No way I'm telling you the nightmare of being with him. I was a lousy, lazy drunk who got caught in his ruse of loving me. He stole most everything I had, racked up charges on my credit card, destroyed my apartment while I was in jail because of him... and it only lasted four months of living together. Talk about unmanageable! And stupid... mostly stupid."

"So is Fox his name?"

"No, thank God I never changed my name, in *none* of my marriages, actually. And I definitely don't want to be Lela Weinstein."

"Oh, and Jewish!"

"And from New York. Stuart was an asshole like you only find in movies. The ultimate bad guy."

"You've been through some real shit, girl. I'm sorry."

"But now you see why I'd have a hard time entering a relationship with an open, trusting soul. My heart was crushed, and I came away broken. I thought Stuart was all I had... even tried to contact him when I was first sober. Always called him my soulmate."

"Evidently, he was *not* your soulmate. In fact, I *know* he wasn't.

"Like you would know!"

"He wasn't your soulmate – because *I am!*"

I snapped my head to look at him, my mouth open in a hearty laugh. "Riiiight."

"I'm serious."

"That's what scares me. I'm not even sure I want to date anybody, Gil, much less meet my soulmate! Because there's more." A long silence. "Something I'm still afraid of... big-time."

"I'm listening. A problem shared is a problem halved, ya know."

"Sounds like you're full of AA rhetoric."

Gil grinned a wide one. "That, I am."

I held my breath. "I'm afraid to sleep with a man. Or a woman, for that matter. Because I've slept with so many."

"Whoa! Where'd that come from?"

Tears seemed to erupt from the center of my gut. *Oh, God! What am I doing?! I'm going to tell him about my Shame, the Shame rooted in my soul, about my promiscuity and how I used people! What the hell, Lela?! It's way too early to tell him that, if you ever tell him at all!*

"I'm sorry. A lot of that is fifth step stuff. But I know for me to ever move forward, I have to share that I've... been... well, let's just say I thought that indiscriminate sex would cure my alcoholism. I have to have that upfront." I felt my face burning red, and the annoying buzz of stress between my eardrums returned.

But I heard what he said loud and clear.

"So you think you're unique in that? Using people? Serving ourselves? Do you think other alcoholics are virgins? Pure and kind in their drinking days? Come on... you're not telling me anything I wouldn't otherwise assume."

I sat frozen in time, my body unable to move. *He doesn't care? He thinks it's normal? And all this time, I've beaten myself up... for nothing?*

I sat in disbelief, unraveling years of feeling shitty about myself. I "saw" this happening, like thread unwinding from a bobbin. When the end of the thread appeared, the air exploded from my lungs. I felt some kind of freedom that I'd never felt before.

But don't let him see you cry, Lela. Don't let him know how much he's affected you today, or how much you love him already.

I said, "I'm done. Let's go," and stood, massaging my butt that had gone to sleep on the concrete surface.

Gil also stood. "I understand your pain, Lela, I think. As you grow in sobriety, you'll forget the past stuff and focus on the future. Right now, you're afraid of relationships because you've been hurt so badly. And something tells me it wasn't just Stuart who broke your heart."

I twisted my lips sideways, grimacing agreement. "Right."

He took my hand, and we walked silently toward his car. He opened the car door for me like my dad had always done for my mom. I'd gone from feeling like an idiot to feeling like a queen.

My Shame was gone, my heart was open. Because I'd found my soulmate.

I knew it before he closed the door, when he bent down to peck a kiss on my lips.

<<<<<<<>>>>>>

FADE TO BLACK
CHAPTER 44

He brought the movie with him. "Oh, you're just going to love it, Lela!" Gil's broad shoulders wrapped around mine in a hug not meant as a caress, but a quick greeting. So far, Gil had been "behaving himself" according to my rules of going slow and keeping our pants on.

He still looked at me too dreamily and complimented me too much, but I was becoming okay with that. More than okay, in fact. Gil made me feel like an empress. And somehow, he could do it without being the least bit condescending.

It'd been one helluva fun week with him; he took a day off to make sure he could make it to the Memorial Day potluck at the club, and we'd taken *two* long walks on "our" shady path with a white gazebo in the center. We made *The Sound of Music* jokes in the gazebo, with Gil twisting and twirling like a girl, serenading me on bended knee... the whole deal. I hadn't laughed that hard in a long time.

But to invite him to my place was a big step. A big, big step. We'd kept everything in public, and mostly in groups, but tonight would cross that fine line into "real relationship." I felt ready, but scared. But also not scared.

"Regular Coke for you, right, Gil?"

"You have some?"

"I bought it just for you. I remember things. It's what you always order, and I noticed. Me? I'm a *Diet* Coke person."

"And I noticed *that*, so there!"

"So that makes you the winner of this contest?" I laughed.

'You are correct, Ms. Fox."

"The frozen pizza will be ready in exactly eleven minutes... yay! Eleven is my lucky number!" Gil's face screwed into a question mark, but I ignored it, not ready to tell the details.

I continued, "Then... after the pizza, we'll pop in the movie. What did you bring? I'll warn you: I'm extremely picky about movies. I don't like the shoot 'em up stuff, or the super-hero stuff, not even girly romance comedy. I'm kinda weird because I like–"

He interrupted as if I'd finished talking, quite rudely, I thought. "Well, I didn't know what you liked, so I just brought my favorite movie of all time. I've watched it probably eight times." He was rummaging around in the Walmart bag he'd brought. "Here it is! *A Bug's Life!* It's a Pixar movie!"

"Oh. My. God."

"What? You don't like it?"

"I was just trying to tell you that I prefer kid's movies! And here you are – a big, strong, muscle-bound man – confidently waltzing in here with a kid's movie! I love it!"

I laughed hysterically, shocked that Gil could be so burly and sensitive at the same time. "I have a child-man, just like me!" More laughing, more than Gil understood, it seemed, because he looked at me with a wrinkled brow. But I kept talking. "I love it! It's so damn charming! You are just... perfectly awesome, Gil Justice!"

When he realized I was serious, Gil's face took a funny, exaggerated, cocksure stance. "That's me, alright! Perfectly awesome!" He dropped the persona as fast as it came. "It's not exactly true, but if *you* think I'm awesome, then it's 100 percent true."

He looked at me with an assured grin and winked. The light caught it just right, and his incredible blue eyes sparkled as if lit from behind.

I felt like I should lean forward and kiss the hell out of him, but stopped myself. "Let me show you my dog's latest trick." Pork Chop had been by Gil's side the whole time because my big, strong man had talked baby-talk to the dog and been so attentive to him. "Watch this! He howls when I do, but, well, it's not quite a howl."

336

"What do you mean?"

"Just watch." I locked eyes with Pork Chop and threw my head back with my mouth in a large "O." Starting with a low volume, I howled like a coyote would howl at the moon. Pork Chop chimed in immediately, but his "howl" was more like a continuous bird's chirp. So stinkin' cute! Gil laughed and went crazy with pets and praises for Choppy.

"You've got a good one, Lela. I wish I could have a dog, but with my work hours... it's just not possible. So I think I'll just borrow yours."

"No way. I'm not sharing."

"Okay, just for tonight." He put Pork Chop between us on the sofa, cooing to him and rubbing his back from head to tail.

"I think, Mr. Justice, that you like my dog more than you like me." I was teasing, but my cheeks turned red with embarrassment.

Gil grinned. "Oh, no, babe. Not *near* as much as I like you." I continued to blush, embarrassed, and feeling stupid. Gil hadn't taken his eyes from me. "And I like it with your cheeks get all pink when I say things like that."

"Hey! You're cheating! You're *trying* to make me blush. That's not fair!"

A noise outside caused Pork Chop to jump down from the sofa and stick his nose through the blinds on the sliding glass door. Taking advantage, Gil scooted closer to me and rolled his strong arm around my shoulders to pull me close. I ended up with my head on his shoulders, smelling his manly cologne.

"What cologne, Gil? It smells heavenly."

Gil hooted a laugh. "Dial soap and regular ol' shampoo! Cologne is too girly for me." We both turned at the same time... and ended up nose-to-nose. I gazed into his eyes as he smiled and kept eye contact. Oh, wow – those baby-blues became soft and vulnerable. He asked, "Can I kiss you?"

"Please. Yes, please."

"We'll burn the pizza."

"Screw the pizza."

– THE END –

<<<<<<<>>>>>>

SNEAK PEEK AT BOOK 7
SERENITY: HAPPY, JOYOUS, AND FREE

CHAPTER 1: Fun & Games

"Okay, here's another one: mountains or beach?"

I hesitated. "Gil, that's not a fair question. A Tennessee girl has to say 'mountains,' but in truth, there's nothing more peaceful for me than floating in the waves at the beach. I used to spend *hours* there when I first got sober, floating and thinking, thinking and floating."

"Because you're an over-thinker."

"Everybody thinks so, but *I* think–"

"Gotcha! You're thinking about thinking! Yep, a double-triple-multi-quadruple over-thinker. That'll get you in trouble someday, Lela."

"*Not* thinking will get *you* in trouble, Gil! You're so laid back that it's scary sometimes."

We teased each other while playing what Gil called the "Get to Know Each Other Game," a series of A-or-B questions, each requiring an explanation. The afternoon sky held a brilliant sun, especially as we stood high on a ridge outside of Rockville, home of the area's famous fire-watch tower.

We'd climbed the wooden steps to the tower, four stories above ground, ooh'ing and aah'ing about the view of a zillion shades of green. The scenery in the undulating hills and valleys of East Tennessee was unmatched.

"God's Country," most call it, just fifty miles east of America's most-visited national park.

"Okay, Gil... yellow or green?"

"Blue."

"That wasn't an option, you ditz." He shrugged, but I wanted his reasoning. "And you choose blue because...?"

He mumbled and grumbled, trying to avoid answering the question, it seemed. I prodded him again, and then he spoke in jet-speed. "My eyes, right?"

"Bluest eyes I've ever seen." I smiled. True, Gil's eyes had always mesmerized me. The outer rims of the irises were a rich navy-blue, the interior a bright azure with navy flecks. The curious right eye, with a smaller pupil, looked the dreamiest, focused with a loving gaze that sent me to the moon. *Dreamy eyes... a romantic boyfriend. What more could I want?*

He said, "Here's one for you: your favorite number."

"Easy! It's eleven, and you knew that! You're a cheat!"

"Yes, I know about your eleven mystery, your connection to Dude. But I was hoping you'd say four."

"Why four?"

"Husbands."

"What the hell are you talking about?"

"I hope to be husband number four."

Laughing, I asked, "You'd take a three-time loser?"

"Only if it was you. Do you have any idea how much I adore you, girl?"

"A million mountains worth?" I asked, opening my arms to the scene below. Smiling broadly, he put both hands on my hips as we stood on the wooden floor of the tower. Then he gently pulled me forward. "As much as the curls on your happy head."

My grin was so broad it almost hurt my lips. "Happy head. You'll never live that flirty pick-up line down, you know."

"Just keep smiling about it, babe. It's the memory of what started this fantasy romance."

We swayed and gazed at each other, but I wasn't giving up on the game. "Question... clocks: digital or analog?"

"Analog, as any good railroader should answer."

"How many in your collection of railroad watches?"

"Nineteen."

"Isn't it 25 years as a railroader? So why just nineteen?"

"Pawned a few in my gambling days."

I nodded. *Yep. An alkie is always desperate for money, but a gambler's need must be worse.*

"Did you gamble your paycheck away, too? You still don't save one red cent of what you earn, so I guess back then, you were even *more* irresponsible with money?"

"Hey, now! 'Irresponsible' is a fightin' word, Chicka. But, yeah, I was big-time irresponsible. Caused a lot of problems in my marriage."

The conversation waned as my mind wandered. I imagined being married to a gambler and how devastating and expensive that must be. He'd be even worse about frivolous spending than he is now! Talking to my boyfriend about money was like arguing with a brick wall, though I'd given up on arguing. It wasn't *my* money, right?

He and I were on different ends of the money-management spectrum. I was saver; he was a spender. For me, paying a late fee was equal to blasphemy; to Gil, it was just part of the monthly bill.

I dismissed Gil's financial recklessness easily, though. I laid blame on what must be his leftover "gambler's mentality." Although four years clean from compulsive gambling, he was less than a year out of bankruptcy and still struggling. At least that's what he'd insinuated; he didn't talk much about it, and more than once, he told me it was none of my damn business.

All was well, but in the big picture of the Gil-and-Lela future, the differences in our budget attitudes gave me pause. Such a big issue, and one that could build up and blow up quickly.

But it wasn't a day to bring up problems. It was all about the "Get to Know Each Other" game, and I continued the questions. I asked, "So are the watches valuable? And you were that desperate?"

"Hell-yeah! The horses were running, and I thought it'd be my day. Then again, I thought *every* day would be my day."

"You know, I'll never understand compulsive gamblers, even though I definitely understand addiction. The consequences come so quickly with gambling."

"But the payoff is always in the next race. Over and over again, all day, every season, every waking second. You get the picture."

"I'm scared of it, the fear instilled by my parents. Mom's father, a good-for-nothing alcoholic, gambled her mother's inheritance away, and Mom's still pissed about it."

"I can't imagine your mom ever pissed anything! Such a proper lady." He paused a beat. "But so out of touch..."

"Watch it now... you just don't know her."

"You and your dad... the way they still dote on each other. You had one helluva strong example. Is that why you rebelled so much?"

"I suppose. My parents were strict, not so much with rules, but with expectations. I knew I could never be the pure and upstanding daughter they wanted." I shrugged. "The only solution to being so inadequate was to become a drunk. And I was damn good at it."

"For 27 years, right?"

"Yep. So much Shame within those years. But for many of them, I was normal. I mean, high achiever and almost functional."

Gil chuckled, "I started *and* ended dysfunctional. Don't know how I kept my job. But, in the old railroad days, the guys covered for their drunk coworkers."

"That's still crazy-unbelievable to me."

"It's definitely not like that anymore! But enough of that... I have more questions for you, my dear Lela."

"Shoot."

"Funny greeting cards or lovey-dovey ones?"

"Funny ones."

"Ice cream: chocolate or vanilla?"

I chuckled. "Neapolitan."

With a broad smile, my boyfriend said, "You're very complicated. Did you know that?"

"Does that make you want to run from the challenge?"

"Quite the opposite. I remain intrigued."

Undaunted, I continued the game. "Okay, I have one, since we're old. Arthritis or broken bones?"

"Never broken a bone in my life."

"No shit?"

Gil talked over me. "Arthritis is another story. My right knee is basically bone-on-bone already, or that's what the doctor says, and that was ten years ago. It's worse now."

He switched from massaging his knee to reach across his body, manipulating his left shoulder. "Plus, my damn shoulder's bothering me again lately. But, hell, every joint in my body is a mess, to tell you the truth. It's not easy walking on those rocks around the tracks. Probably why railroaders retire at age 60."

"But with full benefits, right?"

"Right."

"You're blessed to have those union benefits."

"Worked my ass off, so they owe me. At least that's the way I see it!"

"You definitely work a lot. I miss you when you're gone."

"A railroader's schedule sucks. Breaks up a lot of families, so I hope you can keep an open mind."

"I'm not going anywhere. But you've destroyed my nine-to-five mentality."

Gil threw his head back and laughed. "Nine to five! Har, har, har."

I rubbed my nose against his as we stood face-to-face. "So, are you just going to stand there?"

"Oh! You want to sit?" He turned away, looking over the edge of the tower's railing to scout the picnic tables below.

Smiling, I pulled hard on a belt loop to turn him back toward me. "No, I don't want to *sit!* I want you to *kiss me.*"

Gil exaggerated surprise. "Me? Kiss the one who loves beaches instead of mountains?" I laughed at his antics. "One who spouts five-syllable words and prefers purple – a *secondary* color, as you point out. One who cheats at Rummy and put her sponsor to sleep during a three-hour fifth step?"

I'd giggled throughout his teasing remarks. "Yep, that's the one. Put 'er there, pard'ner. Right on the ol' kisser."

"Gladly." And kiss me, he did... a long, loving one.

During the kiss, I marveled about our budding relationship. No doubt, I was head over heels in love with the intriguing AA guru named Gil Justice.

After the follow-up smooches, I said, "I still feel like I'm on a fantasy carousel, Gil. Our three months together have been a whirlwind, but the happiest time of my life."

"Ditto, girl. My Lela is perfection, and I'm a lucky man."

"We've spent every waking hour together, you know? Either at meetings or at my apartment, right? And, sorry, babe... I've *tried* to like your place, but I just can't. It's a depressing dump."

He smiled broadly. "I never fixed it up. Somehow, I still feel like it's temporary. And your place is awesome."

I asked, "Speaking of you in my place... you're still set for watching my dog next week?"

"Pork Chop and I will have fun. And I made a Plan B with our crazy friend Corncob. If I have to pull an overnight trip, he'll pop by to care for that sweet red dachshund, the Long-haired Alcoholic. That's what the people at the West 40 AA club call him, did you know that?"

"Yeah, and it cracks me up. But the dog *is* calm and quiet in meetings, hasn't pissed the floor, and loves everybody."

Gil's beaming grin spread his mouth beautifully. "Pork Chop is a *good* alcoholic, but he needs to get started on some step work."

I laughed long and hard, feeling grateful that Gil loved my dog so much. Pork Chop was like our child, and I'd miss his sweet face while I was gone... maybe as much as I'd miss Gil's vibrant smile.

Missing them or not, I couldn't turn down the opportunity to go on the trip; it was cheap, and another friend had canceled at the last minute. The opportunity fell in my lap for a reason, I believed.

With a teasing smile, Gil warned, "Just don't meet some hot beach bum or run off to join the circus."

"That's exactly what I'm planning to do, so be prepared," I teased him back.

I'd be hitting the waves on a beach trip with "da' gulls," a handful of the women I knew in my former Rockville life, but this time they'd bring their boyfriends and/or husbands. The party-hearty girls had gone another direction; Jilly and Debbie Doo-Doo had gone AWOL. But this core group of eight... we had a long history together, and the fact that I no longer drank would be a non-issue.

At least I hoped it wouldn't be an issue.

Destin, Florida, our favorite Panhandle beach, would host our now-less-rowdy crowd for the first week of the cheaper off-season, September 9–15, 2001. My sister Jennifer and her beau, "Boring Boris," as I called him, would arrive in the evening of our first day.

Only half-deserving of a vacation, I'd barely made the deadline in finishing the user manual for my client Quadrix software, and I'd been half-ass poking around to ready the training classes. Distracted by Gil and the West 40 club, my work ethic had waned. A surprising turn, because "work, work, work" had been pounded into my brain with the jackhammer of my father's words and example.

But as Gil had pointed out, I wasn't as silly and tough as my father. I used to be, but in those days, I'd swayed toward the Goody-Two-Shoes persona of my mother. Such a change! I'd rebelled against her ways when I was younger, but I had to admit that I'd become conservative, quieter, more accommodating, and definitely more serene as my mood stabilized.

As if he'd been following my thoughts, I said, "See, Gil," I said, "I don't think I'm manic at all. I believe it's just pure happiness. More and more, I don't think I need Bi-Polar meds, and maybe didn't ever."

"If you say so. I haven't known you crazy."

"Yet!" I laughed, "Mood stability can be boring sometimes. And the only time I feel depressed is about work."

Gil had no response. I stood, swaying with him, and wondering if a little mania could be a good thing.

CHAPTER 2: The Day it Happened

The beach was perfect for the first two days. The scorching heat in northern Florida had receded a bit for the fall season, presenting a warm, glowing sun that didn't fry your brain. Some of the guys drank beer on the beach in the afternoon, pulling from a well-stocked cooler, but their drinking didn't bother me. Plus, I had people making sure not one drop of alcohol passed my lips. My sister was watching, for sure.

The first morning, wanting the full crowd gathered at our beach house pool, I ran to the side-yard bungalow to wake up Jennifer and Boring Boris. Man-oh-man, she got soooo pissed at me! It never occurred to me that some people think vacations are for relaxing and sleeping late; I saw the week as an opportunity to have fun at all hours of the day and night.

And just because I was sober didn't mean I couldn't party. I swung with the best of them, dancing and laughing. We had a blast for two solid days.

But Tuesday morning was different. As usual, we'd gotten up early, banging pots and pans to scramble eggs, and to watch the morning news. Yeah... 40-something folks do that.

It was Tuesday, September 11. We saw the first plane crash into the tower in New York; we saw the first replay after it hit. Then we saw the live feed of the second plane crash into tower number two. Silence; only gasps filled the room.

My tears came unannounced, dripping from my jaw as newscaster Brian Williams explained the significance of the terror attack. It was surreal, more than a surprise, but an attack on the soul of America. Nothing like that had ever happened.

To the side-yard I went, maneuvering the path to wake Jennifer and Boring Boris for the second day in a row. I knew she wouldn't be pissed once she understood the magnitude of what had just happened.

They sprung from bed when I shouted through the door. "There's been a terrorist attack!"

Then, to the living room with Jennifer and Boris in tow, I stepped into the bathroom to lose my breakfast. The diameter of my esophagus was the size of a decimal, and I wore my stomach on my sleeve.

Later, taking my seat in on the sofa, I watched as they replayed the scene dozens and dozens of times, stabbing me in the heart with each rotation. Especially haunting were the people who dove out of the windows to escape the fires. My brain fell with them, it seemed, splattered, scared, and dead.

It took twenty minutes to come to my senses.

We didn't have reliable phone reception in the house so I rushed to the balcony to call my son, Bo. Thank God, he answered. Of course, I knew he wasn't in New York but safe in Rockville as a happy TSU engineering student... but there was something about that day that urged people to call their loved ones no matter what.

I talked to Bo for a half-hour, much longer than we'd ever stayed on the phone, but I couldn't bring myself to hang up. I couldn't stop telling him how much I loved him, how proud I was, how much hope I had for his future. He cried, too, and got off the phone only to take a call from his dad. So we squeaked goodbyes, promising to see each other soon.

I lit another cigarette and called my parents, who'd slept late and had only seen the replays for the past five minutes. Mom answered and apologized for not being the first to call... so like her want to protect her children, no matter how adult we were. She and Daddy had sat in silence, she said, flabbergasted and clinging to each other. Their reaction was the same as other couples across America on that day.

The day the world changed.

Jennifer made me hang up with Mom so she could call her. As the older sister, she had the right to be bossy, but that day, there was more to it. I felt thankful in accommodating her wishes. It was a day to love unconditionally, coming face-to-face with a monumental change in American life.

My third call was to my sister Karen and her husband John, thankfully safe at home in Jackson City, a hundred miles north of Rockville. Neither Karen nor I said a word, just cried together, sniffling. As usual, we each knew what the other was thinking, and laughed when I said, "I love you, too" when she hadn't spoken yet.

Thank God for Karen, for something to laugh about. Then minutes later, she had to go with a call-waiting from Mom.

Fourth, I called Gil, who'd also just awakened and was watching the endless replays of the crashes into tower two. The skies of New York were black with smoke, and live shots of people running from what would later be called Ground Zero haunted me, squeezing my emotional well dry.

"Gil, are you okay?" I asked.

"Are you?"

"I'm safe. Freaked out. I talked to Bo." Retelling the conversation with my son sent racks of sobs through my body, my broad shoulders pumping up and down. Gil cooed with assurances and wishes of happy thoughts, never asking me to calm down or stop the tears. It was a day to cry.

Like the charmer he was, Gil worked to soothe me, and I let him.

My last call was to Vickie, my sponsor. She was at work, but nobody was working, she said. The staff members were in the conference room, watching TV with rapt attention. She, too, had called her parents, boyfriend, and bevy of friends.

After I convinced her that I was fine, she poured her heart out to *me*. Vickie's life was in a state of flux, and that day, she couldn't handle it in her usual matter-of-fact way. Vickie had recently broken up with a long-time boyfriend when the sonofabitch came clean that he didn't want kids. The problem: Vickie wanted kids more than anything, and he'd promised her that he did, too.

So Vickie left to pursue her dream of a family and was seriously dating another man who shared the vision. But that day, Vickie ached with the need to call her ex, "the love of her life," as she said. In fact, she'd dialed six of the seven numbers twice, crying with Shame. My heart went out to Vickie, and I lulled her as best I could.

After our group finished with their calls, we slowly gathered beach bags and coolers, sauntering across the street to the shoreline. The waves hadn't stopped, the tide came in as if nothing had happened. But everything else had changed.

We were all quiet on the nearly deserted beach. No rambunctious jumping with the Frisbee, no raunchy jokes or flipping each other with wet towels. A day of contemplation. All I knew was that I couldn't wait to get home and hold Gil in my arms.

Life is precious, Lela. Why do you keep playing hard to get with Gil? Let him move into your place like he wants to do. You're ready... and he's MORE than willing. You've prayed to Dude enough times, so you'd know if it was a bad decision.

The sun shined brightly, adding sparkle to the sand, and I couldn't help but smile. Life goes on, after all. Make the most of it.

This man... Gil Justice... he's a gem, sparkling bright in the sun like the sand. He's your soulmate, your one-and-only. Starting now, give him all of you. Give him ALL Lela Fox has to offer.

LIFETIME # 8: The Transition

Another 180-degree turn for Lela Fox; another Lifetime begins. The official transition happened when I let my guard down and whole-heartedly gave myself to the serenity of being sober and joyous, and letting Gil Justice be a part of my life.

It wasn't that I simply changed boyfriends; it was also a change in mindset. I'd met my soulmate, and to question it was against everything I'd believed about love and relationships.

Gil was the only man who promised me upfront and without hesitation: " I will always put your needs first." He said, "I happily welcome the challenge of being like your father, to treat you like he treats your mother." And, of course, that's exactly what I wanted, and what I'd searched for all my life. Gil promised it... so why would I worry? Why not dive head-first into what felt so right?

He respected and protected my vulnerabilities, and he was calm. Sober-minded. Wise. A voracious lover. As a bonus, he had a stable income, a long-term work record. That, too, was a safety net.

Our lives would be picture-perfect, I envisioned. And the red flags could be dealt with later; they were just innocent trouble spots in what was otherwise a perfect union.

We'd become the royalty of our AA club, West 40, appointed two of the movers and shakers of recovery in Rockville. Though Gil had asked many times when I wanted to make our love official with a wedding ring, I didn't want to be officially married – not again, please! But our union was permanent in my mind, 100 percent.

How could I know the end would be so horrid?

~:~:~:~:~:~

I can pinpoint the exact moment of transition to Lifetime #8. It happened when Gil was ironing clothes, if you can imagine a man doing that. He'd completely moved in with me and Pork Chop, and we were in the middle of an argument... at least *I* thought we were still in the middle of it. But Gil was finished arguing; he'd stepped back to give me space to cool down.

The problem: I was still off my meds, and cooling down from angry moments took hours, sometimes days. Gil decided to speed the pace of my cool-down with an instant fix. He said later, he'd decided to "charm my pants off," but it had nothing to do with getting naked.

Sitting in my office as steam came from my ears, Gil serenaded me from the back bedroom as he ironed his shirt. He sang opera – loud.

> "Oooh, my dear Leeela! She is so angggry...
> But her darling Gilllll is in love with her stilllll"

He was into it big-time, and he was a great singer. My smile started at the second line of the "song," and slowly grew to a howling laugh. Yep, a new-found love had defused a situation when Lela Fox was mad – that had *never* happened before.

In previous Lifetimes, most people, husbands included, had just called me a hothead and walked away. Or yelled back at me. Or, in Stuart's case, called the police.

But Gil made it funny.

He made me laugh, even when I felt like stabbing him, and with each laugh, I fell deeper in love.

The opera song knocked down the rest of the walls I'd built around my heart and my soul, exposing the "real me" to the world. I was incredibly happy – ecstatic, in fact. Being so naturally happy disguised a manic spike in my Bi-Polar rollercoaster, and others, including my family, agreed that I seemed stable and understandably joyful.

But Lifetime #8 would take several twists and turns, and require more courage than I could've imagined. And, if you want to be technical about it, the Lifetime was truly a progression of six A-to-Z changes.

Pack your bags and come along for the ride.

– END OF SAMPLE –

<<<<<<<>>>>>>

MORE ABOUT ME

After my on-and-off career as an advertising writer, and twelve years as a certified picture framer, I retired and began writing for fun. My tidbits landed in AA's *Grapevine* magazine and a few online journals, then a story about my dog was featured in *Chicken Soup for the Soul*.

Hmmmm...

As if meant to be – about a week later, an author-friend challenged me to write and publish a full book. "Just one rule," he said, "Write what you know."

I had no idea of writer's terms then, and I took his advice too literally. I thought "writing what you know" meant writing your life story. I found out later that writers mean, "Based on what you know... which can be any genre." Big difference.

But I was hooked. The words came easily, so I spent the next three years writing my life story, which became seven top-selling books.

I instantly jumped into it and spent the next years happy and – dare I say – organized? Anyway, what you get is my story.

And I hope to help – both newcomers and old-timers.

I am beyond surprised by how many readers love the series. The story is just me telling my story... nothing earthshaking, but I thank you for liking it.

With the series complete, I'm now writing mysteries under my pen name Patty Ayers. Updates to come.

I live in East Tennessee with a panoramic view of the Great Smoky Mountains and a sense of serenity in every corner of my little condo. If I'm not writing, you'll find me tinkering or playing tug-of-war with my distinguished editor, Stormin' Norman the Schnauzer.

Combining creativity with my OCD, I also have a side biz called *KID'S ART IN STITCHES,* where I embroider children's drawings in hot, bright colors.

By the grace of Dude, I've been sober all day long.
I wish you the same.

<<<<<<<<>>>>>>

MORE BOOKS

Find out what happens!

Next up: SERENITY

See all books on my Amazon Author Page:
amazon.com/author/lelafox
and find me on **lelafox.com**

Do you like the book? Tell the world!
A review helps me so so much, and takes just a minute.

Made in United States
Orlando, FL
18 July 2023

35225506R00202